Partial Knowledge:

Philosophical Studies in Paul

PAUL W. GOOCH

University of Notre Dame Press
Notre Dame, Indiana

Copyright © 1987 by
University of Notre Dame Press
Notre Dame, Indiana 46556
All Rights Reserved

Library of Congress Cataloging-in-Publication Data

Gooch, Paul W.
  Partial knowledge.

  Bibliography: p.
  Includes index.
  1. Bible. N.T. Corinthians, 1st — Criticism,
interpretation, etc.   2. Religion — Philosophy.
I. Title.
BS2675.2.G66   1987   227'.206   86-40589
ISBN 0-268-01567-8

Manufactured in the United States of America

FOR PAULINE

Contents

Preface

This book is the product of philosophical activity practised on a biblical writer. Something of what this means may be found in the first chapter, but here I want to say briefly how the work came about and to discharge some debts of gratitude.

Since my academic training is more philosophical than anything else, no one could tell from my education when I began to be interested in Paul; and my own memory cannot answer that question. Nor do I know precisely when that interest turned philosophical: one's mental life does not seem to care much about temporal correlates in the world of datable events. Nevertheless the approach taken in this book first took written form shortly after I had completed my doctoral dissertation on Plato. As a *post partem* diversion I decided to work out an issue in the philosophy of religion — the metaphysical status of resurrected persons — by applying to a text of Paul the type of philosophical questioning I practised on Plato. The result, published in a small journal, *Crux*, in 1971, was my initial attempt to explore the possibility that Pauline resurrection is compatible with a view of persons as disembodied after death. A decade later this thesis was more fully developed in *Religious Studies*, in 1981, and now, recognizing that such an uncommon thesis needs to take detailed account of Paul's text, I have written a new piece on the same theme, set in wider context, for this book.

Along the way I had become interested in ethical questions in Paul, happily encouraged by Peter Richardson when he was at Scarborough College. He and I wrote companion articles on the strong and the weak in Paul for *Crux*, 1975–76, and on Paul's accommodatory dictum "all things to all men" for the *Tyndale Bulletin*, 1978. Both topics have found their way into this book, entirely reworked from their earlier manifestations. The other studies presented here have not had the benefit of descent from primitive forms, except for my investigation of 1 Corinthians 7, which appeared in the *Journal of Religious Ethics*, 1983, and has been expanded and revised as chapter 4.

Now to discharge with pleasure those debts. Many of the ideas in these studies took shape because I had to read something to an audience, and am I grateful for opportunities to read to the Canadian Society for Biblical Studies, the Society of Biblical Literature, the Society of Christian Philosophers, Tyndale House in Cambridge, and the "D" Society of the Divinity Faculty at Cambridge. The Division of Humanities, Scarborough College, University of Toronto, gave much support and understanding during my term as chairman. Most of the book was written while I was on sabbatical leave, 1982–83, for which I thank the university and my college. I am pleased to acknowledge the help of a leave fellowship from the Social Sciences and Humanities Research Council of Canada. And I am grateful to the Master, President, and Fellows of St. John's College, Cambridge, for welcoming me so warmly as Commonwealth Fellow that year: without the fellowship of hall and chapel my time in Cambridge would have been merely good.

The book is gratefully dedicated to Pauline Thompson, my wife. Not only has she shared her love with heart and mind; she has also shared in friendships and experiences with which these studies are associated. So she knows why, in dedicating the work to her, I think of David Mosher in connection with chapter 1, of Peter Richardson and chapter 6, of my brother Peter and chapter 5, and why the memories of my father and my niece Rachel belong with chapters 3 and 7.

The notes to each chapter use for the most part shortened references; for full details of publication the Bibliography may be consulted. Because an analysis of Paul's terminology is important, I have sometimes needed to cite bits of Greek, but readers not knowing Greek will be able to follow the argument. The English translation used throughout is the Revised Standard Version, though other translations are called upon in discussing specific passages. Insofar as possible I have tried to reflect in word choice that there is "neither male nor female" in philosopher, theologian, and reader, but on occasion examples and phrases appear in the masculine gender because inclusive language or feminization would have been worse rather than better — as the phrase "weaker brother" readily demonstrates.

CHAPTER ONE

Introduction: Paul and Philosophy

"Beware of philosophy." Colossians 2:8

This book is a series of philosophical studies in Paul's writings, chiefly the letter known as 1 Corinthians. Each study may stand on its own: each deals with a separate problem as it relates to a particular text in the letter. Those interested in only one theme or piece of text will not therefore do great violence to the whole by tearing apart what may be only loosely stitched together. Nevertheless they may be sufficiently intrigued by the notion of a philosophical study of a biblical writer to skim through this Introduction, in which I offer some explanation of what I am up to in the rest of the book. For although many people have been trying to understand Paul for a long time, and trying to do philosophy for an even longer time, the attempt to practise philosophical reflection on Paul is not common. It could be dismissed as unnecessary for theology or unworthy of philosophy: but before that is done, it may be helpful to work at some questions concerning the nature of the entire enterprise. I remark first on Paul's relationship to philosophy, then reflect on what these studies are and are not, and finally comment on how they are stitched together.

I. PHILOSOPHY AND PAUL

It is difficult not to begin with the blunt warning to the Colossians: beware of philosophy. But it is too easy to shout the warning down as anti-intellectual prejudice, or to excise it from the Pauline corpus with the scalpel of critical scholarship.[1] For suppose we have here Paul's true attitude toward philosophy: then that hostility might be thought to bear upon our undertaking. At the very least it seems paradoxical — if not perverse — to practise upon an apostle what that apostle explicitly rejects. For some, who think that by this rejection Paul opts out of the business of rational discussion, it will be perverse to treat his writing as seriously

1

open to philosophical investigation. Others may regard the attempt less harshly, but still think it somehow inappropriate: it may perhaps be like giving someone of one faith the funeral rites of a different faith. And those for whom Paul holds authority in the Christian faith will feel more deeply the embarrassment of using a proscribed device upon the proscriber himself. For such reasons, and also in order to demonstrate at the beginning how these studies approach Paul's text, we must look more carefully at the warning.

It is first necessary to discover what it is that the Colossians were being warned against. *Philosophia*, of course: but since Colossians 2:8 contains the only reference to philosophy in Paul's writings,[2] we will have to learn about it from its immediate context. That involves a good deal of work, as a glance through commentaries will show. But it is clear from the second chapter of Colossians in particular that Paul is concerned about opposition in Colossae, opposition not so much to his own position and authority as to the claims of Christ's gospel. Some group or other is advocating practices incompatible with the gospel and propounding beliefs that deny its truth. Paul thus writes of the wisdom and knowledge available in Christ because there is a danger of the Colossians' being led astray with beguiling speech (2:4). He wants them not to be preyed upon by philosophy, which is only empty deceit deriving from human tradition and the elemental spirits of the universe, not from Christ (2:8). In place of Christ the Colossians are being offered false abasement, angel-worship, visions (2:18) — in short a self-made religion (2:23).

Now imagine readers of such language who are untutored in other respects about the ways of philosophy. If they were given some ability to reflect on Paul's Greek, they would quickly conclude that philosophy was a bad thing indeed, worse than an embarrassment to faith. For they would reason as follows. Paul associates philosophy with two negative verbs: to be misled (*paralogidzomai*, 2:4) and to make prey of (*sulagōgein*, 2:8). The second means to kidnap, to carry off a victim by force; but its use here is metaphorical in that the struggle is for the beliefs of the victims. That is why the first notion, of being misled or deluded, is important: people usually change their beliefs as the result of persuasion rather than force.[3] So the activities of the opponents at Colossae were aimed at deception. They employed specious arguments (*pithanologia*, 2:4)[4] and hollow trickery (*kenē apatē*, 2:8) in order to generate a series of beliefs and practices that reflect merely human teaching (2:8, 22) instead of the wisdom disclosed in Christ. Whatever its specific content, this teaching involved speculation about and worship of angelic beings, and so set itself up as a rival religious system.[5] If this is what *philosophia* means, it must be dangerous. Its methods are unscrupulous, and it replaces Christian teaching with unbridled cosmological speculation. For our untutored readers philosophy can hold nothing of value for faith. One must guard against it, as truth must be guarded from error, and its use on Paul could only be destructive.

Nevertheless our imaginary readers have begun to reason about the matter. If their curiosity should grow a little, they might well pick up other translations of Colossians 2:8, and that would lead to unexpected results. The Revised Standard Version (RSV), like the King James Version (KJV), preserves the English word "philosophy" in its rendering of *philosophia*, but they would quickly discover that other versions have expunged it. They will read of "hollow and delusive speculations, based on traditions of man-made teachings" in the New English Bible (NEB), and more colorfully of "intellectualism or high-sounding nonsense" in J. B. Phillips's paraphrase. If that strikes them as too colorful, they may consult the *Translator's New Testament* (TNT) for its advice, and read there of "false and shallow ideas based on man-made tradition." The Jerusalem Bible (JB) will restore the familiar word, but in its phrase "some second-hand, empty, rational philosophy" they may well find more to surprise them. Sensing their need for help, they will go to the commentators. They will find that some authors, far from denigrating philosophy, place the term in quotation marks to keep them from assuming that Paul meant to refer to philosophy as normally understood. In fact they will be told explicitly that what was offered as "philosophy" in Colossae "had nothing in common with the critical thinking and discerning knowledge of Greek philosophy, except the name."[6] Or again, from another commentator, by *philosophia* we are to understand a "theosophical system," a claim to "master the secrets of the universe" through esoteric knowledge.[7] Still another renders 2:8 as "do not allow yourselves to be victimized by humbug masquerading as philosophy"; for Paul was not hostile to all philosophy but "only to the fantastic angelology which is disqualifying itself by that name at Colossae."[8]

So the untutored opinion was not merely vague and imprecise; it was entirely wrong. Paul is not against philosophy after all, but only against "philosophy."

Now this is a little surprising, because translators do not usually alter so fundamentally the sense of the terms in their texts. It is true that many commentators now regard some statements in 1 Corinthians as coming from a letter from Corinth to Paul, so that Paul simply quotes their words instead of delivering his own opinion.[9] Such added punctuation makes a great difference to interpretation. But of course it cannot be added at whim; so on what grounds is the sense altered in Colossians 2:8?

It is hard to believe that the commentators think Paul a great friend to philosophy in places other than Colossae. He never mentions the subject or names any philosophers in his other extant letters. Even if some philosophical or semiphilosophical vocabulary can be discerned in his writing, we cannot be sure that he cared very much about the philosophers of Greece and Rome. In fact, the opening chapters of 1 Corinthians contain a critique of worldly wisdom that many readers have thought damaging to philosophical endeavor — so much so that chapter 2, below, is devoted to this problem.

There must be another reason, then. The change from philosophy to "philosophy" is made, I think, because translators and commentators regard philosophy itself as something other than whatever they believe the Colossian opponents practised. If they do not spell this out, they may be forgiven a difficult task: but presumably they work with a notion of philosophy as an activity concerned above all for right reasoning. They might say that its aim is to make clear the truth about the world, including truths about human nature, morality, and society; and truths about God and God's relationship to humankind. But even this elementary understanding of philosophy is double-sided. On the one hand, no one would wish to denigrate the concern for truth and right reason. At the same time, not everything that is proclaimed as truth is really true: so there is on the other hand the sinister side in which pretensions to truth beguile the mind through the appearance of wisdom. Any collection of beliefs about the world, God, and humankind could dignify itself by wearing the name of philosophy, just as any catalogue of remedial recipes might claim the name of medicine. The commentators thus preserve the good side of philosophy by labeling the object of Paul's hostility "philosophy" rather than truth or right reason.

This is an attractive explanation for their punctuation. It is strengthened by the observation that Paul on occasion picks up the language of his opposition in order to give it different content,[10] and it is not unthinkable that he himself would have used quotation marks around *philosophia* in 2:8 had the technique been available to him. The explanation accords with Paul's addition of the words "vain deceit" alongside *philosophia*, so that his meaning would be "guard against being captured by that 'philosophy' which is empty deceit," instead of the untutored assumption that he meant "guard against being captured by philosophy, all of which is really empty deceit." Further, the explanation justifies translations that run the two terms together, rendering *philosophia* by "speculation" or "ideas" (though "intellectualism" and "humbug" do stretch the sense). I must add, however, that the Jerusalem Bible's "rational philosophy" remains curious. If its translators do not want us to glory in unreason, they nonetheless strongly suggest that faith should hold the rational suspect — unless they believe that Paul would not condemn a *first*-hand, *non*-empty rational philosophy (whatever that might be).

But what if these commentators have not properly understood the situation in Colossae? After all, the evidence on which our reconstructions of early Christian communities are built remains incomplete and susceptible of conflicting interpretations. Indeed, Professor M. D. Hooker has argued that there is no need to posit a *system* of false teaching in Colossae; and if this is so, then perhaps we are moved away from particular pieces of speculation toward a more general content for *philosophia*.[11] Further, someone might remind us of the point made three paragraphs back, that Paul is not especially encouraging about philosophy. It remains possible, then, that our untutored readers were not wholly mistaken. Perhaps Paul seriously intended to warn his readers against the enterprise of philosophy as he conceived it, regarding philosophers as those who build mere facades on cardboard foundations. The way to truth is not through philosophy: its reasonings must be deposed, as must everything that lifts itself up against the knowledge of God, and all thinking has to be brought to surrender in obedience to Christ.[12]

This possibility must be entertained here, not because it is necessarily the best explanation of Colossians 2:8, but because it returns us to the question with which this section opened — the possibility of a philosophical investigation of themes in Paul's writings. Nevertheless, though it provides a stronger version of Paul's hostility to philosophy, that fact need not embarrass our investigation. For there is a sense in which the warning of this version may be right, and another sense in which it could never be right. The different senses derive from two ways of construing philosophy already recognized in the brief account above. The first emphasizes the search motivated by love (*philia*) of truth; the second stresses the wisdom (*sophia*) that is the goal of that search. In the first way, then, philosophy is preeminently an activity. Its concern is with right reasoning, clear-headedness, problem-solving; it loves truth and is the enemy of confusion and falsehood. It may be practised on a wide range of human intellectual endeavors, investigating methodological issues and assessing types of reasoning. Yet in another way, philosophy is the product of such activity in particular times and places. It yields up conclusions, either piecemeal as solutions to problems or more comprehensively in systems designed as coherent explanations of reality. Philosophers build philosophies and proclaim them to be true. But, as all students know, philosophical solutions compete with each other, so that no reasonable person could believe all that philosophers have written. And because no person of faith should be asked to do what a reasonable person cannot do, it seems that there may be a point to the Pauline warning. Philosophers themselves tell their students and readers to be on guard against other philosophers; indeed it is periodically the conviction of some thinkers that previous philosophy has so misconstrued its problems that the whole enterprise requires a fresh start. "Beware of philosophy" was preached first to Colossae, but philosophers to our own day have added their "amen."

I do not claim of course that this is how a Pauline disapproval of philosophy is to be interpreted historically. If there was a strong suspicion of philosophy itself in Paul's mind, it would be related to his perception of the incompatibility of the claims of philosophy with the truth of the gospel, not to any notion of how philosophy reforms itself. Still, that is not necessarily an intellectual embarrassment. One good reason for suspecting a particular philosophical system is its inability to accept or account for beliefs that one holds to be more evidently true than the system in question. Whether Paul's warning was directed against a falsely dignified "philosophy," or against all philosophies without room for God, the warning may be sound. It is not the voice of unreason that speaks here.

At least, it is not unreason's voice as long as Paul does not intend hostility toward philosophy in the first sense. For were he to attack, not this or that philosophy, but the very enterprise of right thinking, our embarrassment would be severe. He could never be right about that, and the strength of this claim must be emphasized. The point is not about what Paul in fact did, although I think it historically proper to believe that Paul wanted to reason rightly, to avoid the false and love the true. He speaks of knowledge and wisdom, and works at establishing claims through argumentation. The point is rather that he could not have done otherwise without destroying logical integrity and intelligibility. For it is not in any of us to hold on to what we believe to be false; to accomplish that feat we must resort to the devices of self-deception. At the very least, then, we must convince ourselves and others that we love the truth. But this means that the enterprise of philosophy is a fundamental human activity: we must all beware of shoddy reasoning and muddled-mindedness. To counsel otherwise is to be willing to believe a lie; and to provide arguments against philosophy in this sense is to land in contradiction, for it would require one to give good reasons why good reasons should not be given.

I conclude that the warning to the Colossians, though blunt, should not be heard as a protest against rational inquiry. Insofar as Paul's writing uses argument upon themes open to philosophical investigation, his writing may be examined with the tools of philosophy. Far from being perverse, this kind of scrutiny is necessary, for one can buy immunity from philosophical assessment only at the price of unintelligibility. If Paul would not approve of philosophical studies in his thought, his disagreement would best be founded on the difference between his own claims and the deliverances of particular philosophies. The real embarrassment between Paul and the activity of philosophy will lie only in a refusal to examine the meaning of his language, the scope of his terms, or the implications of his arguments. But because there is no historical evidence for that kind of attitude on Paul's part, and because not even his readers most suspicious themselves of philosophy are stubborn to that degree, I conclude that there are no impediments to my philosophical investigations in Paul's writings.

For some the supposed impediment of Colossians 2:8 will have been forced in the first place. Nevertheless the discussion is useful. Our untutored or embarrassed readers may be just straw men. But even if this is so, the point to consider is not the ease with which they are toppled, but how it is that the stuffing is taken out of them. For what we have been up to is itself philosophical. We have just engaged in a specific piece of reasoning about a Pauline text in order to make general claims about Paul and philosophy, and that reasoning has made use of philosophical distinctions and arguments. Although we have tried to take account of historical information and theological claims, in the end we have decided the case by reflecting on what would follow from Paul's decision to regard philosophy in one way rather than another. And in the process we have learned a little about philosophy as activity as well as product, and how it may be related to faith.

II. Paul and These Studies

It is now time to say a little more about what these philosophical studies are and are not. Since my chief interest in this section is to abort certain misconceptions about the enterprise, I begin with the negative.

It is natural to assume that a study of Paul and philosophy will be concerned with the philosophical systems and schools of Paul's time and his relationships to them. That kind of study belongs to intellectual history, an entirely respectable discipline that may well have insights to offer Pauline studies. Crucial to its success is the question of what Paul knew about Greco-Roman philosophy, or (less stringently) what general philosophical influences may be discerned in his writings. Various proposals have been mounted and debated, and some light on Paul discovered from this source. His style has been compared to that of Cynics and Stoics; and a recent major commentary on Galatians places Paul squarely in the tradition of Greek rhetoric and apologetic.[13] His ethical teachings are said to have parallels with those of the Stoic writers Musonius Rufus and his pupil Epictetus.[14] Some of Paul's imagery may reflect a similar source, for instance his use of the athletic metaphors of struggle and discipline.[15] Or his notion of conscience may have Stoic roots, since it is not an Old Testament concept.[16]

Although such studies of Paul's relationships to philosophy in his day deserve attention, this book does not take that approach. There are two reasons for this, the second more compelling than the first. The first is a personal observation. It strikes me that, when all is said and done, one still needs little of the *content* of ancient philosophy in order to read Paul. Perhaps it is significant that the most fruitful investigations have concerned themselves with philosophical style, broadly conceived: for when one searches for evidence in Paul of the fundamental metaphysical, epistemological, and ethical concerns of philosophy, or for the most important building blocks of philosophy, philosophical concepts and vocabulary, there is not a great deal that can be brought to the surface for clear inspection. Nor is it obvious that whatever survives scrutiny will require us to believe that Paul had anything approaching a professional interest in, or detailed acquaintance with, philosophical schools and systems. (It is not necessary to say that this would not be surprising. How much do philosophers today, all of whom know about Paul, know of his thought? How much do theologians, all of whom can speak about logical positivism, know of philosophy?) So if one does not view Paul as doing in substance what his philosophical contemporaries were doing, or as paying much attention to them, then one does not write a book on the relationships between Paul and the philosophy of his time. That is not to say that interesting comparisons could not be made between what Paul was up to, and what philosophers were up to, especially in ethics. Nor is it to claim that my observations are hardened beyond possible revision, and that is why I offer a second, stronger, reason for the approach this book does take.

Suppose in the luxury of imagination that a hundred major historical problems about Paul have been solved. Scholars have celebrated their agreement over issues about Paul's text, relative influences upon his thought, the nature of opposition to his teaching, the shape of early Christian communities. Expressions like "Hellenistic Judaism" and "protognosticism" have been spelled out with care in the light of indubitable evidence. An impossible dream, granted. But what is interesting about it is that such a state of affairs would not itself guarantee the end to every kind of disagreement about Paul. Scholars would still argue — not over the "facts," as they might put it, but over what it all *means*. For (to put it another way) the task of interpretation would still remain. Though it is not easy to say what interpretation is, we might express it crudely as follows. Not all the historical information we desire could ever disclose exactly what went on in Paul's mind: to know that we should have to become Paul himself. Because we are who we are, we can approach Paul only through his writings and other sources of information about his actions and beliefs. But it is impossible to do this from outside our own time and identity. Interpretation must attempt to close the gap between Paul's mind and our own minds. But since the distance always remains, and Paul's readers come and go, the interpretive task is never complete. Moreover, the task has important philosophical dimensions when practised on a writer like Paul, for he touches on issues of philosophical importance. Even when we think we have reliable historical information, we need to ask how his concepts relate to our categories of thought and expression. Even if we believe we know what he was attempting to argue, we must ask whether his desired conclusions follow from his premises. Besides, when we read Paul we look through layers of other interpretations and must continually ask ourselves whether his text supports in fact what rival readers claim it supports.

Although I shall soon speak more specifically about philosophical practice upon Paul, it is enough for now to recognize the interest of philosophy in the processes of analysis, interpretation, and assessment of argument and reasoning. That interest is not satisfied by the discovery of sources for or parallels to Paul's thought, important as those issues are in themselves. And they *are* important; otherwise we will practise interpretation upon defective material. So I have attempted to be sensitive to these matters in the studies that follow. Nevertheless the crucial issues for philosophy are those not finally determinable through historical investigation alone; and that is the reason that compelled me to focus on the meaning and implications of Paul's text rather than on intellectual relationships with his philosophical contemporaries.[17]

Another possible misconception of the aim of this book requires a comment. Someone may believe, not that Paul was a professional philosopher in the Greek or Roman sense, but that he was nonetheless a powerful thinker with a vision of the world, humankind, and God. So a philosophical investigation of Paul's thought would take as its aim the discovery, refinement, and reconstruction of a philosophical system from the writings of Paul. If Paul did not write in a philosophically systematic way, that does not prevent the skilled reader from working out the vision: after all, philosophers have to do the same sort of thing with Plato's dialogues in order to develop a comprehensive Platonism. Such is the confidence of one writer a life span ago:

It is safe to say that though Paul was not consciously working out a philosophy of religion and of religious history, every such philosophy that will command the ultimate assent of thoughtful, earnestly ethical men must be constructed along the lines which he has laid down, and incorporate the great ideas that lived in his mighty brain and glowed in his throbbing heart.[18]

No doubt the sensibilities of present-day journal editors would remove the anatomical references: even then, however, it would not be safe to say all this. For I doubt that Paul was a crypto-philosopher, an unconscious philosopher, or a manufacturer of enough philosophical blocks for experts to assemble into a recognizable shape. It has often been pointed out that he was not a systematic writer at all; but what is decisive for the matter is not the lack of system but the lack of philosophical content. A philosophy must be comprehensive, with something to say on the major themes of metaphysics, epistemology, practical philosophy, and the like. It must moreover attempt to argue for the truth and consistency of its claims, even if they are not packaged in neat and ordered fashion. Paul, in contrast to Plato, does practically nothing of this, which makes the comparison inapt.

It does not follow that philosophical theology will have no relationship to Paul's thought, or that Paul does not impinge upon the philosophy of religion. My studies demonstrate otherwise, I trust. But they do not expect to find answers to a complete range of philosophical questions in Paul, nor do they assume that there are enough lines for a Christian philosophy to be traced in his thought. Rather, their description as studies *in* Paul is deliberate: they pick up a series of philosophically interesting problems from 1 Corinthians, without pretending to be either exhaustive or systematic.

So this book does not ask the questions of intellectual history or attempt to create a comprehensive philosophical vision for Paul. Moreover, it would be misleading to regard it as an exercise in theology or philosophy as they are usually practised. Many of the Pauline themes that interest New Testament theologians are absent, or at least muted: there is nothing of Paul's soteriology or christology, little about law or spirit, something of eschatology but not a fully orchestrated account. This is because the controlling mood of the studies is philosophical.

Nevertheless, this book will not look like the sort of study that philosophers of religion write these days. There is no discussion of arguments for God's existence, no assessment of the coherence of theism, no exploration of the meaning of religious language or religious experience. In a sense the direction of this book is against one strong current in contemporary philosophy of religion: these studies focus on basic texts of early Christianity, whereas other philosophers have broadened their interests to include a variety of religions in their discussions of philosophical problems.[19] All the same, the problems worked on here are recognizably traditional, set for the philosophy of religion by the Judeo-Christian tradition. They concern epistemological questions, such as the character of our present knowledge of God and the relationship between faith and reason; problems in metaphysics, such as the nature of resurrected persons and their relationship to God; ethical issues, such as the role of authority, or the interests of other people, in determining the right thing to do. What is unusual is that these philosophical concerns are treated, not on their own, but in close relationship to Paul's text.[20]

This means, then, that the philosophical aspect of these studies reflects not so much the *products* of philosophy as its *activity*. Philosophy is used as a tool upon an important biblical text in order to expose facets of its meaning. Part of the activity may be called conceptual analysis, in which a puzzling term is made to disclose its meaning through an examination of the ways in which it is used. We did that with *philosophia* in the previous section; and in the following chapters I take on such concepts as "conscience," "love," "body," "worldly wisdom," and the like, in order to determine how Paul's Greek might relate to the understandings we have of such concepts in our own language.

That kind of analysis is important for clear understanding, but it is only one philosophical task. Paul also engages in arguments: he gives reasons, for instance, why one should sometimes refrain from a permissible action. Even when all the relevant concepts are sorted out, there remain the issues of the cogency and validity of an argument, and its applicability in a variety of circumstances. Philosophical activity thus includes this kind of assessment, and it is practised on several texts of 1 Corinthians in the following studies. Furthermore, philosophy asks about the consistency and compatibility of different beliefs; it is interested in what follows from what, what does not follow but does not contradict, and what cannot follow at all. Much of the argumentation of this book is of this order. It asks, not only about the consistency of Paul's beliefs, but more especially about the relationship of Paul's text to beliefs held by others, including philosophers of religion. For example, it is often believed that religious ethics is a matter of obedience to authority. Does an analysis of Paul's method of argument in 1 Corinthians 7 support this belief? Or again: Paul writes of a resurrection body, but qualifies his language in interesting ways. Is the notion of a disembodied resurrected person incompatible with his text?

Though neither pure theology nor pure philosophy, these studies will have implications for Pauline scholars, for theologians, and for philosophers of religion. Those concerned primarily with the question of what Paul is about will find that philosophical tools have a familiar feel: they themselves ask about the behavior of concepts and the consistency of claims in Paul. Where they come to conclusions different from mine, it may be because of a disagreement over particular facts, or a decision to take a different interpretive move. Nevertheless, as a nonspecialist in this field I have been interested to see if the understanding of Paul's text can be advanced even where historical claims are not finally settled. And if such understandings as I offer here — say, of Paul's use of ethical authorities or his critique of worldly wisdom — are faulty, then I hope Pauline scholars will ask for a better practice of philosophy instead of deciding to throw its tools away.

There are implications for theologians and philosophers as well. It is a familiar feature of the academic landscape that as one moves through systematic and philosophical theology and over to philosophy of religion, the detailed study of Paul's text is left further and further behind. Naturally enough, scholars have their own territories. But the attitude of theology toward reason, for example, has deep roots in Paul's writings. So my analysis of the scope and function of reason within faith as it might relate to the Pauline critique may speak to this fundamental issue; and my characterization of our present knowledge of God in chapter 7, below, may bear upon the very nature of the theological enterprise. Likewise philosophers of religion might find their problems reshaped through a close examination of the meaning and implications of Paul's text. My reflections on wisdom suggest a role for reason within faith, which, though as old as Augustine, tends to be forgotten in disputes between natural theology and fideism. The discussion of resurrection not only exposes tensions between theology and philosophy but also calls for more philosophical work in the development of a logically consistent Christian eschatology. The analysis of ethical authorities raises doubts about the adequacy of a simple ethic of commands — doubts reinforced by the demonstration, in the studies of the weak and of accommodation, that Paul's ethical principles require careful interpretation rather than straightforward imitation or obedience. Finally, an appreciation of the imperfections of our present knowledge may call for a reshaping of our understanding of love and may speak to the problem of evil.

But I have said too much and too little about what these studies are and are not. In that I have only illustrated points of contact between philosophy, theology, and Paul's text, I have not adequately described their many interrelationships, nor defended against all objections the practice of philosophy on this subject matter. In another way, though, my comments may be too much. Readers will find their own ways into this material: they will, I hope, discern relationships and implications not evident to me. For that reason they should seek not to be influenced too strongly by this Introduction. If its recipe seems wrong—the ingredients faulty or mixed improperly—I beg them nevertheless to prove the pudding in the usual way.

III. SOME COMMON THREADS

Finally, to leave eating for sewing, I promised some comment on how the studies are stitched together.

Most obvious is a formal feature. All these studies deal with 1 Corinthians, and in being stitched to that letter they enjoy a kind of unity. However, such formality does not help a great deal, for the unity of 1 Corinthians itself is problematic. It is a collection of advice, comment, and reaction from Paul to a variety of issues, generated in part by a letter from the Corinthians to him and in part by a separate report on problems within the community.[21] Nevertheless for my purposes this has two advantages. First, the range of topics dealt with is philosophically promising: it embraces epistemological, ethical, and metaphysical problems. Secondly, the variety emphasizes the analytic character of my approach, which focuses on specific philosophical questions rather than attempting to build a systematic account. For that reason this book is not a philosophical commentary on the letter as a whole; indeed, I have deliberately placed the study of 1 Corinthians 15 immediately after the investigation of 1 Corinthians 1–4 to stress this fact. I do not mean by this that the letter itself should be broken apart to feed any interest whatever. On the contrary, I argue strongly in chapter 2, below, for holding the first four chapters together, and my chapter 5 aims at a coherent account of 1 Corinthians 8 and 10. Still, the guiding conviction that Paul is not a systematic philosopher in disguise prevents this book from achieving systematic unity.

Are there any other ties between the studies, perhaps threads in the warp and woof instead of stitches at the seams alone? The studies do share a stronger methodological unity. They worry the text for its meaning, but not always in the same way. Sometimes I exhibit purely formal features of Paul's language, as in my chapter 4; sometimes I look for formal clusters of concepts, as in chapter 2. Or again, literary aspects, such as irony (chapter 2) or metaphor (chapter 7), play a role in interpretation. But whatever techniques seem appropriate for specific texts, the approach is persistently philosophical. Always the motivating questions are puzzles about Paul's meaning in connection with some philosophical problem posed for or within faith; always the solution requires us to expose his reasoning, chart the use of his concepts, assess the implications of his claims for various alternatives.

Two other kinds of thread are common to the studies, and each asks for brief remarks. The first will have been visible already, and may be found woven through the language of succeeding chapters. It is the recurrent pattern of speaking from within faith to the issues addressed in the book. So it might be legitimately asked whether my arguments require faith, and Christian faith in particular, before they can get off the ground. In answer I shall acknowledge freely that much of my concern is with philosophical perplexity and resolution for believers, who wonder how faith should sit with reason, how they are to speak of resurrection, love God with limited understanding, obey with intelligence in situations where principles or authorities compete for their allegiance. And unless readers have some interest in the Judeo-Christian tradition,[22] they may not find the motivation to work through studies in problems such as these. Nevertheless this thread can be pulled from my language without unraveling the very fabric of the studies. For one thing, those with another faith, or without faith, may ask similar kinds of questions by doing a little mental translating or rephrasing. And for another, one needs to believe nothing on faith or religious authority in order to assess the validity of the reasoning I engage in here. The employment of philosophical tools is neutral with respect to faith, even though faith may have a vital interest in the beliefs upon which reasoning is done and in the conclusions reached. Moveover, there are reasons why both believers and nonbelievers should engage in such activity. In illustration, it can be argued that it is better that (say) Platonists and non-Platonists work together at Plato's text. For Platonists, wishing to defend Plato, will not abandon arguments that are difficult or seem inconclusive. But because their commitment can mist their vision, they need the colder eye of the critic to keep them honest. The uncommitted, for their part, may lack the motive to win as clear an understanding as may be possible — so they will want to listen carefully to the defender. For similar reasons the critic is invited to these studies.

Finally, consider the second pattern of thread common to all these studies: the theme of partial knowledge. It is openly displayed in the final chapter of this book, as I explore the implications of Paul's description of our present knowledge of God as puzzling and indirect. But it is also the conclusion of chapter 3, for there I argue that a philosophically and theologically adequate account of resurrection sets limits on our knowing and speaking of life after death. And there is another manifestation of the pattern of this theme. Time and again I argue that, even within the context of a faith that accepts the biblical text as serving revelation, the text is not sufficient for understanding or obedience. If the commands of God, the teaching of Jesus, and apostolic advice all help the believer know what to do, this knowledge remains inescapably partial, because it always requires interpretation and application. If it is right not to cause my brother to stumble, that is only a partial truth, in that it is also right for me to exercise my freedom, and right for him to learn to see that. Again, accommodation to others is only justifiable in part: in certain circumstances, to accommodate would be morally or theologically wrong, even dangerous. Nevertheless this strong thread should not be weakened into skepticism or agnosticism. As I argue in chapter 2, reason must not be banished from faith. Faith strives for understanding; and when it has not attained it, it still presses forward in hope. Where its reflections remain puzzling, it holds to the promise of that light in which it will know, and be known, face to face.

That, however, is only at the end. I start in the next chapter with the claim that reason, and therefore philosophy, has nothing to do with the understanding available to faith. My Introduction has come back to its beginning; so it is time to move on.

CHAPTER TWO

Faith, Wisdom, and Philosophy: 1 Corinthians 1–4

> Nobody, under the guidance of nature, has ever made such progress as to come to know God. If anyone puts forward philosophers as exceptions to this, I reply that in their case especially there is a conspicuous example of our weakness. For you cannot find one of them who has not constantly fallen away from that principle of knowledge which I have already mentioned, to wanderings and misleading speculations. They are mostly sillier than old wives.   John Calvin, 1546

Relationships between faith and reason have often been difficult, and in their long history Paul has occupied an important place. Although the role of reason in human knowledge of God is not a major theme of his writings, Paul says enough to provoke in his readers some interest in the question, and of all passages in his letters the opening chapters of 1 Corinthians have been especially provocative. It is true that the first chapters of Romans have some bearing on the issue, but there Paul is more interested in lack of faith despite the knowledge of God he assumes all human beings to have.[1] In 1 Corinthians, however, he takes on human wisdom itself, arguing that the cross of Christ has nothing to do with fine words or the world's wisdom; indeed those who put their faith in human wisdom are completely wrong, fools in God's eyes. Where there is wisdom available to faith, it rests not on wise words but on the revelation God has provided through the Spirit.

We do not know exactly how Paul's readers in Corinth took this, for the theme is not treated in his later correspondence with them. Long generations of later readers, however, have regarded Paul as mounting a critique of philosophy so damaging that faith must regard philosophical activity as religiously illegitimate. It is beyond my task here to chart the history of this interpretation, but an illustration may be found in Calvin's words cited above, from his commentary on these chapters of 1 Corinthians.[2] Nor can I hope to account for the wider dispute between faith and philosophy, which may be read elsewhere.[3] Instead my focus is on Paul's reasoning itself. I want to know what follows for the relationship between philosophy and faith from Paul's text. That many Christians have invested Paul's attitude toward reason with authority may provide context and motivation for a study of this nature; but that point plays no part in the argument. I want rather to illuminate Paul's meaning and to assess the implications of his claims.

The study proceeds in several sections. Although the major part concerns Paul's critique of wisdom, I begin with a consideration of the first four chapters of the letter as a whole. There is a natural inclination, encouraged by commentaries that analyze bits of the text, to carve out sections of the letter dealing with a particular theme. Sometimes that works. But 1 Corinthians is not a systematic treatise, and its unity is a special problem for scholars. Although questions about the structure and language of the passage are not highly philosophical, they are crucial for an adequate interpretation; so I propose to treat the development of theme and the character of the language in chapters 1 to 4 as an important issue. In the light of this treatment I shall move to Paul's critique of the Corinthians, and then more centrally to his critique of wisdom. This central section contains four parts: I review general questions about faith and reason; then I go through Paul's arguments. From these arguments emerge two issues: the nature of worldly wisdom and the religious impotence of reason. The final section of the study states my conclusions about faith, wisdom, and philosophy in 1 Corinthians 1–4.

I. Structure, Language, Theme

In order to treat 1 Corinthians 1–4 as a whole, I begin with questions of its unity. Most commentators acknowledge that the chapters form a unit in response to information received by Paul from Chloe's people,[4] but there seems little agreement about internal unity of theme and coherence of structure. Certain features of Paul's writing have suggested to some a lack of careful construction and only weak connections between the subsections of the passage. There are marks of hasty composition: perhaps Paul dictated without bothering to correct.[5] And the emotional level, especially in chapter 4, is very high. When one thinks in addition to the number of different topics treated, it is possible to see why Hans Conzelmann thinks that 1:20–4:21 is "not a unity, neither in style nor in content."[6] Its boundaries are marked for Conzelmann only formally, by parenetic style in Paul's opening and closing exhortations.

Within the section, however, the only unity comes from an underlying theological concern with the cross of Christ.

John Hurd has pointed to marked differences between Paul's comment on oral reports about Corinthian problems and his answers to written communications from the Corinthians. When replying to a question they have written about, he is systematic, calm, and persuasive;[7] but his reaction to news of divisions or immorality is angry, black-and-white, condemnatory and authoritative.[8] Chapters 1–4 fall into the latter group. We shall see, however, that Hurd's blanket characterization is too simple a description of the passage. It might also suggest a lack of sustained argument on Paul's part, though Hurd does try to discern a thematic unity by positing an alternation and then an interweaving of the two topics of quarreling and of wisdom throughout the section.[9] C. K. Barrett uses these two concepts in the heading for his section, "Wisdom and Division at Corinth," though for him "the underlying subject matter" is the "Gospel, and the calling, responsibility, and duty of those who preach and those who hear it."[10]

Such themes are of course present, but that assertion does not by itself show how they work coherently together to control the language and concerns of the section. A rather different approach follows H. St. John Thackeray's suggestion that the passage has the same flavor as the homily on wisdom in the Book of Baruch; it is reminiscent of a sermon preached on the ninth of Ab, a fast day with a prophetical lesson from Jeremiah 8:13–9:24. W. Wuellner has worked out in some detail an analysis of the Old Testament quotations Paul uses, in the light of such sermon patterns. Although this approach may help explain Paul's context, its greatest disadvantage is that it makes the end of chapter 3 the climax of the passage, and chapter 4 an unrelated appendage.[11]

I offer here, then, a different approach. It does not rest primarily upon the topics dealt with or an underlying theological perspective; nor does it propose slicing up the text into newly organized bits. Rather I retain the standard subdivisions, but ask about two characteristics of Paul's writing: its tone or emotional intensity, and the level at which it is aimed, whether specific or more general.

We may leave aside the set formality of the introduction and begin with the section 1:10–16. Every commentator remarks on the abrupt entrance, and the surprisingly strong and urgent appeal for unity in the midst of divisions and strife. In vv. 14–16 Paul falls over his words a little; but by the next section, vv. 17–25, the language, though powerful, is well controlled as he passes to a general questioning of all human wisdom. At v. 26 he becomes specific again, applying what he has said to the Corinthians, though without urgency or anger. He continues to speak in specific terms about his own relationship to them in 2:1-5. Then at 2:6 the discussion takes up a positive view of wisdom, and continues on a general level in an explanatory tone until the rhetorical question at the end of the chapter.

In the next section, at 3:1, Paul returns to the specific Corinthian situation, applying again his teaching about wisdom to them: but his tone betrays an underlying annoyance in his three successive questions in vv. 3-5, as the issue of divisions and strife is recalled. Nevertheless the feeling is controlled as he moves on from v. 6 to explain in his well-known agricultural and architectural metaphors the cooperation between Apollos and himself; the level grows general, the tone didactic, as he develops the metaphors and the theme of judgment. The section ends, however, with a question and a warning, vv. 16-17. Paul then moves back to his earlier critique of wisdom, linking it more pointedly to the Corinthians in vv. 18-23.

Chapter 4 returns to judgment in vv. 1-5; although the language attempts to be explanatory, the tone is hortatory and a little testy. But from v. 6 on, Paul becomes direct, very specific, and accusatory. He employs powerful language with a full range of rhetorical tools, including irony and sarcasm, to bring into stark contrast the conditions of the Corinthians and the apostles. The central issue is the bloated misconceptions about their status to which the Corinthians have fallen prey. In trying to break through their pride, Paul seems conscious of the strength of his feelings: like an exasperated father he tries to justify his outburst by explaining his intentions (v. 14), but even so the passage ends with the language of threat.

From this brief characterization it will be apparent that the emotional intensity of Paul's writing is not uniform throughout chapters 1-4. There is no "unity" in overt tone; but there does seem to be a depth of feeling that binds together the whole passage. It is present at the beginning and the end; but "parenesis" is too weak a description, for Paul is not simply exhorting the Corinthians. He is upset with them, as his opening appeal shows. Yet he controls his strong feelings, allowing them little direct expression until the beginning of chapter 3. They come to the fore again in the questions and warnings at the end of that chapter, but it is not until the stinging irony of chapter 4 that they are unleashed. Seen in this light, the entire section is held together and sustained by an emotion that reaches its climax only in chapter 4; and if this is so, it is to this climax that we must look to understand Paul's true feelings for the Corinthians and his assessment of their condition.

I may now relate the intensity of Paul's language to my second concern, the degree of generality in his writing, and ask how both concerns bear upon the two themes of division and wisdom in the chapters. A glance back at my description of tone in the various subsections will show that Paul's particularly intense feelings toward the Corinthians surface when the level of writing is specific (though that is not to deny the strength of his language in the more general passages). As Hurd reminds us, Paul is reacting to a verbal report about divisions, so we might expect the entire section to be angry, not calm or persuasive. But we may now see why Hurd's characterization is too simple. Paul's initial disclosure that he has been told of divisions in Corinth is specific and urgent, condemnatory, and upset if not angry. The matter of divisions provokes his three questions in 3:3–5, ending with "What then is Apollos? What is Paul?" His answer, that he himself is not unusual enough to warrant either a party following or criticism from anyone other than God, is given in an explanatory manner, in metaphors that work on a general level, and in tones not angry or condemnatory.

The emotional pitch on the subject of divisions starts off high, but falls away in the course of these chapters. On the other hand, the theme of wisdom works in the opposite way. Paul's discussion of wisdom, both negative and positive, is mainly in general terms, containing no actual criticism of the Corinthians until he points out in 3:1–2 that they were (and are yet) unable to share in God's wisdom, because of their condition. By 3:18ff. he has become more direct, applying his critique of worldly wisdom in general from chapter 1 to the Corinthians themselves, though hypothetically. In 4:6ff. the hypotheticals drop away as he finally lets loose his emotion against their conceited wisdom.

I suggest, then, that in 1 Corinthians 1–4 Paul writes passionately at times, and at times more calmly and persuasively. He engages in general critique and explanation as well as in specific condemnation and application. Although he takes his emotional clue from the subject of divisions, something else vexes him more deeply, for his writing on that issue loses its specific and condemnatory flavor. Instead his real concern becomes uncovered in chapter 4: not divisions, but the false wisdom that the Corinthians believe themselves to possess.[12] The force and movement of Paul's writing lands us in chapter 4, and it seems best to take its theme of conceited boasting as Paul's motivating concern in the first four chapters of this letter. This unites the two themes of division and wisdom as symptom and cause, and holds promise for a more adequate understanding of the nature of that wisdom to which both faith and philosophy are related.

Before beginning to see how that promise may be made good, however, I want to approach the issue of the structure of 1 Corinthians 1–4 in a rather different way. Suppose we ask, not about the tone or level of Paul's language, but instead about its vocabulary, in order to discover the key concepts with which he works. This kind of analysis can be quite sophisticated, employing computer techniques to display frequencies of occurrences and even patterns of associations among several terms.[13] Hunting concepts and not just words is, however, more like skilled sport than science (and as with other kinds of hunting raises the problem of what is to be done with the catch). So we shall not do a frequency count (*theos* would come out high), but instead ask ourselves what preys on Paul's mind in these chapters that interests us, and make that our quarry. We are interested in wisdom: but I have suggested that the whole section is pulled toward chapter 4 for its meaning, and there the dominant themes are boasting and conceit. So, as we must not unstitch patches of verses in the whole quilt of chapters 1–4, we must refrain from drawing out only the thread of wisdom language in the passage. Because of their ties with each other, I propose as candidates for the search the concepts of wisdom and foolishness, power and weakness, and boasting. They will have to be considered with care throughout this entire investigation into faith, wisdom, and philosophy. But since we are only at the level of the structure of the passage, we may for now ask just how those concepts cluster together throughout chapters 1–4. A simple way to do this is in a superficial visual presentation.

First we assign labels. Let W stand for terms for wisdom, knowledge, reason, or word (those with Greek will recognize such terms as *sophia, logos, gignôskein, eidenai, phronimos*). F will represent foolishness (*môria*). Power or strength (*dunamis, ischus*) will be P. X will stand for not just weakness but also lack of ability or status: they go together here (*asthenia*, but also *ta mê onta, katargesthai, ou dunami, mataios*). Finally B will stand for boasting and being puffed up (*kauchaomai, phusaomai*).

Next we can assign the appropriate labels to each verse in chapters 1:17 to 4:21 where these concepts are present. We then picture the result in Table 1.

Finally we must decide whether this tells us anything. It is important to realize that we have not discovered the concepts themselves in this display, but only a kind of map for more sustained and systematic hunting. Even the map has its problems: its lumping together of terms for wisdom and word, for instance, requires justification. Nevertheless the display does have some limited value. It demonstrates the pervasiveness of these themes and their interweaving, so that we may be willing to see the metaphor of interweaving as more suited to our five concepts than to the two themes of wisdom and division — especially because the latter theme disappears. The display thus acts as a corrective to more restricted perceptions of the passage, which either focus on wisdom without regard for its associated concepts, or else see only some lines in the pattern instead of the entire complex.[14] Further, it has heuristic value: it shows us that the five themes cluster together in chapter 4 and at the end of chapter 1 as well, with four of the five present near the end of chapter 3.

Although these considerations of structure, language, and movement in the first four chapters of 1 Corinthians cannot themselves determine the full meaning of the text, nevertheless they do encourage us to look to the fourth chapter for our understanding of Paul's intentions and his working out of the themes of the passage. This means that we may well have to read the earlier chapters in the light of chapter 4. Details of plot and characterization in a literary work achieve fuller meaning when reflected upon in the light of the whole story; discursive writing sometimes works this way too, being best appreciated from the vantage point of its conclusions. However, whether we can make substantive gains in our understanding of 1 Corinthians 1–4 in this fashion requires more than these suspicions engendered by the more formal features of the text;

TABLE 1

Occurrence of Five Key Concepts in 1 Cor. 1:17–4:21

Ch.	v.	W	F	P	X	B	Ch.	v.	W	F	P	X	B	Ch.	v.	W	F	P	X	B
I.	17	W	.	.	.	.		11	W	.	.	.	.		20	W	.	.	X	.
	18	W	F	P	.	.		12	W	.	.	.	.		21	.	.	.	.	B
	19	W	.	.	.	.		13	W	.	.	.	.		22	.	.	.	.	.
	20	W	F	.	.	.		14	W	F	.	.	.		23	.	.	.	.	.
	21	W	F	.	.	.		15	.	.	.	.	.	IV.	1	.	.	.	.	.
	22	W	.	.	.	.		16	W	.	.	.	.		2	.	.	.	.	.
	23	.	F	.	.	.	III.	1	.	.	.	X	.		3	.	.	.	.	.
	24	W	.	P	.	.		2	.	.	.	X	.		4	.	.	.	.	.
	25	W	F	P	X	.		3	.	.	.	.	.		5	.	.	.	.	.
	26	W	.	P	.	.		4	.	.	.	.	.		6	.	.	.	.	B
	27	W	F	P	X	.		5	.	.	.	.	.		7	.	.	.	.	B
	28	.	.	.	X	.		6	.	.	.	.	.		8	.	.	.	.	.
	29	.	.	.	.	B		7	.	.	.	.	.		9	.	.	.	X	.
	30	W	.	.	.	.		8	.	.	.	.	.		10	W	F	P	.	.
	31	.	.	.	.	B		9	.	.	.	.	.		11	.	.	.	.	.
II.	1	W	.	.	.	.		10	W	.	.	.	.		12	.	.	.	.	.
	2	W	.	.	.	.		11	.	.	.	.	.		13	.	.	.	.	.
	3	.	.	.	X	.		12	.	.	.	.	.		14	.	.	.	.	.
	4	W	.	P	.	.		13	.	.	.	.	.		15	.	.	.	.	.
	5	W	.	P	.	.		14	.	.	.	.	.		16	.	.	.	.	.
	6	W	.	.	X	.		15	.	.	.	.	.		17	.	.	.	.	.
	7	W	.	.	.	.		16	.	.	.	.	.		18	.	.	.	.	B
	8	W	.	.	.	.		17	.	.	.	.	.		19	W	.	P	.	B
	9	.	.	.	.	.		18	W	F	.	.	.		20	W	.	P	.	.
	10	.	.	.	.	.		19	W	F	.	.	.		21	.	.	.	.	.

so it is to the content of Paul's writing that we must now turn. We begin then at the end, with Paul's full-blooded critique of the Corinthians in 4:6–21.

II. PAUL'S CRITIQUE OF THE CORINTHIANS

To this point in the letter Paul has expressed disapproval of the Corinthians because of their divisions (1:10–12) and chided them for their immaturity (3:1–4). In order to reduce possible grounds for split allegiances, he has emphasized the cooperative venture of Apollos and himself, explaining that the full assessment of each man's work and worth is in the end God's prerogative (3:5–16; 4:1–5). Although the themes of foolishness, deception, and boasting enter at the end of chapter 3, it is in chapter 4 that they receive full attention.

Paul starts by saying that he has discussed himself and Apollos so that the Corinthians will not be puffed up one against the other.[15] The passage (4:6–21, RSV) reads:

> [6]I have applied all this to myself and Apollos for your benefit, brethren, that you may learn by us to live according to scripture, that none of you may be puffed up in favor of one against another. [7]For who sees anything different in you? What have you that you did not receive? If then you received it, why do you boast as if it were not a gift?
>
> [8]Already you are filled! Already you have become rich! Without us you have become kings! And would that you did reign, so that we might share the rule with you! [9]For I think that God has exhibited us apostles as last of all, like men sentenced to death; because we have become a spectacle to the world, to angels and to men. [10]We are fools for Christ's sake, but you are wise in Christ. We are weak, but you are strong. You are held in honor, but we in disrepute. [11]To the present hour we hunger and thirst, we are ill-clad and buffeted and homeless, [12]and we labor, working with our own hands. When reviled, we bless; when persecuted, we endure; [13]when slandered, we try to conciliate; we have become, and are now, as the refuse of the world, the offscouring of all things.
>
> [14]I do not write this to make you ashamed, but to admonish you as my beloved children. [15]For though you have countless guides in Christ, you do not have many fathers. For I became your father in Christ Jesus through the gospel. [16]I urge you, then, be imitators of me. [17]Therefore I sent to you Timothy, my beloved and faithful child in the Lord, to remind you of my ways in Christ, as I teach

them everywhere in every church. [18]Some are arrogant, as though I were not coming to you. [19]But I will come to you soon, if the Lord wills, and I will find out not the talk of these arrogant people but their power. [20]For the kingdom of God does not consist in talk but in power. [21]What do you wish? Shall I come to you with a rod, or with love in a spirit of gentleness?

We have already noted the passion of Paul's language and his use of rhetorical tools to attack the Corinthians. Here we need reflect only on the most striking and effective of these tools, the irony strongly present in vv. 8–10.

I have included v. 9 as ironic, but that demands some explanation. Paul uses the image of theatrical spectacle in the arena not to liken life to a contest or drama[16] so much as to express vividly the world's regard for Paul and other apostles: they are the poor wretches at the tail end of the show, already condemned to death, without intrinsic rights or value, and good only as sport for depraved appetites. The irony does not lie in an intentional inversion of terms describing the treatment the apostles have received, for Paul goes on in vv. 11–13 to elaborate the list of their sufferings; the world really does perceive and treat them this way. Rather the irony is akin to dramatic irony, but in a complex manner. Irony on the stage depends on the fact that the audience has privileged knowledge: it may know the true identity of a character when others in the play do not, or see more about a situation than some of the personae are allowed by the author to appreciate. But Paul's image reverses this: it is the spectators who do not realize the true identity of the apostles. Worse, in an ironical twist Paul makes God the author of this exhibition — though of course for Paul this is not the true denouement of the drama, for only in the eschaton will the divine authorial purposes be finally exposed.[17] And the irony works also against the Corinthians, who seem to be exalting certain leaders in the church: they do not understand that apostles are not to be found at the head of the procession or indeed that God has arranged it so for God's own purposes. The irony of v. 9 is thus one of misunderstood role and mistaken identity, with not just the world but the Corinthians themselves implicated as spectators ignorant of the truth.

Reasons for implicating the Corinthians are to be found in vv. 8 and 10, where the irony is overt and difficult to distinguish from sarcasm.[18] Paul's words are stinging, but they are not straight invective; they depend for effect upon the ironical position and self-perception of the Corinthians. This is best appreciated in light of his earlier comments at the close of chapter 1 (1:26–31, RSV):

²⁶For consider your call, brethren; not many of you were wise according to worldly standards, not many were powerful, not many were of noble birth; ²⁷but God chose what is foolish in the world to shame the wise, God chose what is weak in the world to shame the strong. ²⁸God chose what is low and despised in the world, even things that are not, to bring to nothing things that are, ²⁹so that no human being might boast in the presence of God. ³⁰He is the source of your life in Christ Jesus, whom God made our wisdom, our righteousness and consecration and redemption; ³¹therefore, as it is written, "Let him who boasts, boast of the Lord."

Although I earlier characterized this as a specific application to the Corinthians of Paul's questioning of worldly wisdom (p. 18, above), it does rest on more general claims. Paul begins in v. 26 by reminding the Corinthians of their own status, but he regards their particular calling as a specific instance of the general pattern of God's activity. If the point is that no human being whatever (and not simply no Corinthian) may boast before God, then Paul's intention must be a nonlocalized claim: God chose what the world regards as foolish things, weak and despised things, things without status, and indeed without any substance or being. The claim employs heightened language rather than philosophical terminology (Paul is not expecting philosophical discussion about how God might be said to choose something that lacks any kind of existence whatever): God chooses the nobodies of this world.

Returning to chapter 4 we find that Paul's pointed description of the apostles places them unambiguously among those called by God. They are fools, weak and dishonored (4:10); they are "low and despised" (1:28) in that they are reviled and persecuted (4:12); and indeed, worse than nobodies, they are the filth and scum of the world (4:13).¹⁹ The description is enlarged: they are hungry, thirsty, naked; they must do manual labor; they are mistreated and unsettled. Exactly how these misfortunes relate to apostolic biographies is secondary; what is primary is Paul's unsubtle placing of the Corinthians in the reverse categories of this picture. They, in contrast with the apostles (and Jesus' followers in general),²⁰ are glutted, rich, even royally positioned; they (to revert to the specific terms of 1:26) are wise, strong, honored.

The irony of Paul's words in vv. 8–10 is therefore unmistakable. It works pointedly by turning inside out the accurate description of the Corinthians in 1:26; and it works implicitly as well: the children prosper, but the father is in disgrace (4:14–15). The Corinthians watch the spectacle of death from the royal box, not knowing the identity of the condemned.

We are now in a position to see how appropriate a tool is irony for the Corinthians' condition. In a word, their problem is self-deception of the prideful variety. They exaggerate their true status and abilities, glorying in themselves. And that is why the concept of boasting is central to the understanding of Paul's critique. I must say a little more about it, in the course of which we shall find ourselves drawing in its relationships among the cluster of concepts considered earlier.

Paul uses two verbs we associate with the concept: to boast (*kauchaomai*) and to be puffed up (*phusaomai*). They are not identical in meaning. In the Old Testament, and in Paul's own language, there is legitimate "boasting" in the sense of rejoicing, exulting, glorying: but where this is legitimate, its ground is always outside the self. One may exult in God (Psalm 149:1) or the Torah (Sirach 39:8) or in the cross of Christ (Gal. 6:14). This positive sense is, however, parasitic upon the basic conviction that the type of boasting human beings usually indulge in is mistaken. They crow about their own abilities to know and to perform, but in the end such conceit or confidence is mistaken and will fail. In a way all of us know this. No one likes a braggart, least of all children, who recognize that it is not fitting (and is perhaps contrary to a sense of justice) to exalt oneself above others. In Paul's context, however, boasters commit more than a social offense. They misunderstand their place in the entire scheme of things. They have succumbed to the primal temptation to become as God without really being able to bring it off, so end up poor know-it-alls/can-do-it-alls, whose self-deception is readily recognized by their fellows. And that is the reason for saying (in the second of the two verbs) that they are puffed up. Glorying, when turned in upon the self, can only inflate its object beyond due proportions.[21] That is why Paul, if forced to glory in himself because his rivals indulge in boasting, will glory paradoxically only in his weakness (2 Cor 11:30; 12:5).[22]

That paradox reminds us of the connections between boasting and strength, for that is what braggarts think they can brag about — their own abilities. But insofar as they are puffed up, they are deceived about those abilities, magnifying their weaknesses into strengths. This deception, rather than any native lack of intelligence, is what makes them also (to bring in another of our terms) fools. The point may be emphasized: the problem is not so much the abilities or inabilities of human reason as the inflated estimate of one's own intellectual powers. In the Old Testament fools are those who have deceived themselves about God (Psalm 14). The fool is also archetypically present in Jesus' parable about the self-reliant boaster who thought he had made his future utterly secure ("Fool! this very night . . . "; Luke 12:15–21). Paul's usage concurs in this understanding of foolishness. In 2 Corinthians 10–13 he remarks several times how foolish it is for him to boast (11:17, "I speak as in folly in this confidence of boasting"). Of course precisely because they are deceived, fools think themselves wise. As they inflate their weakness into strength, so they puff up their mind to wisdom, in the process closing off the possibility of learning the truth from others.

This, then, is Paul's critique of the Corinthians. Boasting is their fundamental problem. Whatever the justice of this charge,[23] or whatever the content of the Corinthian inflated consciousness or the particular manifestations of their pride, surely this minimal conclusion makes good sense of 1 Corinthians 1–4. That Paul was troubled by their conceited self-deception explains the control and release of emotion in these chapters; it may help us see why the issue of divisions as such fades into the background as the cause of strife is exposed; it makes appropriate the sharp instrument of irony to deflate their consciousness; and it provides a pattern within the concept of boasting into which the major themes of foolishness and wisdom, weakness and strength, may fit.

Unfortunately Paul's attack is more sharp than sustained, and we cannot expect from him a full elucidation of the condition of self-deception or even a careful elaboration of its moral or theological critique. He is content to expose the puffed-up conceit of the Corinthians as forcefully as he can, hoping perhaps to shame them into a more sober frame of mind.[24] Nevertheless there is something to be said in behalf of Paul's critique beyond the historical judgment that he did not much like what he thought he saw in Corinth. The braggart and know-it-all is a resident of all countries and communities, not just Corinth. Self-deception is as perennial a problem as human nature can grow, and its exposure has been a special concern of philosophy from the time of Socrates on. And not philosophy alone. Often the most effective exposés of human pretension come from the unmasking mirror of art. That of course opens other worlds, but it may be instructive to allow ourselves a small glimpse.

I have in mind the way in which Shakespeare redraws some of Paul's lines in *A Midsummer Night's Dream*. For in some ways Bottom is Corinthian, not Athenian. His self-confidence is apparently without limit: he gives the orders to the leader, anticipates all difficulties, knows all answers, can in his own eyes play all roles equally well. His fellow mechanicals admire him and let him rule among them to our amusement. But the comedy is heightened when Bottom is translated from his lowborn world and magically metamorphosed into the half-ass that in the wider context of the play his station and conceit require him to be. Titania, queen of the fairies, is made through a distillation dropped in her eyes to fall in love with the monstrous Bottom, but he glories in her attention through his own deception about his true condition. Shakespeare skirts the edges of dramatic irony with sure skill as he has surface in Bottom's vocabulary intimations of asses and fools, but Bottom never comes to complete self-awareness; the metamorphosed mockery manages to elude him. Nevertheless he is only half-ass: there is something strangely evocative in his mixed-up musing as he awakes with his own head restored:

> I have had a most rare vision. I have had a dream, past the wit of man to say what dream it was. Man is but an ass if he go about to expound this dream. Methought I was — there is no man can tell what. Methought I was — and methought I had — but man is but a patched fool if he will offer to say what methought I had. The eye of man hath not heard, the ear of man hath not seen, man's hand is not able to taste, his tongue to conceive, nor his heart to report, what my dream was. I will get Peter Quince to write a ballad of this dream: it shall be called "Bottom's Dream," because it hath no bottom; and I will sing it in the latter end of a play, before the Duke. Peradventure, to make it more gracious, I shall sing it at her death. (act 4, scene 1, lines 203–17)

Bottom has been touched by a kind of glory[25] for which his own abilities are for once no match: the ear might as well try to see as catch its sounds, the hand to taste as to grasp it.

Whether Paul's irony worked to similar effect upon the Corinthians is difficult to know.[26] Bottom's garbled confession of his limitations nevertheless returns us in theme and language to the earlier chapters of our Corinthian study. Though we may feel the philosophy has been left unharmed by Paul's critique of the Corinthians' boasting, the relationships between faith and philosophy seem much less comfortable in chapters 1 and 2. It is to the critique of human wisdom itself that we must now turn.

III. Paul's Critique of Wisdom

Thus far we have raised the issue of the relationship of reason to faith, and after being guided by the structure and language of our passage to start at chapter 4, we have examined Paul's criticisms of Corinthian boasting. No direct challenge to philosophy has been encountered. But of course that is because we have begun at the end: chapter 1 and 2, though they do not contain the word "philosophy" or indeed "reason",[27] engage our theme much more centrally. Paul's critique is of worldly wisdom, developed around at least four concerns. First, he mentions "words of wisdom" and "wisdom of word," so that he is commonly thought to be critical of rhetoric. Secondly, there is much talk of foolishness, and the language of boasting appears: as a glance at our rough mapping in Table 1 reminds us, wisdom is tied up with other features of the human condition. This suggests a critique of illegitimate conceit, false knowledge. Nevertheless a third focus of concern, particularly in chapter 2, is the human inability to know the things of God at all. That gives rise to the fourth, the positive knowledge available to faith, which, because it comes only through revelation, cannot be generated by human reason.

The question of rhetoric is best left to one side, to be treated in Appendix A of this chapter. We shall be led back to the concern with boasting in due course; but before beginning on these issues we ought to reflect a little more on the philosophical question lurking in the third and fourth concerns. Put simply, it is this: What place, if any, ought reason to occupy in relation to faith, especially in a religion like Christianity, which claims a revealed cognitive content? Our attention will have to be given to what the question involves rather than to a definitive answer, partly because an adequate answer is not easily produced, but mainly because our ultimate interest is in the bearing of Paul's text upon the answers that can be given. After thinking about this, in part ii we shall go through chapters 1 and 2 in some detail, from which will arise two major issues: in section iii, the nature of worldly wisdom, and in section iv, the impotence of reason in religion.

i. Faith, Revelation, Reason

Note first that faith and reason have often been contrasted by believers themselves, because they yield different kinds of knowledge. Human reason and experience provide truths about the sphere of humankind and of nature; but revelation is required for theological truths since their source lies in God alone. It does not follow, of course, that all items of revelation are things inaccessible in principle to human reason, for God may as a concession to the weakness of some of us reveal truths discoverable by keener minds. God simply saves us some trouble in so doing. Still, the central truths of the Christian faith have been held to have been revealed in the strong sense; they are not the possible products of human reason or reflection upon human experience. God has revealed them to us by the Spirit (to anticipate a phrase) either (as earlier theological generations held) as propositions in scripture or (as modern theology has proposed) by assisting our reflection upon divine activity in history.[28]

Fortunately the interests of this study can be satisfied without addressing the many-headed questions that emerge from the idea of revelation. It is enough that the idea in some form, such as the one sketched, has enjoyed both long life and some popularity among Christian believers. For from this picture it is possible to turn the contrast between faith and reason into a competition, so that human reason is set at odds with the truth of God. This may happen when unbelievers assert that sound human reasoning discloses as false certain items of revelation held by the believer; or when (as we shall see in chapter 7, below) evidence from experience shakes the believer's own confidence in the truths of faith.

When this happens, one possibility for the believer is to accept as inevitable the irreconcilable competition between God's revelation and the deliverances of human reason, and to settle the conflict by the victory of faith. For the sake of a label we may call this position radical or extreme fideism, and typecast as its proponent the person (encountered more often in books than in life) who rejoices in absurdities because they demonstrate the extent of his or her commitment to God. The label is often affixed by nonbelievers to those they think should be embarrassed by the contradictions perceived in faith, but who shrug off these logical difficulties.

Most believers find sufficient trial of faith in daily life without adding the burden of accepting outright absurdities, so they have sought for rapprochement between reason and revelation. This might be accomplished by allowing reason a legitimate role to play on the edges of faith, as it were. Though impotent to produce the full content of revelation, reason might establish the truth of minimal beliefs upon which faith may be built. There have been disputes of long duration about what is to be included in a list of those beliefs, but the candidates have usually been claims about the existence and nature of God. Reason, it is said, may be able to tell us that a supreme being exists, whose activity mirrors an ordered intelligence and whose nature is personal and moral. Even if some people learn these things through revelation, they (or at least others) could achieve the same results with their unaided natural abilities; and for that reason this enterprise is termed "natural" theology. Various images may be used to express the way natural theology relates to revelation. Reason may provide a foundation for faith; or it may be thought of as a pedagogue to lead us, not to Christ (because the doctrine of the incarnation must be revealed), but to a partial understanding of God.

Natural theology has not enjoyed unquestioned success, especially in the last few centuries. Its critics (and they include believers as well as nonbelievers) have claimed that the desired conclusions do not follow necessarily from the premises natural theologians have set out; or if they do follow, that the premises themselves are not impervious to reasonable doubt. And earlier in this century a more radical attack was launched in the charge that the entire business was doomed from the start because its language was either meaningless or incoherent. This may account for the fact that many philosophers of religion on the side of believers have spent their time arguing that it is *not ir*rational to hold theistic beliefs. To use Alvin Plantinga's phrase, they have attempted to show that "natural atheology" is no more successful than natural theology.[29]

As followers of debates and students of philosophy appreciate, it is easy to reach a stalemate in this kind of argument. One way out for faith may come in the interesting work being carried on in the ethics of belief, as we come to understand more clearly how the right to hold ungrounded beliefs applies to religious faith.[30] But because this is not the place to pursue that line, I want instead to raise another possibility for the relationship between faith and reason.

We may come at this possibility by changing the spatial metaphor from our previous picture: reason is no longer placed at the edges of faith or as its foundation; instead it is asked to play a role within the very territory of faith. Insofar as it is not called upon to pass the final verdict on the truth of religion, or even to establish the minimal conditions of religious belief, its task is relatively modest. But it is important nonetheless. For the claims of a religion like Christianity, which appeals to both revelation and history, are complex and not always transparent. Within faith itself there are concepts requiring elucidation; subsets of beliefs that need to be related to each other and to more central beliefs; ethical principles, embedded in particular situations, that must be extracted and applied to new circumstances.

There does not seem to be a widely known label for this view. One with some currency is "moderate fideism," used for the position that reason, though not capable of giving faith, may be used to establish the reasonableness of beliefs within faith.[31] The tag is not perfect: it may suggest on its own a less than wholehearted commitment; and it does not say how the basic fideism of the position is moderated. But it will serve us adequately enough, especially if we add the reminder that faith is moderated *rationally*, by the active support of reason.

A final comment before our return to Paul's text. Although I have isolated some possible stances toward faith and reason, the actual approaches of believers may not fit neatly into these slots. Further, it is possible to combine certain features of some of these views. One type of natural theologian, for instance, may also seek rational understanding of the content of faith, whereas others could hold that, having made a reasonable commitment, they are called upon only to trust revelation,

not to argue about it (labelers might call them "internal extreme fideists").
More rationally moderate fideists may employ reason outside faith to
counteract charges of irrationality, or to establish that their fundamental beliefs are indeed fundamental, held without further argument by
epistemic right. It is even conceivable that radical fideists could work
at natural theology for some extrareligious motivation, as long as they
are not bound to believe or not to believe on the basis of their results.

ii. The Cross, Revelation, and Human Wisdom

Having reflected on some religious attitudes toward reason and
revelation, we now take ourselves back to 1 Corinthians for Paul's critique of wisdom. The main text for investigation is 1:17–25 (the text of
vv. 26–31 may be found above on p. 25):

> 17For Christ did not send me to baptize but to preach the gospel,
> and not with eloquent wisdom, lest the cross of Christ be emptied
> of its power.
>   18For the word of the cross is folly to those who are perishing,
> but to us who are being saved it is the power of God. 19For it is
> written,
>   "I will destroy the wisdom of the wise, and the cleverness of
>   the clever I will thwart."
> 20Where is the wise man? Where is the scribe? Where is the debater
> of this age? Has not God made foolish the wisdom of the world?
> 21For since, in the wisdom of God, the world did not know God
> through wisdom, it pleased God through the folly of what we
> preach to save those who believe. 22For Jews demand signs and
> Greeks seek wisdom, 23but we preach Christ crucified, a stumbling-
> block to Jews and folly to Gentiles, 24but to those who are called,
> both Jews and Greeks, Christ the power of God and the wisdom
> of God. 25For the foolishness of God is wiser than men, and the
> weakness of God is stronger than men.

Although 2:6–16 presents a more positive view of wisdom available to
faith, it nevertheless depends on a critique of human or natural wisdom,
so should be considered at this stage. It occurs after Paul explains at the
beginning of chapter 2 that he did not preach to the Corinthians in
"plausible words of wisdom," so that their faith might "not rest in the
wisdom of men but in the power of God":

> 6Yet among the mature we do impart wisdom, although it is not
> a wisdom of this age or of the rulers of this age, who are doomed

to pass away. [7]But we impart a secret and hidden wisdom of God, which God decreed before the ages for our glorification. [8]None of the rulers of this age understood this; for if they had, they would not have crucified the Lord of glory. [9]But, as it is written,

> "What no eye has seen, nor ear heard, nor the heart of man conceived, what God has prepared for those who love him,"

[10]God has revealed to us through the Spirit. For the Spirit searches everything, even the depths of God. [11]For what person knows a man's thoughts except the spirit of the man which is in him? So also no one comprehends the thoughts of God except the Spirit of God. [12]Now we have received not the spirit of the world, but the Spirit which is from God, that we might understand the gifts bestowed on us by God. [13] And we impart this in words not taught by human wisdom but taught by the Spirit, interpreting spiritual truths to those who possess the Spirit.

[14]The unspiritual man does not receive the gifts of the Spirit of God, for they are folly to him, and he is not able to understand them because they are spiritually discerned. [15]The spiritual man judges all things, but is himself to be judged by no one. [16]"For who has known the mind of the Lord so as to instruct him?" But we have the mind of Christ. (1 Cor. 2: 6–16)

Perhaps the most striking feature of the writing in both passages is the series of stark contrasts Paul sets out. John Hurd's characterization (p. 18, above) of Paul's response to rumors from Corinth as "black-and-white," although too simple for the whole of chapters 1–4, does hold for Paul's treatment here (the topic is not, however, the rumored divisions but wisdom). To the black side are assigned those who are wise and clever: they are of "this age" (1:20; 2:6) or of "the world" (1:20, 21; 2:12); are "natural" as opposed to "spiritual" (2:14, 15); or are simply "human," "men" (1:25; cf. 1:29, RSV; 2:13). They are perishing (1:18) and their wisdom is being destroyed by God (1:19); they think the cross foolishness and stumble over it (1:18, 21, 23; 2:14). On the white side are those who are called (1:24, or are chosen: 1:27, 28), who believe (1:21); they have received the Spirit and are "spiritual" (2:10, 12, 15), so that they have wisdom (2:6); they are being saved (1:18, 21), knowing both the wisdom and the power of God (1:24; cf. 1:30). The black-and-white categories are determined differently in the two passages, however. In chapter 1 it is the cross of Christ that divides the two groups, one thinking this event and its proclamation foolishness but the other recognizing in that foolishness God's strength and wisdom. In chapter 2 the two classes are determined by their ability to accept the revelation of the Spirit of God; this makes the difference between those who have knowledge of God and those who do not.

Faced with this dichotomy, we may think it not difficult to guess where Paul would assign faith and where reason. It looks as though reason is denigrated by his account. Does it not think the cross foolish? Knowing nothing about God, is it not impotent to save? Revelation is required for that saving knowledge, and the only appropriate response is faith.

So we may guess. But without Paul to ask, we have only his text; and from that text we should not jump too quickly to such a conclusion. There is an obstacle against our doing this: in these chapters Paul talks not about reason per se but about wisdom. It is clear that he deprecates a certain kind of wisdom and advocates another kind; but what is not yet clear is the role that reason may play in either.

Further, there is the question of what Paul understands by wisdom (*sophia*) in these passages. This is a question for the New Testament specialist, and one on which opinion is seriously divided. It takes little time among the commentators to realize just how difficult it is to make progress on some of the historical problems involved in coming to an adequate understanding of the situation in Corinth addressed by Paul. Some speak rather generally of Greek philosophy and rhetoric as his targets,[32] and if this is so, perhaps (depending on Paul's perception of philosophy) reason is implicated in his critique. But other commentators think that the wisdom in question was more religious in flavor, perhaps an early version of the blend of metaphysical speculation and religious enthusiasm that became known as gnosticism.[33] Still others are unhappy with this as a conclusion: the historical evidence is not sufficiently strong, and the hypothesis of gnostic elements is unnecessary, because Paul's text can be explained from an Old Testament and Jewish background.[34] The debate about Corinth is only one part of the larger question of the appropriate setting from which Paul is best read, and I am unable to contribute to that discussion from within. Nevertheless it is worth noting here that any proposal to give restricted content to "wisdom" in 1 Corinthians 1–2 may have the effect of softening Paul's critique. This kind of interpretive move is sometimes made to help modern digestion of an ancient text: for example, some commentators now suggest that Paul was not really condemning homosexuality as the twentieth century knows it, but rather the pederasty of the ancient world. In similar fashion it may be proposed that Paul was not "really" attacking human wisdom or reason in 1 Corinthians 1–2. Instead his intended targets were particular philosophies, or sophistry, or religious speculation, or false wisdom based on competitors to revelation.

Perhaps; but then again, perhaps not. Even if we conclude that reason is not finally implicated in Paul's critique, we are forced by the text to face squarely the issue of the generality of that critique. Historical investigation about the content of wisdom in Corinth, though of value to some points of interpretation, ought not to be assumed to settle the question of the scope of Paul's attack.

For it is hard to maintain that the language of 1 Corinthians 1:17–31 applies only to a certain brand of wisdom. The phrase "in wisdom of word" may refer to rhetoric (as discussed in Appendix A), but the idea of wisdom is not technical or associated with particular schools or practices in what follows. Partly this is so because Paul begins in v. 18 not with wisdom but with *foolishness*, and in a sense this acts as clue to the concept of wisdom in the passage. Paul says that those to whom the preaching of the cross is folly are perishing: but of course the cross might be folly from different points of view, unified not by a common doctrine of wisdom but only by their shared disdain of the cross. In fact, Paul's repetition in v. 21 of the theme of foolishness is followed by an explanation of something like this point: the folly is for both Jew and gentile, though for different reasons.[35] Further, it does not seem to matter who is included among the wise (Paul uses several terms, some quoted from the Old Testament,[36] to embrace rather than restrict: the wise, the clever, the scribe, the debater, vv. 19, 20); the point is that God has made the wisdom of the world foolish (v. 30). There is a fundamental irony in worldly wisdom, like the irony of the theatrical image in 1 Corinthians 4, which explains the paradoxical language of v. 25: what the world thinks foolish is actually wisdom seen from divine perspective; and what the world thinks wise is ultimately foolish, amounting to nothing. But if that is Paul's point, any wisdom that is worldly, regardless of its specific content, will share in the same irony.

In the second passage the theme of worldly wisdom persists, though the term "age" is used in place of "world" in vv. 6 and 8 (as it had been in 1:20). Whoever the "rulers of this age" are,[37] it is not simply their wisdom or lack of it that is criticized. Instead the critique blankets everyone: human ignorance of divine wisdom is so pervasive that not even rulers can know it.

However, in the rest of chapter 2 it seems to me that Paul's critique rests on a different and broader base. No longer is he claiming the irony of worldly wisdom; he is rather insisting that even among those who are of the Spirit and not of the world (the approved, not the disapproved, party) there is no possibility of knowing God apart from revelation. And if this is so, there are even stronger considerations against any interpretation that narrows the critique to some particularized type of wisdom. For Paul's text implies beliefs about our basic cognitive equipment, not just its employment in particular times and places.

That this is so may be seen from a rereading of 2:9–16, where half of Paul's purpose is to point to an epistemological divide between humankind and God, which we cannot cross. That is the burden of v. 9: the things prepared by God are not available for human perception or conception. When Paul says these things have not surfaced on the human heart, *kardia anthrôpou*, he means human beings per se, not just "worldly" ones. Sometimes *anthrôpos* has a pejorative flavor in Paul (as in 3:3–4, where the RSV adds "ordinary" and "merely" to bring out the evaluative force of the term), but at other times it refers indiscriminately to any member of the human race, categories and classifications aside (e.g., 4:1, where substitutions like "anyone" or "everyone" in English and a range of Greek pronouns are perfectly acceptable). This indiscriminate use occurs again in v. 11 of our chapter: as only the spirit in a human being knows the things of that human being, so only the Spirit of God knows the things of God. Some commentators take v. 11 to be a version of the "privileged access" doctrine[38] (reading it as "who among all human beings knows the things of this particular person except this particular person's own spirit"), but the verse must work together with v. 12. It is not simply that just as individuals have private thoughts not known to others, God has private thoughts too; rather, if human things are known only to human knowers, divine things are known only to God's Spirit. Paul's language suggests an analogy, but his main point is to draw a thick and heavy line between things human and divine, and to place the things of God squarely outside the limits of human knowing. His closing adaptation of Isaiah 40:13 in v. 16 emphasizes this: Who has known the mind of the Lord, who instructs him?

One other phrase requires comment. In v. 14 Paul says that the "natural person," *psuchikos anthrôpos*, does not receive the things of the Spirit of God.[39] Paul's addition that these things are folly to such a person reminds us immediately of chapter 1 and worldly wisdom. Most commentators, however, see the adjective *psuchikos* (which Paul contrasts with *pneumatikos*, "spiritual") as descriptive of the human state apart from God, without the further moral and religious evaluation of human sinfulness or worldliness.[40] The term *pneumatikos* will be considered in chapter 3, below, in the study of the resurrection body, but if commentators are right about *psuchikos* here, then Paul's point in v. 14 is a restatement of the material we have just considered: our natural cognitive abilities do not extend to knowledge of God. On the other hand, the reversion to the notion of folly is gratuitous in the immediate context. The whole burden of the argument in chapter 1 as well as in chapter 2 requires us to associate foolishness with worldliness. It may be that in Paul's mind the "natural" person of v. 14 would also in this context be "worldly," so that although the connection is unstated, it is still to be understood.

It is nevertheless still only half of Paul's purpose to expose this epistemological gap between humankind and God. The other half is the claim that the gap has been bridged, from God's side and in our direction, by the Spirit. Thus, to say that the things of God are outside the limits of human knowing is to emphasize the boundaries of our own intellectual activity, not to deny that with God's help we can come to knowledge otherwise inaccessible. The things of God can indeed be part of human knowledge, but only as graciously given (*charisthenta*, v. 12) or as revealed (*apekalupsen*, v. 10).

Although we shall have to reflect further on the content of this revelation, here it should be stressed that Paul does not mean by revelation some noncognitive experience. There is therefore a pronounced difference between Paul's meaning and Shakespeare's intention in having Bottom misquote Paul's v. 9. Bottom's mixed-up language portrays in both form and content the inexpressibility of his dreamlike experience, whereas for Paul the source of revelation is not experience but God the Spirit, and what is revealed is wisdom (*sophia*, vv. 6, 7), which can be communicated in language (*lalumen*, vv. 7, 13).[41] The words of communication are taught by the Spirit, it is true (v. 13); but they are words serving interpretation (v. 13) and investigation (v. 14) rather than expressing nonrational ecstasy.[42] The fact that they are not the product of human wisdom returns us to our earlier theme: the language of the spiritual may be human grammar and vocabulary, but the source of the knowledge (*didaktois* is important) is not human nature.

All these considerations lead us to the conclusion that Paul, far from particularizing this or that wisdom in 1 Corinthians 1 and 2, launches a double-pronged attack. From one side he argues that people who are worldly-wise have misunderstood the cross and thought it foolish, whereas from the other side he claims that no human being at all can know the things of God apart from revelation. This is not to deny that particular problems with wisdom or revelation in Corinth might have provoked this critique from Paul; it is, however, to insist on the generality of that critique.

But if Paul's opposition to wisdom cannot be softened by restricting his target to particular brands and expressions, does it follow that 1 Corinthians 1–2 pits faith unalterably against reason? If believers were to seek advice from Paul about the proper use of intellect, or critics ask for an authoritative statement of the tradition's attitude to reason, would they be forced to conclude (as many have) that extreme fideism is the best description of the apostle's teaching?[43]

The short answer is: no. Paul's critique does not entail irreconcilable opposition between faith and reason. A larger answer, with argument and explanation, is nevertheless required, and best proceeds by considering separately the prongs of Paul's attack. We turn now to a closer examination of worldly wisdom, which raises again the question of the structure of 1 Corinthians 1–4; after that we shall consider the second prong, which cuts more deeply into human cognitive abilities. So we have two questions before us. What is worldly wisdom? Is reason religiously impotent?

iii. What Is Worldly Wisdom?

To this point we have noted that in chapter 1 Paul does not condemn reason per se, but only wisdom that is worldly. The notion of what is "worldly" has been left unexplicated, though as applied here to wisdom it seems to have something to do with foolishness and boasting; and an appreciation of the interrelationships of these concepts looks important to an understanding of the text. By the end of section II, above, we were able to understand how these concepts applied to the Corinthians. And it will be remembered that the language of weakness and strength, boasting and foolishness, also appears at the end of chapter 1 (see Table 1). But we have left unresolved tensions between Paul's critique of the Corinthians and his critique of worldly wisdom: the black-and-white language of chapters 1 and 2 denigrates worldly wisdom, not those who, like the Corinthians, are being saved. They are later criticized, it is true: but what bearing does that have on the criticism of the world?

In section I, above, I suggested that, because the language and movement of chapters 1–4 pushed us on to chapter 4 to discern Paul's intentions, the earlier chapters might best be read in the light of his working out of their themes in chapter 4. It is time to put chapters 1 and 2 back together with chapter 4, and with the beginning and closing sections of chapter 3 which also contain the themes highlighted in Table 1. It turns out that a better appreciation of the relationship between Paul's two critiques will help us understand the worldly character of wisdom.

What we discover when we reflect on all the passages dealing with wisdom, foolishness, weakness, boasting, and strength in the light of the full treatment of chapter 4 is a deliberate mixing of the clear categories Paul has set out in chapters 1 and 2. Look at it this way. Suppose instead of criticism for divisions in 1:10–16 we had some neutral or even complimentary words from Paul, leading to his theme of the cross over against worldly wisdom in vv. 17b–25. We would then find no undertones of criticism in his placing the Corinthians within this theme in vv. 26ff.: by reminding them that they are themselves particular examples of God's choosing the humble to bring human boasting to an end, he is locating them on the right side of the two groups he has set up. The two categories are continued in chapter 2, as we have seen: there is the worldly, but also the human and natural, which must be opposed to the spiritual. Our expectation, again were there no earlier criticism, would be that Paul should apply this to the Corinthians by rejoicing in the knowledge of God that they have been given through the Spirit (cf. 1:5). But that does not happen. Instead chapter 3 begins with this statement (3:1–4):

> But I, brethren, could not address you as spiritual men, but as men of the flesh, as babes in Christ. [2]I fed you with milk, not solid food; for you were not ready for it; and even yet you are not ready, [3]for you are still of the flesh. For while there is jealousy and strife among you, are you not of the flesh, and behaving like ordinary men? [4]For when one says, "I belong to Paul," and another, "I belong to Apollos," are you not merely men?

The jealousy and strife of the Corinthians have prevented Paul from imparting to them the spiritual wisdom he has described, giving point to his words in 2:6 that he speaks this wisdom only "among the mature." Though they are chosen and are being saved, nevertheless they are "fleshly" (if not "natural") and act in all-too-human fashion.[44]

This is not the only mixing of categories in these chapters. So far the Corinthians are still on the right side of things in terms of chapter 1 (if they are immature, they still remain immature Christians, not the worldly-wise), but by the end of chapter 3 Paul is beginning to change that. We saw earlier (p. 19, above) that at vv. 16ff. the tone strikes a warning note, and Paul reverts to the language of chapter 1 in his admonition in v. 18. For the first time he brings the possibility of worldly wisdom right into the Corinthian camp with his "If anyone *among you* thinks he is wise":

> [18]Let no one deceive himself. If any one among you thinks that he is wise in this age, let him become a fool that he may become wise. [19]For the wisdom of this world is folly with God. For it is written, "He catches the wise in their craftiness," [20]and again, "The Lord knows that the thoughts of the wise are futile." [21]So let no one boast of men. For all things are yours, [22]whether Paul or Apollos or Cephas or the world or life or death or the present or the future, all are yours; [23]and you are Christ's; and Christ is God's. (1 Cor. 3:18–23)

Again the problem of boasting emerges in the context of God's judgment on the folly of worldly wisdom — and the Corinthians are warned against it.

We know, of course, the end of the story in chapter 4. There are no hypotheticals; Paul charges the Corinthians directly with the conceit and bragging that are the marks not just of "fleshly" or immature believers but of the deprecated worldly wisdom of chapter 1.

This means that we must read the black-and-white language of chapter 1 in double fashion, with one eye focusing on the surface of the text and the other reading its words in the different light of chapter 4. With the right eye we see two clear-cut categories; but with the left we watch the condemnation of folly and boasting turning back from the worldly-wise onto the Corinthians themselves.

If this appreciation of the ways in which the themes of false wisdom and boasting work throughout chapters 1–4 is at all correct, these themes must color our reading of the chapter 1 critique of wisdom. For it is linked deliberately in Paul's text with the critique of Corinthian boasting, which we have already considered. This strongly suggests that what is wrong with wisdom in its worldly guise lies in self-deception, inflated conceit, bragging — morally and epistemologically undesirable conditions or activities.

In fact a glance back over the language of chapter 1 confirms that Paul understands by "worldly" wisdom not the sort of knowledge the natural theologian is interested in but the swollen epistemic condition of conceit. This accords with several features of the passage. It explains why Paul is anxious to preserve true wisdom in God and in Christ, who is made wisdom to believers: so although all worldly wisdom, and not just some of its instances, is condemned, not all wisdom is worldly. It explains the emphasis upon foolishness, and the demands of the Jews and Greeks for the wrong sort of thing: they are not in Paul's view honest seekers, but people who, thinking they know already, dismiss the cross as nonsense. Further, the verbs describing God's dealing with this kind of wisdom make sense when it is seen as conceit: God destroys (*apolô*, v. 19) wisdom, abolishes (*katargêsê*, v. 28) those who think they are something. Paul later talks of the destruction of knowledge in 1 Corinthians 13:8ff., a topic to be considered in my chapter 7; but here it is not reason or knowledge that is done away with, but worldly wisdom as pretense to knowledge. Likewise God shames (*kataischunê*, vv. 27, 28) the wise, a treatment appropriate to those who think they know when they do not — as Plato recognized when he had Socrates deal with conceit and stubborn ignorance as barriers to knowledge.[45] Finally, that worldly wisdom is indeed conceit is recognized by the climactic condemnation of boasting at the end of chapter 1: God's purpose in bypassing the wise is not the subversion of reason but the elimination of all bragging in God's presence.

I conclude that Paul's target in 1 Corinthians 1 is the same condition he attacks in chapter 4: human intellectual conceit, the puffed-up consciousness of the cocksure, which prevents knowledge of the self as well as of God.

There are important consequences of this view of worldly wisdom, to be seen immediately in three areas. Textually, this view permits an adequate reading of 1 Corinthians 1–4, holding together Paul's critiques of the Corinthians and of wisdom. Theologically, it provides some content for the notions of the "world" or "this age" in the passage. Commentators are sometimes content to leave discussion of these terms at a fairly formal level: the "world" is fallen creation, a sphere completely opposed to God and under God's judgment. It is easy, then, to regard all human activity as corrupted by worldliness; and for some it is only a small step from a comment like "God's standards for assessing men are different from those of the world" (citing 1 Cor. 1:26ff.)[46] to the belief that human canons of rationality are also deprecated because they do not belong to God's sphere. Such a formal description of the "world" may not be false, but it leaves out the reason why worldly wisdom is opposed to God, a reason supplied by our reading of the passage. Paul does not say here that "fallen" reason is impotent in itself to know God; rather whatever impotence there is to be found in chapter 2 belongs to the Christian as well as the worldly sphere. The worldly-making feature of "wisdom" is not its general fallenness, but its misuse of reason in conceit and pride. Further, this misuse is not restricted to the sphere of fallen humankind: although Christians are not for Paul any longer in the sphere of the "world," they nevertheless may exhibit intellectual conceit. Perhaps this understanding of "worldly" in 1 Corinthians 1–4 can be called "functional" instead of sphere-related: it emphasizes the misfunctioning of human knowing in the moral and intellectual vices from which incompletely redeemed people are not yet free.[47]

The third area of important consequence is of course the philosophical. Having affirmed that Paul's critique of wisdom is not a critique of reason per se, we are now in a position to conclude that his first-prong attack is against the misuse of reason resulting in self-deception and boasting. Whether Paul's text can allow reason a legitimate role to play in our knowledge of God must be considered in the next section; but for now we may content ourselves with the observation that Paul's condemnation of worldly wisdom does not directly attack philosophy.

In affirming this I am conscious of the objection that Paul himself might disagree with this claim. After all, he makes such a strong demarcation between the world and the cross that it is easy to imagine him condemning all the epistemological strivings of perishing humanity as so much garbage. His cherishing of the Corinthian nobodies tempts us to fantasies of Paul overturning study carrels in the philosophical libraries of the world, and even more sober historical judgment leaves us little room for thinking that he valued the philosophical movements of his day.

Nevertheless were the historical Paul or the Paul of our fantasies to meet us over the text of 1 Corinthians 1–4, we could put the matter this way. Given that the root problem with worldly wisdom is its conceited pretense to knowledge, it does not follow that every use of reason is condemned; and insofar as philosophy is concerned with the correct uses of reason, it cannot follow that all philosophical activity is rendered illegitimate by his attack. Paul's critique cannot be brushed aside: pride is both a moral and an intellectual vice, destructive of moral relationships and epistemological possibilities. And certainly philosophers may be conceited, and particular philosophies the products of vain speculation. But philosophy itself, however defined and however poorly practised, remains intimately concerned with right reasoning. It cannot be intelligibly claimed to be inherently prideful; though an utterly human activity it does not have to be "worldly" in the Pauline sense.

Further, I suggest that philosophy should not merely escape Paul's critique of worldly wisdom; it should also come to its aid. As I commented at the end of section II, above, philosophy has an interest in the exposure of self-deception and conceit, and instruments to operate upon diseased thinking. Not all philosophy takes this approach, it is true; and there are significant disputes about what is and what is not healthy among our beliefs and actions. Nonetheless from Socrates' day to our contemporary concern for clarity and consistency, a significant mode of philosophizing has been the *therapeutic*, and it is this activity that can serve faith.

So worldly wisdom, though opposed to the true knowledge of God, is opposed not as philosophy against faith but as human conceit that shuts itself up against truth. Paul's critique of such wisdom requires the opposite of an irrationally extreme fideism; it asks for right reasoning and for the cognitive modesty appropriate to all human intellectual activity.

But this conclusion, though important, does not answer all the questions about faith and reason surrounding our text. What of Paul's second prong, cutting into our cognitive capacities more deeply? Does Paul's discussion require the conclusion that reason, however therapeutic its uses, can never by itself produce knowledge of God? When he says categorically, "the world by wisdom did not know God" (1:21), surely his denial should be linked with his discussion in chapter 2 of the natural inabilities of the human mind to know the things of God. If philosophy is not utterly condemned, is it not at least pronounced sterile? To answer, we must consider our second question in light of the earlier discussion of chapter 2 (pp. 35–37, above).

iv. Is Reason Religiously Impotent?

In that discussion of Paul's second prong of attack I concluded that his critique was of human knowledge *as* human, not as fallen or worldly; and that in his view the things of God are not known by any person other than the Spirit of God. This draws the heavy epistemological line between humankind and God, a line crossed only in revelation given to us by the Spirit. But at that time we also noted that the content of revelation deserved investigation, and it is to this content that we now turn.

The issue is not a minor one. For unless we raise it, there may be a natural assumption that Paul means by "the things of God" truths conveyed in what philosophers sometimes term "theistic" propositions, claims that make or depend upon some reference to God. For Paul, all such propositions would be revealed, and his claim would amount to a denial of the possibility of natural theology. Natural theologians, to preserve their enterprise from Pauline disapproval, would be forced to limit the content of revelation in chapter 2 to the central truths of Christian faith, such as the incarnation, the trinity, resurrection, and the like.

When we turn back to the text from these wider concerns, we are immediately puzzled by what Paul does *not* say or do with the content of revelation. Although the phrase "the things of God" is so indefinite that it appears to allow any theistic proposition, and thereby to include preeminently the central truths of Christianity, in fact it becomes very difficult to say exactly what Paul had in mind. I confess to three perplexities.

The first is over Paul's lack of examples of revealed truths, and their absence in his pattern of argument throughout the Letter to the Corinthians.[48] In addition to calling the content of revelation "the things of God," he uses expressions like "what God has prepared for those who love him" (2:9), "what [God] freely gives to us through the Spirit" (2:12), and "the mind of Christ" (2:16). Almost any Christian belief could be included under these descriptions. But if the content is indeed fairly clear and includes important Christian doctrines, it is curious that Paul does not invoke revealed truths to give instruction or settle disputes later in this letter. He does express a conviction in chapter 7 that his opinions about marriage are supported by the Spirit — but he does not claim that they are revealed, nor (as we shall see in chapter 4, below) are they given the weight of revelation in his uses of authority there.

More perplexing is the apparent conviction of Paul that the Corinthians themselves do not yet share in this revealed knowledge. Having discussed the wisdom available to the spiritual in chapter 2, he expresses regret in chapter 3 that the immaturity of the Corinthians, evidenced by their fleshliness, prevents their being spoken to as spiritual (3:1–4; 2:6). They have been given milk, not meat (3:2). And yet they are called and chosen of God; they are being saved; they do have the Spirit and the gifts of the Spirit (1:7; and chapter 12). My perplexity over the possibility that some may be Christians without this revealed knowledge is shared by commentators, but they handle it in different ways. C. K. Barrett, for instance, thinks there is no special content to revelation beyond the word of the cross, but simply an elaboration of that word; Robin Scroggs argues strongly that the difference between the kerygma and Paul's esoteric wisdom teaching is clear-cut.[49] However the matter is to be resolved, it is beyond dispute that the content of spiritual revelation in 1 Corinthians 2 cannot be the basic propositions of the Christian faith. More likely is the suggestion that the mystery that Paul speaks of among the mature is the entire eschatological plan of God for humankind.[50] Just as one can know enough to become a member of a community without ever understanding completely the life, functions, history, and direction of that community, so one can become a Christian without entering into the wisdom revealed to God's people.

We must be careful about the conclusions we draw from these two perplexities. We might think that because what is revealed is, according to 1 Corinthians 2, esoteric or at least nonbasic to Christian faith, the fundamental items of faith do not depend upon revelation but can be known in some other way. Though such a stand is compatible with the text, it is not positively supported by it; and without that support we must move cautiously. Though Paul gives no statements about the wider scope of revelation in discussing spiritual wisdom in 1 Corinthians, he may well limit his discussion here for reasons determined by his context. Certainly in Galatians he insists that the gospel itself, not just wisdom for the mature, is given by revelation rather than human teaching (1:11–12). Even there, however, it is not clear how much in the articulation of Paul's gospel rests on revelation. But, given these cautions, we may still conclude with confidence that 1 Corinthians 2 itself does not require the view that all theistic propositions have revelation as their source or ground.

This conclusion is strengthened by a third perplexity. It is a puzzle much larger than our text allows us to solve, and only some of the more obvious pieces can present themselves for attention here. It concerns Paul's relationship to Judaism and to the law in particular, and it arises in the following way. In 1 Corinthians 1, Paul denies that the world can know God through its wisdom, and as we saw (page 35 and note 35) he includes Jews among those who think the cross folly and who therefore fail to know God. Yet surely Paul did not mean to deny that the law, and the Old Testament in general, yield knowledge of God. Further, although the agency of revelation in chapter 2 is the Spirit, the restricted content of revelation—spiritual wisdom for the mature—leaves untouched any knowledge of God that may be available through the law. To repeat the point just made above, the fact that the Spirit reveals some things to some people does not preclude others from knowing something about God in another way; and that some knowledge of God is in fact available must be preeminently true, even for Paul, by reason of his own Jewish heritage. Those who have not received the revelation of the gospel are not therefore in complete darkness about God.

We may pursue this briefly by contrasting Paul's attitude toward worldly wisdom in 1 Corinthians 1 with his attitude toward the law. It is sometimes said that our text treats wisdom or philosophy as an addition to the gospel, in the same way that keeping the law adds to the gospel; and both thereby pervert the word of the cross. Just as one does not need the works of the law to be justified, so one does not need wisdom.[51] Perhaps: but setting out a parallelism between law and wisdom obscures a radical difference between them. Without venturing too deeply into the currents of contemporary discussions on Paul and law,[52] we may recognize that for Paul the law had an important historical role to play in human knowledge of God and ultimate salvation. Although Moses is not as significant for Paul as is Abraham—in that Abraham was justified by faith apart from the law[53]—still the law given through Moses is not intrinsically bad or worthless. It is not "sin," but is rather holy, just, and good (Rom. 7:7, 12), even spiritual (7:14). By it is sin made recognizable (Rom. 3:20ff.). It is true that in his Letter to the Galatians Paul has a less favorable evaluation of the capability and effect of the law, and he calls the Galatians foolish for wanting to put themselves again under the law after having been made free in Christ (3:1). But that is the foolishness of their immature attitude, not the foolishness of the law itself. Even here the law performs the important task of preparing the way for faith in Christ (3:24).

Paul never says that God in Christ has destroyed or abolished the law, or has made it foolish nonsense. If it is now redundant, it is because Christ has fulfilled it (Rom. 10:4). Yet none of this language could apply to wisdom in 1 Corinthians 1: this wisdom is deprecated, destroyed, brought to nothing, and exposed as foolishness. The wisdom of the world has no redeeming features, in either the popular or the theological sense of the term. Law, however, is propaedeutic for faith in Christ and provides content for our knowledge of God even if it is not completely potent for salvation.

By now we have no difficulty in understanding why Paul treats wisdom in this fashion: because by worldly wisdom he means the products of conceit and boastful pride. Prideful reason may distort the gospel, but intellectual activity itself is not automatically an addition to or perversion of faith. Our text, taken strictly, makes reason impotent only to deliver those products of revelation that form spiritual wisdom for the mature. Paul has here given no grounds for concluding that *all* knowledge of God must come about through revelation apart from reason. Indeed, it is possible that reason might play a role analogous to the preparation for faith afforded by law. This role would be only analogous, for the law is itself a product of revelation. Nevertheless our text does leave open the possibility that knowledge of God which is propaedeutic for faith, though not sufficient for salvation, may be obtained by reason. If Paul does not believe this, he has not argued that case in 1 Corinthians 1–4.[54]

IV. FAITH, WISDOM, PHILOSOPHY

It remains to consolidate and conclude. It has been the burden of this study that those who deny the religious legitimacy of reason on the basis of 1 Corinthians 1–4 must find different grounds or illustrations for their view. By itself this text does not force its reader to deprecate reason or to banish it from the domain of theology; instead, when its critiques are fully run, there is still room for philosophy as propaedeutic to faith and therapeutic for it.

The passage does not applaud philosophy or offer encouragement to its practice. The reasons for this belong to Paul's understanding of philosophy in its relationship to wisdom and the Corinthian situation, and I have left to New Testament scholars the task of throwing light on these historical problems. But whatever faults the Corinthians suffered from, Paul cannot be criticizing them for the very use of reason in the service of faith. For we have seen that, however content is assigned to worldly wisdom, Paul's critique cuts not at reason itself but at its inflated pretender — intellectual conceit. This permits the rationally moderate fideist to introduce reason into the realm of faith, where it may serve correct thinking upon the content of religious belief. Its customary employment has been mainly in philosophical theology, understood as the attempt to work out traditional philosophical issues within a Christian scheme of understanding.[55] However, there is nothing to prevent the use of philosophical tools to chart the language, expose the arguments, and assess the implications of biblical texts. The rationally moderate fideist may also work on the edges of faith by defending the intelligibility and cogency of Christian beliefs or by attempting to demonstrate that conclusions contrary to faith are not necessarily true. In all these prophylactic or therapeutic uses of philosophy, sound reason is promoted and worldly wisdom destroyed.

What of the positive work of philosophical reason in natural theology? Is there reliable knowledge of God available to human understanding apart from specific acts of divine revelation? Whatever the answer, our study demonstrates that the enterprise of natural theology cannot be easily condemned on the theological grounds of 1 Corinthians 1–4. Paul's strong emphasis upon the need for revelation entails only that the human mind is not able to discover all there is to know of God; it does not demand the radical conclusion that reason itself is impotent to deliver any theological truths at all.[56]

Whether anyone ought to engage in natural theology is of course another matter. My conclusion is not primarily about the religious limits of reason or the desirability of a certain kind of Christian apologetic; it is rather about what does and does not follow from 1 Corinthians 1–4 as to relationships between faith and philosophy. In restricting itself to the implications that legitimately arise from a given text, the study has been a modest one. But because many readers of Paul have invoked this text to equate philosophy with worldly wisdom and to oppose both to faith, or to charge faith with disdain for reason, my conclusion has a modest importance. It is possible, of course, that the study is flawed or mistaken. But of more significance than the soundness of its arguments is what the attempt itself illustrates: that religious understanding requires the aid of philosophical reasoning. That a particular piece of reasoning on a text is inadequate does not invalidate the role of philosophy: it only shows that the task must be done in better ways. It is this conviction that carries us into the following studies of Paul's arguments to the Corinthians. The text — even if it serves revelation — is not by itself sufficient to yield the wisdom that both faith and philosophy seek.

APPENDIX A: WORLDLY WISDOM AND RHETORIC

Because the focus of this study is on philosophy, I have discussed the relationship of worldly wisdom to reason at the most general level.

There are many commentators, however, who see that Paul's critique has something to do with rhetoric. Hence, to reflect adequately the interests of the text, I ought to consider rhetorical expressions of worldly wisdom. I offer the following points.

1. There can be little doubt that rhetoric is under attack. Paul mentions the *sophia logou* as a possible (but wrong) way to evangelize (1 Cor. 1:17; RSV translation, "eloquent wisdom"), and he points out in 2:1 that he himself did not come with superiority of words or wisdom; his speech was not in the "persuasive words of wisdom" (2:4; on the text of this verse, see Barrett, *First Corinthians*). Word and wisdom are linked in these verses, and in 2:13 as well, with the emphasis upon the form of presentation in speech. Paul clearly thought that rhetoric in some form was opposed to the gospel.

Some commentators have suggested that Paul deliberately put aside rhetoric in Corinth, either (1) because he had found his attempt to follow rhetorical or philosophical style in Athens a failure (but see Barrett on 2:2), or else (2) because he did not want to impress the relatively uneducated Corinthians with style, but instead with the power of the cross. In either case the question of the use or abuse of rhetoric is a tactical one; it would not follow from his decision to speak simply in Corinth that Paul thought rhetoric intrinsically bad. But this strains the text a little. Although the opening of chapter 2 does record a deliberate and specific decision on Paul's part ("I determined not to . . . ," 2:2), his statements in 1:17 and 2:13 are general, not limited to his behavior in Corinth. Further, in these chapters "word" is so closely linked with "wisdom" that the form of presentation is implicated along with the content (so Conzelmann and Barrett, on 2:1). Both belong to the "world" and not to Christ.

2. Commentators, of course, wish to resist the implication of a general critique, that rhetoric is inherently evil. So Barrett: "Wisdom is used in a bad sense when it denotes simply the skilled marshalling of human arguments, employed with a view to convincing the hearer. This process is by no means evil in itself, and becomes evil only when it is employed as a substitute for true Christian preaching, and veils the power of the Spirit by its show of human persuasiveness" (*First Corinthians*, 67–68). Unfortunately, Barrett leaves unexplained the relationship between "true Christian preaching" and rhetoric: the notion of substitution might suggest that rhetoric is acceptable in "human" arguments — say, about politics — but not in proclamation where the preacher should never aim to convince.

Calvin works at the matter with some care. He recognizes that, as a God-given art, rhetoric can be sound and dependent upon truth, so that it would not be opposed to the gospel. Paul eschews rhetoric in

Corinth because of the itch there for "high-sounding talk" (*First Corinthians*, on 1:17). Nevertheless Calvin confesses that the critique of eloquence has in some measure "a permanent validity," for two reasons. (1) When human language is "unpolished and unrefined" the majesty of God shines more brightly. (2) The other effect is that human pretensions are exposed and we become more tractable. Yet Calvin is also pulled by his first affirmation: rhetoric when dependent upon truth may serve the gospel "as a handmaid serves her mistress." Moreover there is evidence for this in the fact that the Spirit of God, speaking in scripture, has its own eloquence. This is seen especially in the prophets and a little in Moses; and "even if the writings of the apostles are not so polished, yet a few tiny sparks of it flash out at times there too" (ibid.).

3. This brings us back to Paul himself. If he felt rhetoric to be completely at variance with Christ, we might expect the plainest of styles in his writings. In fact Paul does not expect the Holy Spirit to work with just any words and phrases; he makes good use of rhetorical devices, many in the form of the Greek diatribe (Augustine comments on his style in *On Christian Doctrine*, 4.7; and German scholars in particular have compared his style to the diatribe and other forms: see Conzelmann, Introduction, Section 4, and references there). Nor is Paul alone in criticizing rhetoric while attempting to use language effectively: Socrates in the *Apology* does the same thing, and Plato's *Gorgias* is an especially noteworthy example. All of them, and many others as well, are aware of the power of words to bewitch and persuade apart from considerations of truth. But it is useless to think that truths can be expressed apart from all rhetorical consideration: as sculpture has shape, so words have style.

4. I suggest therefore that the critique of rhetoric in 1 Corinthians 1–2 is best seen as a specific instance falling under Paul's general critique of worldly wisdom. Just as that attack takes prideful reason as its target, so the attack on rhetoric is against the deliberate misuse of words to convince beyond the proper bounds of knowledge. I have distinguished the general target from reason or philosophy by calling it "worldly wisdom," and perhaps the same distinction needs to be made between "worldly persuasion" and rhetoric or style. It need not follow for Paul that all worldly persuasion expresses the speaker's own conceit: presumably he felt his approach to the Corinthians to be solidly based, but he abstained from wise speech because of the conceit it might engender in them.

APPENDIX B: CALVIN ON 1 CORINTHIANS 1–2

Calvin has argued forcefully that reason cannot produce any reliable knowledge of God. Because the view that 1 Corinthians makes faith and natural theology irreconcilable is found in his commentary on these chapters, I assess his argument in light of the understanding of the text advanced above.

Although acknowledging that the text deals with the misuse of clever speech and inflated intellect, Calvin argues that the underlying issue is the very legitimacy of reason in the realm of religion. It is not that human learning is entirely worthless, for all the arts that contain sound learning, depend on truth, and are useful for human affairs in general, are not opposed to religion (*First Corinthians*, on 1:17). The difficulty is that such arts cannot produce knowledge of God. Paul "does not utterly condemn" natural insight or wisdom or education, but he does affirm that "all those things are useless for obtaining spiritual wisdom" (on 1:20). Is this because the human mind is simply the wrong instrument for such a task? Not exactly: in Calvin's view, the situation should have been different. "The right order of things was surely this, that man, contemplating the wisdom of God in His works, by aid of the innate light of his own natural ability, might come to a knowledge of Him" (on 1:21). However, the order is no longer right. Human beings have turned away from the knowledge of God, which they might have enjoyed; ingratitude, perversity, and pride cloud our vision. Calvin employs the language of blindness, and to good effect: it suggests a lack of perception that, in the proper way of things, could have been available. He insists that it is self-inflicted: "It must be put down to our fault that we do not reach a saving knowledge of God" (on 1:21). And it is permanent: we are blind, not merely blinkered or blindfolded. Were it only a matter of disobedience or prideful conceit, we might attempt reform and pay closer attention. It is worse than that:

> Although Paul here tacitly blames human pride for the fact that men presume to condemn as foolish what they do not understand, at the same time however he shows how great is the feebleness, or rather the dullness of the human mind, when he says that it is not capable of spiritual understanding. For he teaches that it is due not only to the stubborn pride of the human will, but also to the impotence of the mind, that man by himself cannot attain to the things of the Spirit. (on 2:14)

Recognizing that it is hard to condemn the genetically handicapped, Calvin leaves us a moment of responsibility when we could have paid attention to God's glory in the works of God. Instead we make only a feeble start before being distracted. As he puts it, "men make progress in the universal school of nature to the point that they are impressed with some awareness of deity, but they have no idea what God's nature is.

On the contrary their thinking immediately falls away to nothing, and so light shines in darkness" (on 1:21). In this context he accuses philosophers of wandering blindly about in their speculations.

In sum, Calvin uses 1 Corinthians 1–2 to portray us as creatures with severe epistemological damage. We ought to have the proper cognitive organs to see God, but collectively we have at first blindfolded ourselves, and then allowed our capacities to atrophy to such a point that we are now blind to any light still available to us. We are worse off than Plato's prisoners: they at least saw images of reality, but the shadows of our philosophical speculations are the phantasms of our darkened minds.

To decide that Calvin was wrong about the human condition would take some skill and not a little self-knowledge. I do not set myself that assignment, but a more humble one. Is he right to conclude this *from our text*, or to use our text to illustrate his assessment of human cognitive capacities? The answer of this study of 1 Corinthians 1–4 must be that Calvin has gone well beyond the limited conclusions required by Paul's discussion of revelation. Our perplexities about the content of revealed Christian wisdom in 1 Corinthians 2 are not resolved by Calvin's assumption that Paul here as good as denies all natural knowledge of God. For Paul's denial has practically nothing to do with natural theology; it deals instead with a restricted number of Christian truths, probably eschatological, whose relationship to basic Christian doctrine is problematic. As we saw, even should Paul widen his doctrine of revelation to include the knowledge of God presupposed by the gospel and available through the law, this still would say nothing about the possibility of philosophical arguments about the foundations of theistic belief. In spite of Calvin, the natural theologian cannot be threatened by Paul's critique of human knowledge.

Lest I misrepresent Calvin, let me end with the assurance that he did think that philosophers could find a place in the kingdom of God. He rightly observed in his remarks on 1 Corinthians 1:27 that shepherds are the first to be called to Christ; then afterward come the philosophers. I do not dissent: but I hope to have shown that Paul may allow the wise to teach shepherds to watch the skies expectantly; and that, when both have worshiped, the wise ought not to be sent away.

CHAPTER THREE

Disembodied Persons and Pauline Resurrection: 1 Corinthians 15

They questioned what it is to rise from the dead. Mark 9:10

When they rise from the dead they are as angels in the heavens.
Mark 12:25

It was ancient counsel that should we speak no ill of the dead. But all of us who have buried the dead know how hard it is to speak of them at all. It is not that grief may cause us to stammer, though sometimes it asks for silence in place of words. It is instead that felt strangeness of any language of the present about persons who are not just absent but irrevocably past. We continue to speak of them as they were, but to speak of them in the present tense seems a denial of the very meaning of death.

Yet Christians do just this. We claim that our dead are with God, and that on the last day they will rise again. Against our claims, different charges have been brought. One is that we delude ourselves into denying death: we speak of the dead because we are ill. And no doubt many examples may be found of believers who keep their dead alive in imaginations and pictures betraying their own needs. But we are not alone in this and I shall speak no more of it.

Another charge is that our very speaking is ill because is harbors a self-contradiction: one either dies or survives, but never both. But this begs the question. We may be certain that either a thing exists or it does not, but the real question is whether the death of a person is in fact the end of that person's existence. Christian certainty claims that it is not.

The philosophical issues in this claim are many, and most of them are not explored in this study. My concern is not the ground of Christian certainty or all that it entails, but the ways in which the Christian doctrine of resurrection and philosophical claims about the nature of persons are related. For this I need to examine the concept of resurrection, and the first section of the study is a reminder of the distinction between this doctrine and the idea of immortality. The next section sketches the difficulties into which competing views of resurrection fall when they attempt to be both philosophically and theologically adequate. This leads to a fresh look at the ontological implications of Paul's writing about resurrection, chiefly in 1 Corinthians 15, and I develop an interpretation of resurrection that may be termed Pauline without directly imputing it to Paul's own mind. How this view relates to the resurrection of Christ occupies section IV. The last section attempts to assess the adequacy of this understanding of Christian resurrection. It concludes with suggestions for philosophical investigation, and asks about implications for our speaking of the dead.

I. IMMORTALITY AND RESURRECTION

It is possible to speak of the dead if only their bodies have died. By the "dead" we would then mean persons no longer inhabiting bodies, persons who are still themselves but who exist as souls or spirits. The philosophical doctrine expressed in part by this view is known as dualism, and it is almost as old as philosophy itself. In those moving last pages of Plato's *Phaedo*, Socrates drinks the poison that will kill his body to release his soul. But before he drinks he makes light of his friends' concern about his burial: they will be able to bury him, he says with a smile, only if they can catch him before he gets away. Socrates is not his body but something else.

To have any significance for life after death, Socrates' soul must not be simply one of the parts of the person who is Socrates, even a necessary or everlasting part; it must be the essential·thing that Socrates is. But again, to have significance, the soul must not be a thing as fragile as the body. So from the beginnings of philosophy much effort has been expended in discussions of the exact nature of the soul and its relationship to the person. By positing that it is immaterial, one can argue that it is unextended and without parts; that it is therefore logically incapable of dissolution; that it is incorruptible and immortal. Death is defined as the separation of soul and body, and it is defeated by metaphysics: not that human beings do not die, but when they do, their real personal essences persist, because there is no power that could ever destroy them.

No power at all? That claim gives Christians pause, because it comes into conflict with doctrines of God's omnipotence and God's creation of everything other than God. Belief in immortal souls works best when one can affirm that they have always been around; they join up with a body for a time, and then are released. It also goes well with doctrines of cycles of reincarnation. The belief thus had a natural home in the Greek world, preeminently in Plato's philosophy, though of course there were many Greeks who did not accept it. But its connection with Christianity was neither obvious nor easy.

The major reason for this lies in the fact that Christians, following out their Jewish roots, spoke not so much of immortality as of resurrection.[1] Only God is properly immortal (cf. 1 Tim. 6:16); dead human beings overcome death by being raised again. This belief was not universally accepted in Judaism, being denied by the Sadducees (Mark 12:18; Acts 23.8; Josephus, *Jewish War*, II.163–65). Nor is it prominent in the Old Testament. But the conviction that God's power is sufficient to overcome death does grow through the Old Testament period. There are stories of reanimated corpses connected with Elijah and Elisha (1 Kings 17:17–24; 2 Kings 4:18–37; 13:20–21);[2] and Ezekiel's vision of dry bones brought together and given life (37:1–14). Although that vision has to do with the nation Israel, individuals are included, and other prophetic affirmations apply this hope to individuals (Isa. 26:19; Dan. 12:2–3). By the intertestamental period there is an explicit understanding of an eschatological resurrection in which God will bring together even scattered pieces of bodies so that the dead will live again (2 Macc. 7; 14:37–46). And it was this kind of understanding that the first Christians brought to the resurrection of Christ.

In the Judeo-Christian context, then, the emphases are upon God's activity and the raising up of bodies from the sleep of death instead of the persistence of separated souls. The differences between this and the Platonic metaphysical view are so pronounced that it is possible to erect a high wall between immortality and resurrection: Oscar Cullmann did this in his 1955 Ingersoll lecture, "Immortality of the Soul or Resurrection of the Dead?" concluding that the answer to the question in his title is unequivocal: "the *teaching* of the great philosophers Socrates and Plato can in no way be brought into consonance with that of the New Testament."[3]

It would be wrong to place, as some do, all Greeks on one side of the wall, and Jews or Christians on the other, simply because Cullmann's quarrel is with dualism rather than paganism. And certainly as a historical construction the wall was broken down by the church fathers when they attempted to work out doctrines of resurrection in philosophical ways, as Harry Wolfson's Ingersoll lecture in 1956 shows.[4] They asserted, against views of immortality as a natural property of souls, that God alone can grant immortality; but they also argued that God would grant it to the soul as well as raise the body. So they held together the notions of resurrection and immortality. Of course, perhaps the fathers were wrong to do this. If, as Wolfson says, their concept of soul was basically Platonic, perhaps they were infected by dualism, a disease (according to some) from which all right-thinking persons should seek immunity.

We must now consider some of the ways in which this issue has been argued out in recent times, and the impasses to which we have apparently been brought in philosophical and theological discussion.

II. ARGUMENTS AND IMPASSES

Insofar as the philosophers of our century have been writing their footnotes to Plato, they have in the main arrived at conclusions contrary to his views of dualism and immortality. The two doctrines do not of course have to go together, it being possible to believe either one without the other; and it is probably true that dualism has been the more obvious object of philosophical interest in recent times, though in its Cartesian, rather than its Platonic, version. There is no need to trace the lines of argument: in one direction there are the materialists, no doubt bolstered to some extent by neurological evidence, who reduce mental states to brain states. There are in another direction those who find no need for separate mental substances, though they still affirm that human beings are not just machines or neurological systems. Some point to the difficulties dualism engenders for theories of agency; some attempt to unravel the complex ways in which our language about human beings depends upon embodiment. Their efforts are not unfamiliar to theologians in the English-speaking world, who know the names of Wittgenstein, Ryle, Strawson. They have heard of ghosts in the machine, and contemporary philosophical discussion about the nature of persons becomes an influence in the judgment that the church fathers were wrong.

This general critique of dualism has found potent application to the concept of immortality. But the argument has not simply been that if dualism is wrong, there can be no immortality; rather, the attack has centered on the very intelligibility of the notion of a disembodied human being, and on the difficulties of identifying souls, in a putative afterlife, with persons who have lived among us in this life. A successful attack on those fronts will mean that, even if dualism were true of present human beings, it would provide no answers for fundamental questions about a community of disembodied persons in another life. The shape and intent of critiques from this general direction have varied: Antony Flew speaks for the antitheist in abandoning all hope for, and intelligible talk of, survival. D. Z. Phillips, as a certain kind of fideist, retains our language but bases it upon a radical metaphysic in which the dead survive only as long as the living keep living to talk about them. A more moderate view is held by Terence Penelhum, who thinks that, although there may be some content given to a mental life apart from a body, the logical difficulties with identity mean that the notion of disembodied survival is absurd. He suggests that a doctrine of resurrection is a more promising approach to the question of survival, though it is not without its problems. Peter Geach holds very much the same view, believing that without the *possibility* of resurrection of the body, any hope for life after death is groundless.[5]

Naturally, this talk of resurrection among philosophers of religion attracts biblical theologians. It is their kind of language, not the foreign tongue of souls and immortality. So from the side of theology, recent philosophical analysis has exposed the two metaphysical sins of the church fathers, dualism and immortality.

While philosophy these days has been carrying out its investigations into our language about persons, theologians have themselves been busy at work on the history and development of biblical concepts. Their discoveries in the field of biblical anthropology (by which they mean the network of concepts having to do with the nature and functions of human beings) have been especially important for the Judeo-Christian understanding of resurrection. Put too simply, most of them conclude that there is no anthropological dualism in the Old Testament. Instead the Hebrew view of persons is overtly physical, as can be seen, for example, in its use of language about bodily organs to express emotions. Because there is inevitably talk of an inner life as well as of bodily existence, most theologians do not claim the Old Testament view to be reductionist or materialist; they prefer to talk of the human being as a "psychophysical unity," with emphasis upon the physical. And they remind us that the doctrine of creation affirms the intrinsic value of the material: there is no need for a dualist desire to escape from the body. We may be dust, but we are dust created by God, to know and serve God and our fellows.

So far, so good. While British philosophers and Old Testament prophets are not easily mistaken for each other, we are assured that their views on the metaphysical status of human beings are happily compatible.

What, then, of resurrection? Here, alas, we fall into difficulties. It is Paul who writes most of resurrection, and one might expect studies of his anthropology to emphasize the centrality of the concept of body (*sôma*) in Paul's view, to invoke the necessary physicality of persons, and to conclude with a doctrine of the resurrection of the body that could link up with our contemporary philosophical views about persons. Our expectations are not groundless, for that is how resurrection has been understood throughout the history of Christian thought, even by the dualistic fathers of the church. They saw Pauline resurrection as the raising from death of embodied persons, and creedal affirmations from earliest times have expressed belief in the resurrection of the body, not simply life everlasting.[6] But our expectations are not sufficiently subtle for modern theology. For it is not now uncommon to deny that resurrection has anything to do with physical bodies; it is instead *spiritual*.

It is, I confess, not always easy to discover what is meant by spiritual resurrection. A nineteenth-century German view seized on the distinction between form and substance, equated "flesh" (*sarx*) with the substance of our present bodies, and argued that since Paul's word *sôma* denoted the "form" of human beings, a resurrected *sôma* would be made of spirit, or "heavenly light substance."[7] Though such a view now holds little interest, a wide variety of scholars subscribe to the opinion that *sôma* is the best word in the New Testament to denote the whole personality, and they are thus able to make physicality incidental to the concept in many of its occurrences (this seems to be the case, for instance, where personal pronouns can be substituted for *sôma* without any loss of meaning, as in Rom. 6:12–14). Then, faced with Paul's "spiritual" body (*sôma pneumatikon*) in 1 Corinthians 15, it is possible to conclude that resurrection is the raising of personalities, and to take the additional step of claiming that these personalities are not physical at all.

The motives for such exegetical and theological conclusions are complex, and so it would be wrong to generalize about them. It is sometimes alleged, however, that the "spiritualizer" of resurrection desires to avoid the intellectual scandal of belief in a physical impossibility — the revivification of corpses. Spiritual resurrection at least allows us to hope without that particular scandal, and it also settles historical scandals about Jesus' resurrection, because that event when understood as spiritual may let sleeping bones lie. Sometimes, as for J. A. T. Robinson, spiritualized resurrection is a fact about the quality of present life and does not really mean the postmortem existence of persons.[8] For the purposes of this study, however, we may ignore attempts to squeeze the eschaton into this life completely. Instead, we must stay with those theologians who conceive of resurrected beings, whether Christ or believers at the general resurrection, as spiritualized personalities rather than embodied human beings.[9] For they bring us to our first impasse. Desiring to escape from the philosophical clutches of a Hume by avoiding miracles, a spiritualizer may run straight into the arms of a Ryle, to be forced to watch his resurrected ghosts fade into unintelligibility. Here our contemporary philosophy of persons triumphs over what it regards as scandal: personal immortality may not mean immateriality of persons.

Shall we summon these theologians to retreat back to firmer physical ground, where resurrected bodies really are bodies and not vanishing shadows of personalities? They will be welcomed by their fellow theologians who refuse to spiritualize resurrection,[10] and also by some philosophers of religion; but I have worries about the implications of such a welcome. The worries are threefold.

I approach the first worry by way of Jerry Cruncher in Dickens's *Tale of Two Cities*. He is a "Resurrection-man," an exhumer and stealer of corpses, and the irony of the term sets our problem. For the irony is not simple: it is not just that what he raises up is dead, without coming back to life; it is rather that, if resurrection means anything, it does *not* mean the straightforward revivification of corpses. That would be reanimation, and a reanimated body would be woken up to the same *kind* of existence it had before, including presumably the business of dying all over again. Yet (and this is the fundamental worry), in the end, this is the best that a philosophy of persons as essentially embodied can offer theology: reanimated corpses turned back into people as we have known them in this life.

I have argued this elsewhere, specifically for John Hick's notion of a resurrection world, which he introduced to serve certain conditions for the eschatological verification of Christian faith.[11] There I concluded that Hick's resurrection world works best where it is as much as possible like our present world in its ontology and epistemology. But the point may be generalized: we best know persons in this life, so in discussions of the conditions of knowing persons and using language about them in another kind of life, philosophy will offer its best where that life is most like this present life. The philosopher qua philosopher is most satisfied, then, with resurrected people who are as much like us as possible.[12]

But that will not do. It is worrisome in that it generates long lists of questions about the detailed characteristics of resurrected bodies, of the sort Augustine deals with in the closing chapters of *The City of God*: questions about the sex and age and size of new bodies, the status of aborted fetuses, and the fate of hair and nails lost from this present body. These concerns found their way into an influential medieval textbook, the *Sentences* of Peter Lombard (4:43,44), and Aquinas wrote on the subject (*Summa Theologica, supp.* q. 80). But surely the right attitude was Calvin's: he refused to explore what he called the "corners" of heaven, believing this to be a "superfluous investigation of useless matters" (*Institutes*, III.25). For the Christian may feel a little like a Platonist who is asked about the Forms of hair, dirt, and mud, and other "trivial and undignified objects" (*Parmenides*, 130c): there is an uncomfortableness about questions concerning haircuts in heaven or artificial limbs in the life to come. The indignity is logical: the questions are not so much superfluous as the *wrong sort* to ask. Full-blooded resurrectionists may call upon contemporary philosophy of persons for aid, but they will find themselves committed at least to the legitimacy of these questions, even if they do not know the answers.

This brings us to my second worry. If we do believe resurrected people to be as much as possible like us, then we have not taken into account the New Testament claim that in the resurrection we shall be changed. Some changes in social organization (e.g., no marriage, Mark 12:25) or even in behavior or character might not affect the basic issues of personal identity and the nature of persons. Nevertheless the type of change Paul has in view in 1 Corinthians 15 is (as we shall see) radical, as radical as the transition from seed to full grown wheat. The long series of contrasts he develops is intended to emphasize not the sameness of earthly and resurrection bodies but their difference. It is this difference that makes resurrection more than reanimation, and stops simpleminded questions about the specific physical characteristics of resurrection bodies; and it is this difference that makes theologically inadequate all philosophical discussions keeping resurrected persons much like the embodied persons we are now.

There is a third worry, more deeply theological in that it concerns our basic relationship to God, not simply an adequate exegesis of scripture. Put as a question, the issue is this: In what way do believers expect to know God in the life to come? In this present life they experience an epistemological gap between themselves and God (see the discussion of 1 Cor. 2 in chap. 2, above), bridged only from God's side by revelation. In the life to come, it might be argued, revelation will be clearer: perhaps revelatory events or persons will be more diaphanous, as it were, so that we will experience God's presence less ambiguously. But it strikes me that there is something wrong with a picture that keeps knowing there of the same character as it is here. For the expectation of believers is, I should think, not that God will do a better job of sending evidence across the gap to us, but that God will instead bring us over that gap. The believer hopes to have faith replaced by sight, to have the epistemological barriers removed. The veil that makes revelation necessary for this life will be torn away, and we shall know God as completely as God now knows us (1 Cor. 13:12; see chap. 7, below). In a word, we shall see God face to face — and (here is why that expression is metaphorical) not because God will be like us but because we shall be like God (1 John 3:2). That we should have to stand in line to see God, wait our turn, have only half an hour with God, or indeed any length of time that ends—all this is foreign to the believer's expectation of being in the presence of God and knowing God intimately. And yet, if we keep our resurrected persons much like those in our present world, I suspect that their epistemological structure and capabilities will be too much like ours to fit them for heaven.

I conclude that the respectable philosophical view of persons as intrinsically embodied, which promised much on behalf of resurrection against dualism and immortality, turns out to be less than helpful to the theologian. The philosophical impasse for the theologians of spiritualized resurrection may not exist for those who insist on the physicality of resurrected bodies, but the price of their comfort is a resurrection world that keeps the kingdom of heaven, if not on earth, then on a reasonable facsimile of earth. This philosophy at least seems to block the way to heaven.

This means that we have arrived at some strange impasses. At first it seemed that a holistic biblical anthropology would suit rather well a philosophy of persons as intrinsically embodied. The spiritualizers among the theologians spoiled that, opening themselves to criticism from those who deny the sense of immaterial immortality. But the physicalists have fared no better: their resurrection world, though philosophically safe, is not adequate. It looks as though it is hard to satisfy in one doctrine of resurrection the demands of philosophy and the requirements of adequate biblical exegesis and theology. Some champions of philosophy will not find that surprising, having suspected all along that Christian eschatology is incoherent, and they will find no need to speak more of it. Among the champions of theology there may be an opposite rejection of philosophy, or at least of the kind of philosophizing that brings us to such impasses;[13] they will warn against seduction by philosophical fashion and continue to speak about resurrection a great deal.

Either reaction may be extreme. I propose that we abandon neither theology nor philosophy as yet, turning instead to Paul's doctrine of resurrection, bringing to bear philosophical as well as exegetical questions upon his text.

III. Pauline Resurrection

The basic questions for this investigation are set from the side of philosophy: What is the ontological status of resurrected persons, in Paul's view? He speaks of bodies: but what are their characteristics, and how do they relate to the characteristics of antemortem bodies, especially in ways that affect personal identity and relationships?

I have already spoken of persons and bodies in the context of philosophical discussion, where they are terms whose relationship is problematic. Philosophers ask whether persons must be embodied, whether a person is more than a living human body functioning in a society, whether any sense can be attached to a disembodied person, whether a community of such bodiless persons is conceivable. All this talk would be foreign to Paul. He did not write about such questions, nor did he use any Greek word that would correspond closely to our understanding of "person." It may be argued that his Hebrew background did not even contain the distinctions necessary to our inquiry: there is no antithesis between matter and spirit in his writings, and indeed he never once uses the Greek philosophical term for "matter": "he was at no time concerned with philosophical distinctions."[14] Does it follow, then, that approaching Paul's text with our philosophical categories is illegitimate?

Not necessarily. We must of course proceed with care, attempting to understand the thought patterns of an author, especially from antiquity, as much in his own terms as possible. And about his conceptual framework we must not make historical claims that would be anachronistic. Nevertheless our present understanding of a text from the past will of necessity be structured by our own concepts and language. Even to deny distinctions in Paul requires that we ourselves operate with them, and the questions we ask of him must be asked in our own language.[15] Our language contains concepts such as person, and distinctions such as embodied vs. disembodied; and they lead us to ask about the ontological status of a Pauline resurrection body regardless of Paul's interest in that question or even his ability to frame it. We need not impute any metaphysical scheme to Paul himself in raising this question; we need only hope that there will be signs in his language, implications in his arguments, to help us decide among the options available to us.

First we should be clear about those options. Although they bear some relationship to Paul's account (in that they take the problem to be the relationship between present persons and resurrected bodies), they are generated from our contemporary philosophical concerns about personal identity through time and our ability to identify others as the same persons over time. They thus bring into closer focus, not Paul's intentions, but the logical and ontological possibilities about resurrection that are open to contemporary readers of Paul before they decide what his text encourages or permits. The first three options relate to the role that is played by the physical characteristics of human bodies in questions of personal identity, and assume that in resurrection as in this life persons are full-bodied beings. The possibilities, then, are these.

1. A resurrected body might be *just the same as* the body in this life, without any change of properties between these two states. A more

technical way of putting this is to say that the antemortem and resurrection bodies will be *qualitatively identical*. And let us suppose that they are *numerically* identical as well; that is, it is one and the same body that has continued into the resurrection from this world. However, it is logically possible to have *two* bodies that are qualitatively identical but in different spaces (the "two peas in a pod" possibility). We can then let 1a represent the possibility that the resurrected body is an exact *replica* of the antemortem body.

2. A second option is that the resurrection body may be the same antemortem body that has *changed* to some extent. How much change a thing can support (e.g., in its parts) and still be the same thing is a familiar problem; and it is related to a parallel problem: our ability to identify something that has undergone a good deal of change when we have not witnessed the process. But leave these aside: we do recognize people who have aged or altered in appearance, and sometimes when we do not, we can be helped toward recognition. It is that sort of change (call it "nonradical") which is a possibility for a resurrected body, and though incapable of precise specification it is a workable notion.   (2a): As in 1a, it is possible that the resurrection body should be numerically different from the antemortem body, but changed nonradically in its characteristics.

3. It is also possible to claim that a particular resurrection body corresponds to an antemortem body when the resurrection body is *radically dissimilar* to the earlier one. If the change is radical, an observer who has not witnessed the process of change will have difficulty guessing that what is now seen is identical with what was known before. We may call this a metamorphosis of the old body, remembering how such things happen in children's tales of fantasy (C. S. Lewis has a good description of Eustace's turning into a dragon and the difficulty of recognizing him in *The Voyage of the Dawn Treader* [Harmondsworth: Penguin, 1965], chap. 6).   (3a): Alternatively, there could be the destruction of the antemortem body and the creation of a separate resurrection body with characteristics radically different from those of the first body. Here questions of identification are stretched to the breaking point, unless we can discover some elements of identity between the two bodies. Dualism attempts one answer in claiming that a soul might be what these two bodies have in common.

This sketch of possibilities is certainly not sufficient to handle questions of personal identity in the life to come: for instance, I have said nothing about other important criteria of identity such as consciousness and memory. But my point is only to sketch possible options, not to flesh out how each of them would have to function.[16]

4. There is, however, a fourth option. The above possibilities all work on the assumption that the resurrection body is physical; but suppose we stress instead of the physical the mental aspects of persons, their self-awareness, feelings, perceptions, and memories. Of course some philosophers will forbid us to talk of personal consciousness without bodies. But if we ask to walk through that impasse in the name of ordinary people and Platonists,[17] we shall be able to argue that it is at least possible that in the resurrection the dead will not have physical bodies at all, but will be disembodied persons. In this case there will be no point to talking about changes, radical or otherwise, in physical characteristics, or about the persistence through change of matter. We shall be asked about identity and identification: but again, since the point of this exercise is the provision of options for interpreting Pauline resurrection, I draw it to a conclusion here.

Our task now becomes primarily exegetical and theological: we must examine the evidence of Paul's text to see whether it will determine a choice among these options or at least encourage movement in one direction rather than another. The weight of scholarship on this issue is so great as to make progress difficult, especially if we have to turn aside for details. I propose therefore to let our options guide the journey, and rather than traversing the whole of Paul's eschatology, to work more carefully through 1 Corinthians 15, with briefer comment on other passages reserved for a separate note.[18]

We may dispose fairly quickly with our first option. It is in effect what we earlier termed reanimation, and although some Jewish eschatological beliefs were of this order, expressing "the crassest materialism and literalism,"[19] Paul's view does not belong there. Even if (as some hold) we cannot be sure that this was not his earliest position in 1 Thessalonians 4,[20] the evidence of 1 Corinthians 15 is unequivocal. It is not just that the dead will be raised: "we shall all be *changed*," he writes (v. 51). And the argument in vv. 35–42, as we shall see, is designed to emphasize the differences between bodies. So there are no good textual reasons for holding on to option 1, or its 1a version either.

Now I might invoke Paul's analogy of seed and fully grown wheat with its radical differences in characteristics between the two states (v. 37), and argue that this makes option 2 unavailable as an adequate interpretation of Pauline resurrection.[21] Nevertheless it could be maintained that this possibility is not far from Paul's mind: he likens the resurrection of Christians to Christ's resurrection (vv. 20, 49), and in the gospel stories the disciples were able to recognize Jesus, though not always immediately (Luke 24). Accordingly we must delay this decision until we have examined the text more fully.

I propose to consider 1 Corinthians 15 in three stages, considering first the wider issue of Paul's argument and language, then focusing on his concept of *sôma*, and finally examining the specific notion of a "spiritual" body, *sôma pneumatikon*.

i. Argument and Language

The structure of 1 Corinthians 15 is too complex for brief comment, but its sections seem to me to be as follows:

(a) vv. 1–11
(b) vv. 12–34
(c) vv. 36–49
(d) vv. 51–58

(a) The first eleven verses are a unit about the gospel, which is the content of preaching and the object of belief (vv. 1, 2, 11). Central to this are the facts of Christ's death and resurrection; and Paul is at pains to enumerate the witnesses of Christ's resurrection, including himself. (b) All this is reminder to the Corinthians: its purpose becomes clear in v. 12, where Paul passes from a statement of fact to the use of this fact in an argument. The argument continues to v. 34, but within this there is some eschatological teaching, vv. 20–28, whose point we shall see shortly. Of the bones of the argument we need only say that Paul is concerned to bring evidence against the assertion of some Corinthians that there is no resurrection of the dead.[22] The evidence is marshaled from among the network of other beliefs Paul assumes the Corinthians to share. Preeminently there is the belief that Christ has himself been raised (see the list of witnesses). A subargument follows: should Christ's resurrection be doubted, Paul argues from counterfactuals he believes the Corinthians would want to deny. For if Christ has not been raised up, then proclamation is empty; Corinthian faith is empty; they are still under the power of sin; their dead are perished; further, the witnesses are all false; and the condition of believers is to be most pitied. A second line of argument begins in v. 29, where Paul appeals to their practice of baptizing for the dead.[23] Finally he points to his own behavior, his attitude to life and danger, as evidence that he shares belief in general resurrection. In all these ways Paul argues, not *that* Christ is risen, but *from* Christ's resurrection and all its implication *to* the conclusion that consistency requires belief in resurrection. But general resurrection does not follow inductively from one resurrection. That is the reason Paul introduces his eschatological teaching in vv. 20–28: to show in the grand scheme how Christ as firstfruits means ultimate victory over death for all humankind.

At verse 35 Paul shifts to the ground of an anonymous questioner. Suppose there is resurrection: But how are the dead raised? And with what sort of body do they come? The second question is answered first, in the next section (c) of the chapter, where Paul discusses in vv. 36–49 the nature and characteristics of the resurrection body. Verse 50 is an assertion after a string of comparisons, and may summarize what has gone before; but it is also transition to the last section (d), Paul's attempt to answer the first question, how the dead are raised. Having discussed the nature of the resurrection body, he is able in vv. 51ff. to assert that they are raised by being changed at the last trumpet. But this section quickly moves to pick up the eschatological terms of vv. 20–28, and the chapter ends with an exhortation reminiscent of its opening verses.

This truncated summary, though inadequate in itself, makes it possible to appreciate one feature of the general structure of the argument that might otherwise be overlooked. The section on the nature of the resurrection body is a subsidiary one, not part of the main line of Paul's thought. It answers what might readily be taken as an objection to resurrection, a metaphysical objection about bodies of the same critical cast as the Saduccean social or moral objection about resurrected marital relationships (cf. Mark 9:23). If we were so minded, we might rearrange the chapter to have vv. 50ff. meet up with vv. 20–28, leaving out the discussion of resurrection bodies, without twisting the major bones of Paul's doctrine. I do not propose that exercise, because the discussion of the objection is still important. But it ought to be seen in perspective.

These comments on the structure of the chapter lead to a point about its language. It is only in the answer to the objection that Paul uses the word *sôma*, never in the main line of argument. Even there, of the nine occurrences of the word, one is in the mouth of the questioner, five are used of nonhuman objects, and only three, all within v. 44, are used by Paul to refer to the resurrection body. Too much could be made of this, so we must wait to assess its significance after we have discussed *sôma* directly. But for now we should remind ourselves of how Paul does speak of resurrection in his main discussion. What he says, time and again, is that the *dead* (*nekroi*) are raised. That, I think, is instructive. For whatever Paul's fleshed-out concept of person, whatever the metaphysics of death or the mechanics of resurrection, surely by *nekroi* he means dead *people*. To say that God is God of the living and not the dead (Mark 12:27) is not to draw a distinction between two states of matter or flesh, but to speak of people like Abraham, Isaac, and Jacob. And to speak of resurrection from the dead is to say something primarily about people, not metaphysics.

Indeed, if we were to draw up a chart listing the occurrences in chapter 15 of *nekroi*, the terms for resurrection (*anastasis* and the verb *egeiretai*), and *sôma*, what would stand out immediately is the *isolation* of *sôma*, not its connection with the other terms. The only time *sôma* is associated with *egeiretai* is in v. 44. In thirteen other occurrences of *egeiretai* the subject is either Christ or the dead: but in v. 44 the subject is not *sôma*. Rather, there is a series of nonspecific uses of *egeiretai* in vv. 42–44, (corresponding to *speiretai*) translated in English by "it is raised," where "it" is a grammatical subject with no corresponding term in Greek and no specific antecedent. We could as properly (though not as idiomatically) translate, "there is raising," which leaves the precise identity of the thing raised a blank to be filled in by other means. So the proper grammatical structure of v. 44 will not let us say that a *sôma pneumatikon* is raised, but rather that the raising up of what is sown is *as sôma pneumatikon*.

Again too much can be made of this. But one comparable feature of Paul's language deserves notice before we settle on *sôma* itself. Not only does he say "we will be changed" (vv. 51, 52) and not "our *sômata* will be changed"; in place of adjectives modifying *sôma* he uses abstract terms, nonspecific general nouns, in vv. 50, 53, 54. This corruptible and this mortal put on incorruption and immortality: *not* our decaying and mortal *sômata* will be rendered incorruptible and immortal. A literary flourish, perhaps? Or is it rather a confession in the very grammar of the passage of something deeper, the inappropriateness of too detailed and literal a specification of what it is that we shall be?

ii. Paul's Concept of Sôma

Since Paul does in fact talk of *sôma* in connection with resurrection, it would be difficult to settle anything purely on the basis of the features of his language and argument that I have noted. His questioner asks pointedly: In what kind of *sôma* do the dead come? It would be perverse to ignore Paul's answer in our deliberation about the ontological status of the resurrection body.

Look first at the way the answer proceeds. Paul invites the questioner to consider two things: first, the great change that is utterly familiar to everyone between one state — seed — and another state of the same thing — full grown fruit — and secondly, the vast spread of the *kinds* of things there are in the universe. The text reads (vv. 35–42a, RSV):

> [35]But some one will ask, "How are the dead raised? With what kind of body do they come?" [36]You foolish man! What you sow does not come to life unless it dies. [37]And what you sow is not the body which is to be, but a bare kernel, perhaps of wheat or of some other

grain. [38]But God gives it a body as he has chosen, and to each kind of seed its own body. [39]For not all flesh is alike, but there is one kind for men, another for animals, another for birds, and another for fish. [40]There are celestial bodies and there are terrestrial bodies; but the glory of the celestial is one, and the glory of the terrestrial is another. [41]There is one glory of the sun, and another glory of the moon, and another glory of the stars; for star differs from star in glory. [42] So is it with the resurrection of the dead.

The emphasis is thus on the *differences* among the range of things that are *sômata*.

Paul's language is not technical, and suggests possibilities for the imagination rather than classifying things into clearly defined categories. Those who think of *sômata* as preeminently used of the human body or of persons must be disappointed here: when Paul refers to the human body in v. 39 he calls it *sarx*, not *sôma*. There are many kinds of *sarx*, but even more kinds of *sôma*: seeds and sun and stars, in fact all things in earth and heaven have their *sômata* given in infinite variety by God; each in its own way has its proper glory.[24]

Apply this now to resurrection. One point Paul makes is that, although human *sarx* decays in death, God's creative power is so richly manifested in the variety of God's work that the poor questioner's imagination need not stumble over resurrection. (Did not Daniel say that the resurrected righteous would shine as stars in the firmament?, 12:3.) But another point is made as strongly. It is not that whatever is resurrected will be of a different order from human *sarx* (as, for instance, sunfish differ from sunflowers or suns). Rather, there is a crucial continuity in the difference, as the controlling metaphor of sowing in vv. 36, 37, 42–44 makes clear. What is sown is the thing that is raised: but we must not limit God's power by attempting to predict how much like this mortal body the resurrected *sôma* will be. In the end it is up to God.

With this understanding of Paul's answer to his questioner, we are able to make an advance on our logical possibilities for the relationship between antemortem and resurrection bodies. We were left between option 2 and option 3, wondering which was a more satisfactory account of Paul's text. Option 1 was abandoned because Paul stresses *change* in resurrection. But now we must ask whether that change may be so great that we must talk of radical dissimilarities between this life and the life to come. I submit that Paul's text does require the possibility of radical change: not only the analogy of the dying seed, but the fundamental stress on God's ability to create vastly different kinds of *sômata*, will move us away from option 2 and its variant, 2a, in which resurrected bodies are still recognizably the same as antemortem bodies.[25]

But what of the fourth option, that resurrection is of persons who are no longer embodied? Does not Paul's very use of *sôma* mean that he has embodied persons in mind?

I think it very difficult to be confident about that. My argument might rest simply on the assertion of many theologians, that *sôma* means the whole personality rather than the physical body. We could then conclude that the theological claims made about resurrected human personalities (e.g., that they are subject to Spirit) may hold of disembodied persons. Suppose, however, that the opposite view is correct: Paul normally means persons in their physicality when he uses *sôma*.[26] Is physicality, then, part of its very meaning in Paul's reply to his questioner?

In fact all the things referred to in 1 Corinthians 15:37-41 are material objects: but the shared characteristics of the referents of a term do not always determine the meaning of the term. For instance, all the things referred to here are also the kinds of things visible to the naked eye, but that is not part of the meaning of *sôma*. So if we ask about the meaning of *sôma* instead of its referents, the case, I submit, is not obvious. The way Paul actually uses *sôma* here is strongly suggestive not of persons in their physicality or persons in their wholeness, but rather of our concepts of "thing" or "individual". Paul stretches the term beyond its customary NT use (where it refers to organic things only), and his argument about diversity works best when the term is considered a "bare" subject, with all its properties (perhaps even its ontological status) to be filled in by God's choice.[27] But the case does not rest there, for Paul goes on to offer some description of the resurrected *sôma* as a *sôma pneumatikon*, and to that we now turn for our third stage of textual consideration.

iii. Sôma Pneumatikon

At first metaphysical blush, the expression *sôma pneumatikon* seems contradictory: if a body is (as it is claimed) irreducibly physical, how can it be spiritual? That, however, is to misconstrue Paul's language, as many commentators have pointed out.[28] Paul wishes to draw contrasts, not describe the stuff of which resurrected bodies are made. The contrasts are strikingly expressed in vv. 42-49 (RSV):

> What is sown is perishable, what is raised is imperishable. [43]It is sown in dishonor, it is raised in glory. It is sown in weakness, it is raised in power. [44]It is sown a physical body, it is raised a spiritual

body. If there is a physical body, there is also a spiritual body. [45]Thus it is written, "The first man Adam became a living being"; the last Adam became a life-giving spirit. [46]But it is not the spiritual which is first but the physical, and then the spiritual. [47]The first man was from the earth, a man of dust; the second man is from heaven. [48]As was the man of dust, so are those who are of the dust; and as is the man of heaven, so are those who are of heaven. [49]Just as we have borne the image of the man of dust, we shall also bear the image of the man of heaven.

We can set out the distinctions between the antemortem state and the resurrected state in a list, placing at its head "natural" and "spiritual" (*psuchikon* and *pneumatikon*) as summarizing terms:

natural	:	spiritual	(v. 44)
corruption	:	incorruption	(v. 42)
dishonor	:	glory	(v. 43)
weakness	:	power	(v. 43)
earthly	:	heavenly	(v. 47)
mortal	:	immortal	(v. 53)

By mounting up these contrasts, Paul is anxious to assert a great change: the natural life we now experience, out of dust, subject to weakness, decay, and death, will change into its opposite conditions. We shall bear the heavenly image. So the meaning of *sôma pneumatikon* must be read in terms of its heavenly origin and function, and the characteristics it shares with the divine.

It is often pointed out that since a "natural" body is not one made out of *psuchê*, so Paul does not mean by a "spiritual" body one that is made of *pneuma*. True: but this truth depends upon Paul's complete silence on the very stuff of resurrection. When we come to raise the question of what he did say, we find all his language straining to point away from the conditions of this life to the glory of resurrection. Does it point away from the physical? From *this* physical body, yes. From the sphere of the natural, yes. To the heavenly realm of God's glory and power, yes. But to disembodied personal existence?

On the basis of Paul's text alone, I find myself unable to give an unhesitating yes to the crucial question that would move us decisively from option 3 to option 4 in the resurrection possibilities. A good part of my hesitation arises from Paul's lack of interest in this issue, so that I must be careful not to make a historical claim about what was in his mind when he wrote. Nevertheless, I do claim that it is legitimate to read what he did write as compatible with option 4, that resurrected people are disembodied but nonetheless real. Remember that most of what Paul writes in the chapter is about dead and resurrected people, not bodies; that he uses grammatically nonspecific forms without clear referents to bodies; that he stretches *sôma* to a "bare" subject; that he keeps pointing away from the natural order to the heavenly. In all this there can be found very little to deny that resurrection may be to disembodied personal life, and much to suggest it.

Of course, this is not all that Paul said about resurrection.[29] But by dealing with some other texts in a separate note (Appendix C) and with Christ's resurrection in our next section, we may move from Paul's text itself to think of some consequences of resisting my conclusion.

Suppose for some historical reason we believe that if Paul had made his mind more transparent, he would have unequivocally asserted a physical resurrection; and suppose further that for some theological reason this is the best way to conceive of resurrection within Christian eschatology. Then there follow two kinds of dissatisfying consequences, one related to philosophical problems about identity and one that concerns the very nature of God.

Come at the first by thinking of the importance of bodily continuity in discussions of personal identity. To know that this is the same person today as I talked with yesterday, there need not be strict qualitative identity between the body known then and the one known now (that is, option 1 above, p. 61). M. E. Dahl recognizes this in his notion of "somatic identity" for resurrection bodies.[30] Aging will make a difference to the man we met in London years ago: the exact stuff of his body then is gone, his appearance altered — but he is the same man. Nevertheless, Dahl's notion will not help resurrection identities. For, as we have seen, the alteration in resurrection is radical. And a theologically adequate doctrine of radical change will throw into confusion our regular tests of bodily identity over time (as we saw with option 3, p. 62). If a very different body (say, six inches taller, ten years younger, and of the opposite sex) claimed to be the London man, we would have a large problem on our hands. Worse, if the body were the body of some strange animal never seen before, Dahl's criterion of somatic identity would be of no help at all. Yet Paul's doctrine of resurrection requires a change this radical, if it is applied to a physical resurrection.

Perhaps we should deliberately tone down the extent of change in order to make the issue of identity more like our option 2, where recognition is possible according to the usual tests. Unfortunately, although this move is open to Dahl and others, the resurrection world it permits is the one built by the philosophers, where epistemological conditions are heavenly only because they are just like those back home. We have come up against that impasse again. Furthermore, any proponent of bodily continuity between this life and the resurrection world must face a related problem. On this view the resurrected body is the same as the antemortem body only where there is spatio-temporal continuity between the two. Suppose that this means that the decayed dust of the old body is refashioned into a new body (of either type 1 or type 3: the difference does not matter for my point). If it is the very dust, then the resurrection world must stand in some spatial relationship to this present world. Heaven will have an address somewhere in the universe. Those who preserve resurrection identity through continuity may not welcome this consequence, but it follows inescapably from their criterion.

We may, however, abandon that criterion. It can be argued that we can recognize the identity of bodies, even after some changes, without always satisfying ourselves about their spatio-temporal continuity: so resurrected persons might well be bodies spatially discontinuous with antemortem bodies without sacrificing their identities. John Hick's well-known stories about resurrection worlds makes use of this possibility, in that dead bodies are buried, whereas, new replica bodies are created elsewhere.[31]

Now assume that this possibility can fend off philosophical objections about its cogency. It still cannot serve resurrection as adequately as might be hoped. For if we have an identical (or nonradically changed) replica body in a resurrection world (options 1 or 2 above), then we do not cross our familiar impasse to a heaven of significant change. So we introduce the more theologically adequate possibility of a new creation, where the old body decays but God re-creates us in very different fashion (option 3). But then the *only* criteria available for identifying resurrected persons as the same persons before death, both for themselves and for observers, are consciousness and memory. Yet these are the very same criteria presumably available for the identification of disembodied persons. The creation of radically changed physical bodies for resurrected persons only complicates the issue of personal identity and adds nothing to it.

These problems with attempts to preserve personal identity by means of physical resurrection bodies lead me to the second kind of dissatisfaction, over the very nature of God. For it seems to me that those who insist on embodied resurrected persons are often influenced by a philosophical view about persons that, in the end, must sit most uneasily in the wider context of Christian theism. At its core is the God who is supremely real but not a physical object at all, personal without occupying space or requiring a body. We shall call God bodiless rather than *dis*embodied, for that suggests a previous embodied state. We cannot call

God a human person: but Christian tradition has insisted that God is nevertheless supremely personal, and it has found such language meaningful in spite of claims that embodiment is what makes people real. If there is scandal for philosophy in Christian theism, it is not so much over immaterial immortality as it is over the very nature of God as spirit. If dualism about persons is unfashionable, this must not make theists forgetful of the essential dualism in the Judeo-Christian tradition between God the creating spirit and the created order.

Of course this is not to say that invoking the concept of God solves philosophical problems. My point is simply that the language of resurrection must not be torn out of the fabric of Christian theism. Since the dominating pattern of that fabric, indeed its very ground, is one who is bodiless being — God — it seems strange to shy away from disembodied personal resurrection to accommodate the interests of some philosophers. The philosophical issues we can raise about resurrection and disembodied persons lie deep in the logic of theism itself, and should be neither considered nor resolved in isolation from our language about God. There are differences between God and other persons, which must be taken into account in our final section; but before coming to that issue we must complete our study of resurrection by considering how this account of a Pauline view fits with the resurrection of Christ.

IV. Is Christ's Resurrection a Pauline Resurrection?

For some, a major obstacle to interpreting Pauline resurrection as resurrection to disembodied personal existence will be their understanding of the nature of Christ's resurrection. They hold that the accounts of the resurrection of Jesus are not spiritualizing accounts: there is an empty tomb; an embodied, empirically accessible person is raised from death. Paul understood Christ's resurrection in this way, and drew explicit links between that event and the resurrection of the Christian dead. To spiritualize Pauline resurrection is thus to alter fundamentally claims about Christ's resurrection. And it seems fair to say that a primary motive among the physicalist interpreters of Paul is the desire to preserve an empirical resurrection in the case of Jesus. Conversely, those who spiritualize Pauline resurrection often appear to believe that this will avoid historical problems about the contents of Jesus' tomb or philosophical scandals about miracles. Disembodied resurrection as a general theological premise makes it possible to reinterpret Jesus' case in nonempirical terms.[32]

This is not the place for discussion of the many critical issues surrounding the doctrine of the resurrection of Christ. I want to fasten attention not on the meaning or truth of that doctrine, but on the supposed connections between sets of beliefs: What does in fact follow from beliefs about Pauline resurrection for beliefs about Christ's resurrection? The answer will, I hope, partly satisfy and partly displease both physicalists and spiritualizers.

It is necessary first to ask whether the question of connection may be settled on textual grounds. Does Paul say enough about the relationship between Jesus' resurrection and general resurrection to tie the two together in ways relevant to our concerns?

It is indeed clear that Paul ties together the fact of Christ's resurrection and the hope of resurrection for all the dead. The references include 1 Thessalonians 4:14; the argument in 1 Corinthians 15:12–34 summarized above; 2 Corinthians 4:14; and Romans 8:11. But contrary to some opinions,[33] there is nothing in these passages to support the contention that *just as* Christ's resurrection was physical, *so* the resurrection of believers will be physical. The emphasis is upon sharing in resurrection, not an ontological comparison between the resurrected body of Jesus and the resurrected dead. Nor will 1 Corinthians 15:49 support that weight: "as we bore the image of the earthly, so we shall bear the image of the heavenly." This no more means physical resemblance than does "the image of God" in Genesis 1:26–27. Nevertheless one Pauline assertion is relevant. In Philippians 3:20–21 Paul writes (RSV):

> [20]But our commonwealth is in heaven, and from it we await a Savior, the Lord Jesus Christ, [21]who will change our lowly body to be like his glorious body, by the power which enables him even to subject all things to himself.

Although there is no explicit reference to death or resurrection here, when the assertion is read in the light of 1 Corinthians 15 we may take Paul to make a clear connection between the glorious *sōma* of the heavenly Lord Jesus Christ, and that into which our present humble *sōma* will be changed.

Because this is the only crucial text on our question in the Pauline corpus, it needs consideration. Suppose we reject attempts to explain it away as pre-Pauline:[34] does it follow, as Gundry asserts, that Paul here unequivocally claims physical resurrection bodies for believers? The argument seems to be the following:

> (1) Paul regards the resurrection of Christ as physical.
> (2) Paul equates the glorious *sōma* of Christ with the resurrected *sōma* of believers.
> Therefore (3) Paul believes the resurrection of believers will be physical.

The conclusion is given added weight for Gundry by the intrinsic physicality of *sôma* in the second premise. But our reflections on 1 Corinthians 15 are pertinent here: that physicality is part of the very meaning of *sôma* in the context of resurrection is not obvious. Suppose, therefore, that we keep *sôma* as "bare" a subject as Paul's language and argument in 1 Corinthians 15 suggest. Philippians 3:21 will then stress that, as Christ was fashioned as a man, humbled, and exalted (Phil. 2:8, 9), so believers will be fashioned from their humble state ("vile body," KJV, is a wretched translation) to the state of Christ's present glory. That is the burden of Paul's assertion, and the metaphysics of both incarnation and resurrection are not in sight.

We, however, find ourselves concerned with a metaphysical question about resurrected persons. Will Gundry's first premise help our enterprise?

I propose to grant this premise, that Christ's resurrection is a physical one. This will not please those who spiritualize anything with the name of resurrection, but it will preserve something the physicalists regard as of great importance. In that the concern of this study is not the truth of the premise but its function in arguments, we might leave the matter there. Nevertheless three comments are not inappropriate.

First, the premise is a much better expression of the gospel accounts of Jesus' resurrection than are any spiritualizing reconstructions. The tomb was reported empty; the disciples thought they met again a real embodied person who could be seen and heard, who ate with them and invited them to try out the usual tests of personal identity. This does not mean the accounts are of a resuscitated corpse alone. They fit more closely my resurrection option 2 above, where there are signficant changes but changes not sufficiently radical to prevent identification.

Secondly, a physical resurrection suits the epistemological conditions of embodied human beings rather well. I do not mean by this that it would be a gracious concession to illiterates or people who have never read their Plato. Evidence and doubt are important everywhere. Something like my option 2, if it actually came about, would be important evidence for the claim that Jesus was not done in by death. But what could count as evidence, for the kind of people we find ourselves to be, for his purely disembodied existence after death? The disciples on one occasion during his life took Jesus for an apparition (*phantasma*, Matt. 14:26). So physical resurrection would, if it occurred, be just the sort of thing required.

Thirdly, if physical resurrection is the way to tell the story of Jesus' defeat of death, then it will be scandal to some casts of mind. But is there a way to tell *that story* that would avoid scandal?[35] The real scandal, as we saw earlier, is theism itself.

Return, then, to the argument which is supposed to conclude with the physicality of general resurrection. We have accepted the claim that Christ's resurrection is physical, and we may accept the claim of Philippians 3:21 that in the general resurrection believers will be changed from their humble state to Christ's glorious state. Still, the conclusion does not follow. For the argument as set out neglects the final stage of the story of the risen Christ: his ascension into heaven. It assumes that, if his resurrection is physical, the only way he could continue to exist is as an embodied being with (to use our earlier phrase) some address in the universe, to which we might apply to see him. That is not only peculiar: it does not fit with the story. After Easter the risen Jesus seems to have been physically present in discontinuous spaces, but nevertheless to have held onto his reality. At his ascension he disappeared from sight, to be physically present no longer.

Make what you will of the story. But if we are allowed to talk of disembodied persons, we might find ourselves conceiving of persons who, while retaining their identity, could move through successive stages of embodiment, disembodiment, and reembodiment. And we could, if we tried, conceive of calling their last move from embodiment to a final disembodied state, after this series, their ascension. That may in fact not be a bad way to tell the story of Jesus.

My point will be plain. The physical resurrection of Jesus is entirely compatible with his disembodied existence, as long as we do not attempt to claim that he was both embodied and disembodied at the same time. His ascension marks the terminal embodiment: henceforth we know him no longer in the flesh. Nothing in the story of incarnation, death, resurrection, and ascension forbids this conclusion, and much in the language of Christian theism encourages us toward it. The spiritualizers of resurrection may be partly pleased after all.

And what of Paul? I have argued that Pauline resurrection may be seen as resurrection to disembodied personal existence without illegitimately forcing Paul's text, regardless of what he himself may have thought on the matter. He may, of course, have been so unconcerned with the metaphysics of resurrection, apart from insisting on its reality, that some will argue against settling the matter from his writing. It would not surprise me to learn that he was in (at least) two minds: wanting to insist on the bodily resurrection of Jesus, but believing in an even greater change between this life and the life to come than was exhibited in Jesus' case. Why else, when answering his questioner in 1 Corinthians 15, does Paul not simply say: the dead come in the same kind of body with which Jesus was raised? Since the Corinthians are reminded of Jesus' resurrection as a basic premise, this could have satisfied them. But Paul sensed, perhaps, that this was not exactly the right answer. That he was in two minds does not, however, entail that his general account must be inconsistent, and my approach does permit reconciliation between his minds, and between spiritualizers and physicalists, as well as attempting to respect the text.

So I retain the advantage of allowing Paul to believe that Jesus' resurrection was in fact physical, something like my option 2. At the same time it can be argued that even if Jesus' resurrection was not initially to disembodied existence, nevertheless his postascension existence as truly personal provides us with a model for the resurrection of the dead within Christian eschatology. By allowing for Paul's own beliefs in physical resurrection we can satisfy one part of the story of the risen Christ and explain Paul's desire to talk of *sôma*; but by paying close attention to the reserve of Paul's language, the ways in which his arguments actually work, and the story of ascension, we may argue that disembodied resurrection is a legitimate conclusion for Christian eschatology.

V. BEYOND BOUNDARIES

It is time in this concluding section to remind ourselves of the problems from which we turned to examine the nature of Pauline resurrection. My account of contemporary theological and philosophical discussion discovered impasses between competing lines of argument over resurrection. The position of the church fathers on dualism and immortality was attacked by theologians with philosophical reinforcements. But the spiritualizers among the theologians were themselves regarded by some of their fellows as less than loyal, in that they abandoned the biblical concept of human beings as essentially embodied and the physicality of Jesus' resurrection. And all the theologians were threatened by philosophers: the spiritualizers, who opened themselves to attack from those who see persons as intrinsically embodied; and the physicalists, who found their philosophical allies offering them only an all-too-earthly heaven.

My drawing out of the metaphysical possibilities of Pauline resurrection and its relationship to the resurrection and ascension of Christ has attempted to reconcile the spiritualizing and the physicalist theologians, though hardly to the complete satisfaction of either. By paying close attention to the texts, I have attempted to preserve loyalty. But have I succeeded in pushing beyond other boundaries that seem to stand in the way of a satisfactory and coherent doctrine of resurrection?

There are concerns more particularly theological with which I have not dealt, and it might be protested that my account of Pauline resurrection as compatible with a disembodied state cannot be harmonized with some of those concerns. For instance, many will claim that an adequate account of Paul's eschatology must not deny a genuinely future day of general resurrection; and it might be argued that if resurrection involves disembodied persons, there will be nothing for God to do on Resurrection Day, for persons will already have been "resurrected" when they die.[36] But this attack has no target. From the view that resurrection will be to disembodied personal existence it does not follow that embodied persons become disembodied at the time of death, that the last trumpet is a series of staccato blasts from the first death on. It would follow only if personal consciousness, memories, and the like, were somehow inherently indestructible, but I have not asserted that. The view still requires God's resurrecting power and allows God to do what God will when God chooses. In fact the attack may be turned around: if resurrection is conceived as physical replication of a dead body (my options 1, 2, or 3), there is nothing to prevent God from making replicas one at a time, so to speak. If one thinks it necessary to have a guarantee against that kind of surprise, the best belief to hold is one in which resurrection stuff is spatially continuous with the stuff of the antemortem body: then having the dust and bones will be assurance that Resurrection Day is not yet.

There are other theological issues within eschatology not touched on here, but for most of them this view of Pauline resurrection will make no difference. An unresolved puzzle might be mentioned, however. How does the view fit with Paul's claim in Romans 8:18ff. that the entire creation is awaiting the revelation of "God's sons" in order to be released from the bondage of corruption into the freedom of their glory? Two comments in reply. First, the puzzle remains on almost any resurrection view, even a physicalist one, if the language is taken literally. Secondly, if it can be shown that it is theologically important to take it literally, one could develop a more complicated version of my view of Pauline resurrection. This would involve two stages: initial resurrection in a "redeemed" physical setting (Easter for all creation), and a final passage to disembodied existence for persons (everybody's Ascension).[37] I do not find myself compelled to run this version, but neither do I rule out surprises.

If I hope that these theological murmurs are stilled for the moment, it is only because we must listen to other challenges. The first will not be difficult to anticipate. You started with a distinction between resurrection and immortality (it will begin), and then had the church fathers keeping both views together. They at least retained resurrection; you on the contrary have ended up only with immortality. For what is the difference between a disembodied person and an immortal Platonic soul?

In reply I may beg to say that this view of Pauline resurrection does not require a Platonic dualism about the nature of human beings as we know them. Someone could in fact believe such dualism to be true and also accept this view of resurrection; but it need not work that way. The resurrection view demands that it is conceivable that in another world persons could exist as centers of consciousness and memory apart from bodies; not that it is true that in this present life persons are composites of two substances, soul and body. For that matter, an idealist doctrine about persons in this life is also compatible with my view; but one is not required by the view to believe such a doctrine. Further, the occurrence of this kind of Pauline resurrection is not the inevitable outcome of any metaphysical theory about human beings. The fathers were right to insist that death is not defeated by metaphysics, but by God's action. For that reason, the language of immortality is still foreign to Christian eschatology. To speak of "immortal persons" is to suggest an imperviousness to nonexistence that is not to be found in my account. The dead still need to be raised from death, though their bodies are not dug out of graves.

However, even if these objections do not raise impassable barriers, there remains a fundamental issue in need of careful consideration. My account of Pauline resurrection has employed the concept of disembodied persons in order to avoid difficulties in physical views of resurrection, and as a way of interpreting both the radical change in resurrection and the ascension of Christ. Nevertheless, this concept is just the one in dispute among the philosophers we met in section II. If the very notion of a person inextricably involves embodiment, then whatever virtues there are in my account dissolve into unintelligibility: people cannot be people without bodies, here or in any world.

As a countermove, I pointed out at the end of section III that the idea of bodiless person seems an inextricable part of the framework of Judeo-Christian theism. Since my thesis about resurrected persons is interwoven with the dominant pattern of this fabric, it ought not to be picked apart on its own. The imagery aside, there is this truth about the interweaving: if someone wishes to deny the strong thesis about the possibility of any bodiless being whatever, this denial of theism itself will destroy my weaker thesis about Pauline resurrection. Nevertheless, theists committed to the coherence of the concept of God do not necessarily have to agree that talk of resurrected disembodied persons makes sense. For they will point to differences, not similarities, in the threads. God is bodiless: but resurrected persons are those who, on my account, used to have bodies, and this will make a difference to their consciousness. Again, it has been argued that a plurality of disembodied persons is not plausible; but of course resurrected persons form a plurality, and a rather large one at that. Or again, because there is no automatic metaphysical right to continued existence beyond death for created beings, this raises the question of what will constitute limits and finitude in resurrected persons if they have no bodily boundaries.

Such concerns force us, I think, to ask about the basic conditions that must be met if we are to have a satisfactory account of resurrected persons. It is not hard to begin to answer. After death there must be individual persons who know and love God, and are known and loved by God: without this there are no resurrected *people*. They must be, in some sense that they can appreciate, the same persons as those who lived as human beings in this life: without this there are no *resurrected* people. That, however, is only a beginning. Philosophical discussion will continue to explore what it is for persons to know and love each other: they require, it would seem, thoughts, feelings, memories; distinctness from each other; ways of acting upon each other; a language in which to communicate; and perhaps other abilities or opportunities. Such conditions may be met in this life by our embodiment in a physical world. Whether they could be met in another world that is not spatial and in which persons had no physical bodies is the question at issue, and philosophers are not agreed on this.[38] Much will depend on what the words mean. If, for instance, "body" means simply "whatever it is that individuates me and makes possible my knowing and loving others," then of course it is patently self-contradictory for anyone to hold that even God could resurrect persons to disembodied existence. In that sense, for me to be at all is to be (or have) a "body." But that does not answer the substantive question that lingers in our thinking about resurrection, the relationship of our present human bodies to the kind of persons that we shall be.

On that question, my account of Pauline resurrection has rejected options 1 and 2 in which resurrection worlds are something like the worlds we know. Those who link the concept of "body" with the very conditions of personal existence may prefer my option 3. If I remain for now with the fourth possibility — resurrection to disembodied personal existence — it will be to emphasize not what we know of that life, but what we do not. Both options may allow radical change, and thus forestall those unworthy questions about the physical characteristics of heavenly bodies, so that heaven may be heaven.[39] But my thesis about disembodied persons takes the further step of dissolving all that is familiar about our present world and way of living: the adjective describing our state is negative, but it places us with God.

That says little of the dead, except that resurrected people are real, and their experience one of glory. We shall continue to talk of theories of resurrection and to philosophize about the conditions of personal existence. But the dead themselves we commit to God. For, after all, that is how it must be, if death is death. The barrier of radical change and disembodiment draws a boundary to our knowledge and to our language. Christians do speak of their dead as with God, awaiting resurrection to glory, and in this their words express confidence in God. But if we shall be so changed, there is little more for our language to describe: ours is not the tongue of angels.[40] Yet trust and fear, longing and hope, remain for our feeble expression. Where are the right words? The boundary remains. Philosophy and theology fail; but in the experiences of art and music and poetry we may find other forms of expression. *Et lux perpetua luceat eis*, we ask for our dead; and Mozart or Fauré fill our words when we cannot say what that light will be.[41] At the close of the day Christians may pray also for themselves, "Lighten our darkness, O Lord." They ask, because the burden of ignorance is not lifted. They have the promise of glory; they dare not ask for more.

APPENDIX C: RESURRECTION ELSEWHERE IN PAUL'S WRITINGS

Eschatological language pervades Paul's writing, and its themes are so strong as to cause some (like A. Schweitzer) to regard them as the key to Paul's thought. On that, and on the question of development within Paul's eschatology (see note 20 to this chapter), there are differing opinions, but these differences do not need to affect our inquiry. The question is one of consistency on one point only: Is there any passage in Paul that would be inconsistent with the interpretation of 1 Corinthians 15 developed here? Or to put it another way: Are there other places in Paul's eschatological discussions that will help us settle on one of the resurrection options set out on pp. 61-63, above? We need to look at passages in 1 Thessalonians, 2 Corinthians, Romans, and Philippians.

1. 1 Thessalonians 4:13–18 says nothing that will decide among our resurrection options. The fact of resurrection for those who are dead in Christ, and the snatching up of those who remain alive, suggest perhaps something like options 1 or 2, in that the language of descent and clouds recalls the ascension in Acts 1. But the possibility of change is not denied, and it would be rash to argue that this text is flatly inconsistent with option 4, especially in light of the interpretation of ascension proposed in section IV of this chapter. Whiteley correctly asserts that the passage is "compatible with almost any answer" to problems about the nature of the resurrection body (*Theology*, 249).

2. In Romans 6–8 Paul stresses the present participation of believers in the death and resurrection of Christ. If there is no future general resur-

rection referred to in these chapters, then they have no bearing upon our question. But Paul need not be read as asserting only a completed resurrection in salvation (contrary to Whiteley, ibid., 254): the future tense of verbs in 6:5, 8 and 8:11, as well as the eschatological expectation of 8:17ff., point to future resurrection and glory (cf. Barrett, *Romans*, on 6:5, and Gundry, *Sôma*, p. 44, esp. note 2). In that case, does Paul's language require a physical resurrection?

Two considerations seem relevant. First, Paul links the resurrection of believers with the resurrection of Christ in the verses just mentioned. At the basic level this linking is a participation in the events of death and resurrection, so that the stress would be on a future fact, not on a detailed description of how it would all come about. But there is the implication of *likeness* as well: in 6:5 Paul says that we shall be joined with Christ in likeness of his resurrection. And 8:17 stresses our sharing in Christ's glorification (the theme of glory is repeated in vv. 18, 21, 30); 8:29 claims that it is God's purpose that we should be conformed to Christ's image. All of this is compatible with the interpretation of 1 Corinthians 15 advanced above, and indeed in Romans there reappears the vocabulary of glory and image. Whether the "likeness" of Christ's resurrection demands a physical body is not clear: perhaps the word means the "image" of death and rising again—that is, baptism (so Barrett, *Romans*, on 6:5). If not, the likeness need not be physical: see section IV of this chapter.

This does, however, raise a second consideration. In 8:11 Paul specifically uses *sôma* in connection with resurrection; and he talks in 8:23 about the redemption of the *sôma* in the context of the groaning of the whole creation. Does this rule out my option 4 by requiring a physical resurrection? I have commented on the issue in 8:23 in section V, above, so here I restrict myself to 8:11. The verse reads:

> But if the Spirit of him who raised up Jesus from the dead dwells in you, he who raised Christ Jesus from the dead will also enliven our mortal bodies through the indwelling of his Spirit in you.

Of course, here *sômata* may mean simply "selves." Paul talks of the raising of Jesus from the dead, not the enlivening of Jesus' body from among dead bodies; hence his interest remains, as we saw in 1 Corinthians 15, in persons. Robert Gundry argues vigorously against this (*Sôma*, 37–46). His view, however, requires that "the body is dead" in v. 10 means not (as we should expect) that the self in its "fleshly" life has died with Christ (cf. Barrett, *Romans*, on 8:10), but that physical bodies are mortal. Although there seems a good deal of stretching in this interpretation, I shall leave detailed criticism to the specialists, observing only that Paul's vocabulary need not always meet rigid standards of precision to be intelligible. Nevertheless, even if we do take *sômata* here as indelibly physical, what Paul says is only that our corpses will be revived. Then the natural understanding is that he means option 1, or perhaps option 2, at most. But no one would feel compelled to argue that 8:11 *denies* change in resurrection just because Paul does not mention it here. We look instead to 1 Corinthians 15 for his developed doctrine of resurrection: and I see no reason why that developed doctrine, including the form in which I have interpreted it, is not to be read into Romans 8:11. By itself the verse will not yield enough to decide upon any options for resurrected bodies or persons.

3. For a discussion of Philippians 3:20–21, see section IV of this chapter.

4. That leaves 2 Corinthians 5:1–10 (RSV):

> For we know that if the earthly tent we live in is destroyed, we have a building from God, a house not made with hands, eternal in the heavens. ²Here indeed we groan, and long to put on our heavenly dwelling, ³so that by putting it on we may not be found naked. ⁴For while we are still in this tent, we sigh with anxiety; not that we would be unclothed, but that we would be further clothed, so that what is mortal may be swallowed up by life. ⁵He who has prepared us for this very thing is God, who has given us the Spirit as a guarantee.
>
> ⁶So we are always of good courage; we know that while we are at home in the body we are away from the Lord, ⁷for we walk by faith, not by sight. ⁸We are of good courage, and we would rather be away from the body and at home with the Lord. ⁹So whether we are at home or away, we make it our aim to please him. ¹⁰For we must all appear before the judgment seat of Christ, so that each one may receive good or evil, according to what he has done in the body.

This passage has occasioned such intricate debate that I cannot begin to deal with it adequately in a few paragraphs; but fortunately not all of its problems impinge directly on this discussion. I draw attention to four features of the text, and raise questions about some of the literature on the passage.

(a) Notice that Paul abandons the concept of *sôma* in discussing the postmortem state. He continues to talk of persons, of course (the passage is written in the first person plural), but not of persons as *sômata* past death. Indeed, in the larger context of 4:7 to 5:10, *sôma* occurs five times, but always with reference to the present life.

(b) It might be said, however, that the imagery of dwellings and clothing takes the place of the concept of *sôma* and does its work. Paul contrasts two kinds of house (*oikia*) in 5:1, 2, picking up a contrast from 4:18. There is on the one hand the earthly, temporary, destructible tent, belonging to the seen and the mortal; and on the other hand the dwelling in the heavens, eternal, not made by hands, and associated with God, life, and the Lord. The verbs having to do with putting clothing on or off (vv. 2, 3, 4) seem to function in the same way as verbs for being at or away from home (vv. 6, 8, 9). It is therefore tempting to see being clothed in a tent as something like being a soul in a body. But more on this later.

(c) If after death one comes to a permanent home, there is a great *change* in one's condition. This is compatible with 1 Corinthians 15, with its emphases upon the differences between the antemortem and the postmortem states. The imagery does not allow for resurrection as the revivification of corpses, or the enlivening of mortal (physical) bodies: here the old is left behind.

(d) Further, there is no bearer of continuity between these two stages except the persons themselves. The concept of *sôma* is not available for this purpose in the passage, nor is there any analogy like the seed from 1 Corinthians 15. Still, this does not prevent Paul from assuming the continuity of persons.

Now the questions.

First, does the passage suppose, as the traditional interpretation has it (cf. Whiteley, 254ff.), an anthropological dualism? It looks as though Paul teaches something here about an "intermediate" state of nakedness, in which a "soul" awaits the putting on of a heavenly body. This gives rise to other questions of eschatological detail: Is this the *sôma pneumatikon*? Is the passage about resurrection at all, or only about the wait until resurrection? Much dispute centers on E. E. Ellis's analysis of Paul's language (in "The Structure of Pauline Eschatology"; for comments, see Whiteley, 255–58, and Gundry, 149–53), which concludes that by the earthly dwelling Paul means not the body but "the securities of earthly existence." Because much of the debate centers on notions of corporeity and solidarity, it might be overlooked that Paul's language need not be read only in the light of corporate vs. individual categories. For it is possible that he is merely contrasting two *environments*: one in which we now find ourselves, and one for which we long. Of course one may push him to individuate these environments, so that each of us has a "home" at present in our physical body. But it is curious that he does not speak of *sômata* in connection with the longed-for environments, and that he refers to it only in the singular. So we may refrain from squeezing too much metaphysics out of the passage by letting Paul remain vague about the environments.

Secondly, suppose we take Ellis's view of the passage, that it is about corporate solidarities in Adam and Christ. Ellis then must say something about its relationship to the parousia: and he ends up claiming that there is no escape from materiality at death, but instead a changed "psychosomatic organism which envelops and pervades the whole personality and finds its fulfillment in the deliverance of the whole man at the resurrection" ("Structure," 43). But is this a conclusion from our passage? Ellis is forced back to 1 Corinthians 15 for this view, because he must hold that 2 Corinthians 5 does not bear upon the nature of resurrected persons. That move, however, simply allows us to argue the case for option 4 straight from 1 Corinthians 15 without reference to 2 Corinthians 5, for there is nothing in the latter text to contradict the former.

Thirdly, a question about C. F. D. Moule's treatment ("St. Paul and Dualism"). Moule thinks there *is* a difference between the two texts. The first uses the language of change and transformation in resurrection; the second speaks of *exchange* of one dwelling for another, of "using up" matter (as Moule puts it). This would permit a view of resurrection to disembodied existence in 2 Corinthians 5, but not in 1 Corinthians 15. Yet must the texts be as different as Moule supposes? The transformation and change in 1 Corinthians 15 is, on my account, of persons, not matter. And the exchange of 2 Corinthians 5 is not of persons (for what would *that* mean?), but of environments. We change from one way of living to another; in exchanging dwellings we are ourselves radically changed.

On any account there will be eschatological puzzles not solved by 2 Corinthians 5. For most of these accounts, 1 Corinthians 15 will be determinative of the nature of resurrected bodies, and therefore not inconsistent with the later text. Only if we insist on a strong body/soul dualism in my point (b), above, does the passage hold problems for my interpretation of a Pauline resurrected person as disembodied; but I have suggested that a weaker reading of (b) as contrasting environments is an acceptable account. Moreover, points (a), (c), and (d) all encourage the view that Pauline resurrection is indeed compatible with disembodied personal existence.

CHAPTER FOUR

Ethical Authorities: 1 Corinthians 7

> Conseillyng is nat comandement
> He putte it in our owene juggement.
> Chaucer

It is not rational to act or believe without justification. Not all beliefs have to be justified in the same way, nor do basic beliefs stand in need of justification by reference to something more basic. Rationality does not moreover require endless processes of justifying commentary on one's behavior. Nevertheless to be reasonable in acting and thinking is to be willing to be guided by reasons, and this means that reasonable beliefs and behavior are capable of justification.

The determined skeptic may argue that religious beliefs are unreasonable: belief in God is not justifiable for rational people. Some believers, for their part, reject the concern for reasonableness as an expression of human pride. That Paul's critique of worldly wisdom does not require the divorce of religion from reason was argued in chapter 2, above, and in the last section of chapter 7, below, there will be some comment on the reasonableness of belief in a loving God in the face of contrary evidence. Now, however, we turn to the question of rational justification in the believer's ethical life. Although there have been different ways of specifying the relationship between faith and morality, believers do insist that their belief in God has something vital to do with their ethics. But this claim, at least as it has been widely understood, has opened them to the charges of immaturity and irrationality. We need first to see how this has come about.

I. AUTHORITY AND JUSTIFICATION

It is well known that moral philosophers find it difficult to reach agreement about the justification of ethical values and actions. Some advance deontological theories of intrinsic rightness and duty for duty's sake;

others propound teleological theories based on the good or bad consequences of actions or rules. Nevertheless, almost all philosophers agree
that ethical judgments are not simply expressions of personal taste or
preference, and that they therefore require justification beyond invoking one's likes or dislikes. Further, there is strong agreement that moral
questions are not to be settled by a simple appeal to authority. It is not
only immature but, more strongly, improper in the logical sense to decide
one's moral values and rules by consulting and obeying a moral authority: far from permitting any rational defense of morality, this drains the
meaning from the notion of ethical justification. Why is this so?

The explanation typically given asks us to imagine someone who
professes to determine ethical values and actions by reference to some
authority, whether person, group, or institution. The right thing to do
or the proper virtue to develop is to be decided in accordance with the
desires or will of the authority, and the authority functions as justification for all moral beliefs and values. But — here is the crucial question —
what is it that justifies the moral values and choices of the authority?
Or to put in another way, the obedient moral agent should be able to
ask what makes it *right* to obey this authority. If one simply accepts the
answer of authority to one's question, then already one is so committed
to obedience that the activity of providing justification is empty: nothing
could count as a reason for disobedience. If, however, it is legitimate
to ask for reasons, then there must be a way of determining what is right
independent of authority. In this case authority may have certain practical functions, but it cannot serve as the logical ground of morality; to
obey it without question would be ethically irrational. It is in the very
nature of ethics to be autonomous in at least this limited sense of being
logically independent of authority;[1] and this independence entails that
it is always appropriate to ask for some kind of justification for ethical
decisions beyond appeals to authority.

Given this understanding of authority and justification in ethics,
it is not hard to imagine how the religious person in the street will appear to the philosophical expert. Within the Judeo-Christian tradition
God's moral authority has been considered supreme, for God's holiness
includes not just distance and separateness from creatures but also perfection and absolute goodness. Obedience to God is an absolute duty for
all categories of believers, and the invocation of divine authority is sufficient religious justification for their actions. Morality for the believer is
thus indelibly *theological*, and it is this character that makes religious
ethics vulnerable to challenge from philosophical critics.

The basic challenge entered the history of philosophy outside the
Judeo-Christian tradition in Plato's *Euthyphro*, where Socrates asks about

the appropriateness of defining pious action as that which all the gods love: Will their love make an action pious, or will they love it because it is pious?[2] The question was easily translated into the language of biblical tradition: Does God command an action because that action is right, or does God's commanding the action make it right? The problem has persisted through the centuries, so that in our own day G. E. Moore, W. K. Frankena, and scores of other writers have discussed the relationship between religious and ethics in these terms.[3] A major point usually made in discussions of the issue is that religious believers are wrong if they think they can justify a morality defined in terms of God's commands; such a religious morality is ultimately arbitrary, not the subject of rational discussion or choice. The philosophical critic sometimes carries the attack further: this morality can be described only as infantile, for it is immature to rest ethics on religion. A standard approach is P. H. Nowell-Smith's characterization of believers. For them, he maintains:

> [Morality is] an affair of being commanded to behave in certain ways by some person who has a right to issue such commands; and, once this premise is granted, it is said with some reason that only God has such a right. Morality must be based on religion, and a morality not so based, or one based on the wrong religion, lacks all validity.[4]

Where moral choice is only a matter of obedience or disobedience to commands, it is natural that rules will be seen as right regardless of consequences, so Nowell-Smith puts religious ethics into the deontological category. But, seeing no virtue in deontological theories, he suspects that the only explanation for believing that rightness is intrinsic to a rule is an immature capacity to figure out reasons for oneself. He then easily links deontology with Piaget's "heteronomous stage" of moral development, where all rules are accepted without question from one's authority. Nowell-Smith is convinced that the religious mentality is essentially a matter of blind, unquestioning obedience. Just as children must grow up to interpret, judge, and modify rules for themselves, so he thinks religious believers should outgrow their ethical dependence upon God.

The assumption that theological ethics is at base a matter of unquestioning obedience is a pervasive one.[5] In its psychological claim it may be true of certain believers, though that proves little: one does not need to be religious to be immature. It is the stronger charge that deserves attention: Is it indeed the case that believers cannot defend their ethics because their morality is obedience to divine authority? There are specific things to be said to specific critics,[6] but also more general arguments in favor of an ethic of divine commands.

For instance, it is difficult to support a contention that obedience is in itself ethically inferior: sometimes it is manifestly wrong *not* to obey a moral authority, just as it is epistemically wrong not to believe some truths on authority though one has not worked them out for oneself, and perhaps could not do so. Some authorities have the right to issue statements for belief or commands for obedience, and one defense of the virtue of religious obedience is that God supremely has this right.[7]

A different line of defense has been taken by Robert M. Adams, who preserves a determining role for divine commands in Judeo-Christian ethics by distinguishing between moral rightness or wrongness, on the one hand, and other values, such as kindness or cruelty, on the other.[8] Anything contrary to God's commands must be ethically wrong for that reason; but value claims, such as that God is loving, are not determined by reference to divine commands. If, beyond expectation, God were to command acts of gratuitous cruelty, believers would not be committed to obedience, because they could not say that these acts were right or wrong; their normal moral concepts would break down.

There will be continued philosophical debate about Adams's view,[9] and no doubt others will defend the believer's obedience to divine commands. But that is not my present concern. For although the issues are philosophically stimulating and religiously important (how could any believer deny the relevance to morality of the commands of a loving God?), the debate tends to ignore a crucial issue: the actual character of reasoning in accepted pieces of theological ethics. Not that philosophers are unaware of the need for additional work. Adams, for example, acknowledges that a divine command theory requires a theory of revelation. Nevertheless it is possible to assume that the primary epistemological task is to justify our knowledge of specific commands, and the primary ethical task is to justify obedience to those commands — and in these assumptions to miss important features of paradigmatic ethical reasoning within faith. To put the matter quite simply: even when believers agree that some command has divine authority, they often find that they must do more than ask themselves about obedience. They must ask, not just how the command is revealed, but what it means to act in accordance with it. The life and structure of theological ethics in the Judeo-Christian tradition may be difficult to capture in a sentence,[10] but surely its ethical argument has been much more concerned with *how* than with *whether* to obey. If this is true, then both the critics and defenders of theological ethics as an ethic of obedience will not accurately reflect the relationship between faith and morality.

It is to explore in part this possibility that I propose an examination of Paul's ethical advice in 1 Corinthians 7. The exploration is only partial. This is only one specific piece of argumentation, preoccupied with issues about sexual and marital relationships: it would be precarious to generalize from it to wider concerns in Paul's ethics, and even more dangerous to permit it to generate broader theories about revelation and theological ethics. Nevertheless the passage is a useful beginning for those interested in a case study of authority and obedience. Because Paul's writings have special status in Christian ethics, his reasoning may be seen as paradigmatic rather than merely typical, and although the issues are specifically focused, they are not trivial. Moreover the very fact that Paul's advice in the chapter has been the subject of immense popular disapproval (if not misunderstanding) may enhance the utility of the text: if this helps us distinguish what he counsels from the underlying justifications for his counsel, our understanding will be advanced. But perhaps the best reason for choosing the chapter is that Paul here explicitly works with authori*ties* to arrive at his ethical advice, forcing us thereby to recognize the complexity of religious obedience.

And so to the text — though not to all the problems it raises.

II. SOME FORMAL FEATURES OF THE TEXT

There are so many problems that spring up from a reading of 1 Corinthians 7 that it is often difficult to discern the lines of Paul's reasoning. If one judges naive (or worse) some of his statements on sex and marriage, then it will be easy to believe that there is no reasoning worth looking for in the passage. Ignoring that, there seems no reasoning in the form of a developed theology of marriage upon which Paul's advice is explicitly based. Moreover, the passage presents historical knots to the reader's understanding. What did the Corinthians say when they first wrote to Paul on these subjects? What sociological factors moved them to consider separation and divorce in their community? What was the nonmarried but potentially charged relationship between male and female to which Paul refers? None of these questions can receive consideration here. Others have dealt carefully with them, and may be consulted for an understanding of the content of the chapter.[11] Since our concern is with the structure of Paul's reasoning, we can permit ourselves some unclarity on specific exegetical points. Indeed we may find virtue in the lack of a detailed theology of marriage, for this permits the issue of authority to come quickly to the fore.

We need the text before us. The RSV is here reproduced, but in order to suppress the specific content and to bring out certain features of Paul's language, I have italicized some of the text, in three categories.

Wherever the English renders an imperative in the Greek, the verb is italicized; value words like "well" or "better" are in italics; and verbs of judging or saying or opining, as well as nouns for commands or opinions, are also in italics. Though crude and in need of qualification in the light of the original Greek, the technique will serve our initial purpose. The RSV reads:

> Now concerning the matters about which you wrote. *It is well* for a man not to touch a woman. ²But because of the temptation to immorality, each man *should have* his own wife and each woman her own husband. ³The husband *should give* to his wife her conjugal rights, and likewise the wife to her husband. ⁴For the wife does not rule over her own body, but the husband does; likewise the husband does not rule over his own body, but the wife does. ⁵*Do not refuse* one another except perhaps by agreement for a season, that you may devote yourselves to prayer; but then come together again, lest Satan tempt you through lack of self-control. ⁶*I say* this by way of *concession*, not of *command*. ⁷*I wish* that all were as I myself am. But each has his own special gift from God, one of one kind and one of another.
>
> ⁸To the unmarried and the widows *I say* that *it is well* for them to remain single as I do. ⁹But if they cannot exercise self-control, they *should marry*. For *it is better* to marry than to be aflame with passion.
>
> ¹⁰To the married I *give charge*, not I but the Lord, *that* the wife *should not separate* from her husband ¹¹(but if she does, *let her remain single* or else *be reconciled* to her husband) — and *that* the husband *should not divorce* his wife.
>
> ¹²To the rest *I say*, not the Lord, that if any brother has a wife who is an unbeliever, and she consents to live with him, he *should not divorce* her. ¹³If any woman has a husband who is an unbeliever, and he consents to live with her, she *should not divorce* him. ¹⁴For the unbelieving husband is consecrated through his wife, and the unbelieving wife is consecrated through her husband. Otherwise, your children would be unclean, but as it is they are holy. ¹⁵But if the unbelieving partner desires to separate, *let it be so*; in such a case the brother or sister is not bound. For God has called us to peace. ¹⁶Wife, how do you know whether you will save your husband? Husband, how do you know whether you will save your wife?
>
> ¹⁷Only, *let every one lead the life* which the Lord has assigned to him, and in which God has called him. *This is my rule* in all

the churches. [18]Was any one at the time of his call already circumcised? *Let him not seek* to remove the marks of circumcision. Was any one at the time of his call uncircumcised? *Let him not seek* circumcision. [19]For neither circumcision counts for anything nor uncircumcision, but keeping the *commandments* of God. [20]Every one *should remain* in the state in which he was called. [21]Were you a slave when called? *Never mind.* But if you can gain your freedom, *avail yourself* of the opportunity. [22]For he who was called in the Lord as a slave is a freedman of the Lord. Likewise he who was free when called is a slave of Christ. [23]You were bought with a price; *do not become* slaves of men. [24]So, brethren, in whatever state each was called, there *let him remain* with God.

[25]Now concerning the unmarried, *I have no command* of the Lord, but *I give my opinion* as one who by the Lord's mercy is trustworthy. [26]*I think* that in view of the impending distress *it is well* for a person to remain as he is. [27]Are you bound to a wife? *Do not seek* to be free. Are you free from a wife? *Do not seek marriage.* [28]But if you marry, you do not sin, and if a girl marries she does not sin. Yet those who marry will have worldly troubles, and I would spare you that. [29]I mean, brethren, the appointed time has grown very short; from now on, let those who have wives live as though they had none, [30]and those who mourn as though they were not mourning, and those who rejoice as though they were not rejoicing, and those who buy as though they had no goods, [31]and those who deal with the world as though they had no dealings with it. For the form of this world is passing away.

[32]*I want you to be* free from all anxieties. The unmarried man is anxious about the affairs of the Lord, how to please the Lord; [33]but the married man is anxious about worldly affairs, how to please his wife, [34]and his interests are divided. And the unmarried woman or girl is anxious about the affairs of the Lord, how to be consecrated in body and spirit; but the married woman is anxious about worldly affairs, how to please her husband. [35]*I say* this for your own benefit, not to lay any restraint upon you, but to promote good order and to secure your undivided devotion to the Lord.

[36]If any one thinks that he is not behaving properly toward his betrothed, if his passions are strong, and if it has to be, *let him do* what he will, he does not sin; *let them marry.* [37]But whoever is firmly established in his heart, being under no necessity but having his desire under control, and has determined this in his heart, to keep her as his betrothed, he will *do well.* [38]So that he who mar-

ries his betrothed *does well*; and he who refrains from marriage *will do better*.

[39]A wife is bound to her busband as long as he lives. If the husband dies, she is free to be married to whom she wishes, only in the Lord. [40]But *in my judgment* she is happier if she remains as she is. And *I think* that I have the Spirit of God.

This rudimentary exercise makes it plain that 1 Corinthians 7 is dense with imperatives: they number almost two dozen. Although it would be a mistake to think that Paul gives ethical advice or instruction in only one grammatical form,[12] it is noteworthy that hortatory verbs are much thicker through chapter 7 than in Paul's ethical teaching in the surrounding chapters of the letter. The discussion of idol-food in chapter 8, for instance, has only one imperative (though we will see in my chap. 5 that there are direct imperatives on the subject in 1 Cor. 10). Further, although there are other places in Paul's letters where imperatives come quickly on each other (Galatians 6 and Romans 12, for example), in such passages there is not the same heightened use of the first person, or the explicit distinction between Paul's own opinion and the Lord's. (Though the figures can mean little, we can count twenty references to the Lord or God if we include Christ and the Spirit, and a total of twenty uses of the first person singular verbs or personal pronouns.) These features confirm the suitability of this text for a study of the way commands are related to authority in paradigmatic reasoning within theological ethics. We ask, then, how authority is invoked by Paul: Whose commands count?

III. THREE ETHICAL AUTHORITIES

The expression "Ethical Authorities," in the plural, appears in the title of this chapter, for its central contention is that at least certain commands in theological ethics receive their authority in complex ways. In 1 Corinthians 7 we find three loci of theological authority: Paul himself, the teaching of the Lord, and the commands of God.[13] Although each could profit from extensive discussion in its own right, my present concern is to determine how they are related to each other. For where there is more than one authority on a given topic, either they say the same thing (and there are no practical problems over the logic of authority) or else they differ. Differences may be reconciled by ranking authorities, or resolved by choosing among them. We shall see that Paul discerns differences and does some ranking, but in no simple manner. I begin with what he says about himself.

i. Paul

Paul considers his own instructions authoritative. He is writing as an apostle to his converts, and he expects that the answers he provides to their questions will be taken seriously. The evidence for this is readily marshaled. (a) On the linguistic level, he uses not only second and third person prescriptions, but in addition several verbs with imperatival force in the first person: "I say" (*legô*, vv. 6, 8, 12, 35, and *phêmi*, v. 29); "I wish" (*thelô*, vv. 7, 32); "I give charge" (*parangellô*, v. 10); "I rule" (*diatassomai*, v. 17); "I give my opinion" (*gnômên didomi*, v. 25); "I think" (*nomidzô*, v. 26; *dokô*, v. 40). The identity of the writer is therefore significant.

Secondly, (b), this is heightened particularly in the verb *diatassomai* in v. 17, translated in the RSV as "this is my rule." The sense of the word contains the notion of ordering or commanding. Paul uses it in 1 Corinthians 9:14 to remind the Corinthians that those who preach the gospel have the right, ordained by the Lord, to support; in 11:34 to promise to settle other questions about conduct at eucharistic meals when he comes; and in 16:1 to apply to the Corinthians his orders to the Galatian churches about the collection for the saints.[14] Paul does more than give advice or counsel in all the churches: he orders or *decrees*, setting out authoritative instructions and expecting things to happen in certain ways because of this.

Further (c), Paul expects that his own choices will serve as an example to others, who should be expected to imitate him. The call to imitate his conduct is issued in 1 Corinthians 4:16 and is repeated at 11:1. Although not explicit in chapter 7, it is thinly disguised in v. 7: "I wish everyone were as I am myself." That Paul believed his own behavior to be an ethical model is evidenced elsewhere in his writings — earlier in 1 Thessalonians 1:6 and later in Philippians 3:17 — so there is nothing unusual in his claiming this authority in Corinth.[15]

Finally (d), Paul reinforces his authority rather pointedly in two places: he provides an opinion as one who is fit to be trusted (*pistos*, v. 25) by the Lord's mercy; and as one who also thinks that he has the Spirit of God in the judgments he has expressed (v. 40). Although these characteristics do not seem to be unique, belonging only to Paul or other apostles, they nevertheless underline the authoritative character of his instruction.

If this were all we knew of the text, we might conclude that Christian morality consists in simply obeying one's leaders, and that therefore philosophical concerns about attempting to justify ethics by appeal to authority had good foundation. In fact, by seizing only on the above

points, I have distorted Paul's view of his own ethical authority. I need
to fill out the picture by adding all the qualifications Paul himself introduces. And I can start with the last point (d), in order to stress that the
only authority Paul claims for himself in 1 Corinthians 7 is the moral
authority of one who is more experienced and mature. In this respect
his language is unlike his defense in 1 Corinthians 9, which rests on the
rights that belong to apostolic authority and the manner in which he has
foregone certain privileges.[16] But there is nothing in principle to exclude
other mature Christians from the role Paul assumes here in his chapter
7: although it is an apostle who speaks, there is no appeal to status.

Again, though it is good to stay unmarried like Paul (v. 8), he does
not expect slavish imitation. Instead he is at pains to stress that all have
their own gifts in this matter (v. 7), so that it would not be wrong to
marry under some circumstances. Paul's readers may not always like the
feeling that marriage may be only second best: but however the text is
interpreted on that score, it ought to be made clear that, in Paul's view,
to marry is an acceptable choice, given the right set of conditions. His
own choice in this matter is not automatically determinative for others,
and point (c) above needs this qualification.

But perhaps the most striking limitation placed on Paul's authority
is seen in connection with the verbs mentioned in points (a) and (b). Some
of them are relatively weak: Paul thinks or believes (*dokô*); he supposes
or opines (*nomidzô*); he wishes (*thelô*). All these are more tentative than
dogmatic.[17] Moreover, there are explicit contrasts drawn between his own
advice and what the Lord has to say, and here a second authority is introduced for our attention.

ii. The Teachings of the Lord

We come upon the subordination of Paul's authority in the intriguing claim of 7:6 that he speaks by concession (*kata sungnômên*) rather
than by command (*kat' epitagên*). The basic distinction between the two
terms is the difference between permission and obligation. Paul uses
epitagê to refer to commands with divine authority in v. 25 and in
Romans 16:26, and never of his own judgments.[18] Whatever the content
of his concession in v. 6,[19] his advice is clearly subordinate to a higher
ruling and is permissible only insofar as it is accommodated to that ruling. This is seen too in his shift from *legô* to *parangellô* in v. 10: he himself
"speaks" to the unmarried (v. 8), but it is really the Lord, not Paul, who
"gives charge" ("gives the ruling," NEB) to the married. Presumably Paul
has in mind the sayings of Jesus about marriage and divorce found in
Mark 10:2–12 with parallels in Matthew 19:3–9 and Luke 16:18.[20]

Although the place of Jesus' teaching in Paul's ethics is a question much discussed,[21] one point alone suffices for our purposes here: Paul treats the sayings of the Lord as possessing more authority on the subject of separation and divorce than do his own statements. In adding to the teaching in vv. 12ff. he is careful to dissociate his words from dominical authority: "to the rest I say, not the Lord." And when he has no "command" from the Lord about unmarried women (*epitagê* again, v. 25), Paul does not manufacture a command on his own, but simply gives his judgment or opinion (*gnômên*, v. 25). In all this there is a consciousness of the special authority attaching to the Lord's teaching, an authority that Paul does not share.

iii. The Commands of God

Although there are twice as many references to "the Lord" as to God, Paul does specifically invoke the authority of God to settle possible disagreements. A different word is used for God's commands in v. 19 than for the commands of the Lord in vv. 6 and 25 (*entolê*, as distinct from *epitagê*), but the main point is logical rather than linguistic: *the only thing that matters* is keeping these commands. It is likewise with the gift and call of God, which seem to function in a way similar to God's commands. For instance, in v. 7 it is the *charisma* of God to each individual that determines for Paul what that person's choice should be, and not Paul's own preferences. Moreover, in the difficult case of mixed marriages between believers and unbelievers, sometimes separation is appropriate and sometimes it is not — but the overriding consideration is God's call to live in peace (v. 15). It is the same with those who find it hard to decide about circumcision or slavery. Christian behavior is compatible with either condition or its opposite, because what matters is that all keep God's commandments (v. 19), remain as they were when they received God's call (vv. 20, 24), continue on as they were called or as the Lord gave them to be (v. 17). If one could maintain to Paul that one's condition and behavior were the result and expression of God's gift and call, that would be justification enough.

Paul seems to run together the authority of God and the authority of the Lord in v. 17 with his parallel construction (*hekastô hôs memeriken ho kurios, hekaston hôs keklêken ho theos*), and he might wish to claim that these were not two separate loci. Nevertheless, I think that his actual treatment does suggest a difference of emphasis. If the commands of the Lord are the sayings of Jesus (or even if they are prophetic utterances on particular circumstances), their content is specific and of necessity leaves gaps to be filled in; but what ultimately fills out the commands is the authority of the gift and call of God. God's authority is thus more pervasive and general, operating at the level of basic principles rather than specific instructions.

This, then, is the structure of ethical authorities in 1 Corinthians 7, with Paul's experience and maturity granting him the right to offer instruction, but with his authority limited by the specific teachings of Jesus or sayings of the Lord, and the more general authority of God. To speak of God's general authority suggests that we have at last arrived at the Ultimate Authority in theological ethics, the point at which philosophers may either criticize or defend an unquestioning obedience to commands. Will they be able to discover that kind of obedience in Paul? I think not.

IV. OBEDIENCE AND INTERPRETATION

Look again at Paul's treatment of authoritative sayings and commands. His qualifications of his own apostolic authority and his appeals elsewhere for justifying reasons demonstrate that he himself cannot be on his own the final model for ethical behavior. But more significantly, in 1 Corinthians 7 we see him fully engaged in the processes of interpretation, extension, necessary modification, and application of the rules and principles he has been given. The question is not the simple one of obedience or disobedience; the crucial issue lies, as we suspected, in *knowing how to obey*. This involves intellectual and moral judgment, not a mindless surrender of will, for it involves knowing what the rules mean and deciding what constitutes their application in a given situation. This can be illustrated at three points in the text.

First, put aside for the moment whatever problems can be generated by New Testament scholars over what Jesus said about divorce. What Jesus did not say, according to the synoptic evangelists, was that marriage could be dissolved (except perhaps by reason of adultery). Yet here is Paul, claiming all the authority of the Lord's instruction in vv. 10–11, but adding a concession that countenances separation between Christians as long as there is no remarriage. Further, in v. 15 he is willing to pronounce on his own that a Christian spouse is not shackled by the marital tie if the unbelieving partner separates. Paul does not discuss the metaphysics of marriage (Jesus' saying that the two are one flesh, yoked together by God) any more than its moral and legal aspects, and some may think that his own counsel is incompatible with Jesus' view. But a plausible rejoinder is that Paul views himself as extending Jesus' teaching into new situations — mixed marriages — not explicitly covered by the original principle. He is careful not to do this on his own, for he adds to his approval of the separation of the unbelieving partner that God "has called you in peace" (v. 15). So the saying of Jesus is stretched into new circumstances with the justification provided by God's call.[22]

Secondly, there is a similar but starker attitude toward the authority of God's commands themselves. I have pointed out that for Paul the only thing that matters is the keeping of these commands (v. 19), yet this pronouncement proceeds from the claim "circumcision is nothing, and uncircumcision is nothing." Paul was hardly unaware of the controversial nature of his position on circumcision; his Letter to the Galatians argues vehemently that circumcision is part of the law from which Christ has liberated us. Yet that law was of course given by God and possessed divine authority. Because it is not appropriate to investigate these themes here,[23] I must content myself with the observation that Paul's placing of circumcision outside the "commands" of God in 1 Corinthians 7 requires a distinction between "commands" and "law," for which an *argument* is necessary. Whatever the success of that argument, its very process involves Paul in the business of interpreting and assessing the moral content of revelation. If theological ethics were simply a matter of acquiescence to authority, Paul never could have written v. 19.

Thirdly, there is a tension, if not contradiction, in Paul's attitude toward the principles generated by God's gift and call. Though these principles are general prescriptions to live in peace (v. 15), to remain and continue on as when one was called (vv. 17, 20, 24), Paul apparently recognizes that circumstances may dictate a contrary course of action. For example: (a) if you were single when called, stay that way *unless* you should get married (I shall not attempt to exegete the reasons of vv. 9 and 36!);[24] (b) if you were married when called, stay that way *unless* your partner separates; (c) if you were called when a slave, stay that way *unless* you are given the chance for freedom.[25] There are further complications that lead beyond the limits of this study: if you are married, be as though you were not, because of the circumstances of the time in which you live (vv. 29ff.). Let it be sufficient to say that the eschatological dimensions of 1 Corinthians 7 offer additional evidence that rules and principles are to be modified in ways appropriate to the circumstances in which they are applied.

We have moved therefore from some impression of the patterns of authority in 1 Corinthians 7 to the recognition that Paul himself is actively engaged in the interpretation and application of sayings and commands he accepts as authoritative. The exact extent of his modification of these commands is not as significant as the fact of modification itself:

Paul's counseled obedience requires the judgment of the believer, not an unquestioned acceptance of rules.

Indeed, we can extend the conclusion further. To this point we have been occupied with the dominating theme of authoritative commands. But although the believer must take full account of theological authorities in reaching moral judgments, Paul also introduces considerations that are not tightly dependent upon any theological justification. To this aspect of his reasoning in chapter 7 of 1 Corinthians I now turn.

V. NONTHEOLOGICAL CONSIDERATIONS

Two features of Paul's argument stand out. We shall come to the second — his characterization of responsible choice — in due course; I begin, however, with the fact that he sometimes justifies his advice without reference to authority of any nature. This is just what we would *not* expect if theological ethics consists in accepting rules or commands that achieve their rightness from God without further argument.

A straightforward illustration of nontheological justification comes in vv. 14–16, where Paul argues on behalf of keeping mixed marriages together. As noted in the first point taken up in section IV above, Paul does not work from a theology of marriage in his counsel, nor does he invoke dominical authority (for he wishes to say that keeping a mixed marriage is permissible and desirable but not always obligatory). Instead he appeals to consequences: there are potentially good results in not separating from an unbelieving spouse. These results are theologically important in that they refer to salvation; but it is the desirability of the results, not divine authority, that justifies the advice.

The same reasoning works in vv. 9 and 36, where the foreseen bad consequences of sexual temptation are sufficient in some circumstances to justify marriage. But perhaps the most striking set of nontheological reasons Paul offers is the trio in v. 35. Immediately upon his controversial claims about the worldly distractibility of the married, Paul adds: I say this for your own advantage (*sumphoron*), for what is seemly (*euschêmon*; RSV, "good order"), and for waiting on the Lord without distraction (*euparedron tô kuriô aperispastôs*). In other words, his advice is given for these purposes, and will be justified by the results they refer to. The first result is directed to the self: his readers will find their own good promoted by following Paul's advice. The second is a reason related to more general values, including esthetic and social values: their lives will be fitting, honorable, attractive. The third, like vv. 14–16, contains a theological element: by so ordering their lives they will be free from the cares and concerns that intrude upon one's sitting down and staying with the Lord. But again, though there is a theological reference in this reason, the justification is not itself theological. The Corinthians are to do this, not for the sake of a divine command, but because it will produce a certain valued experience. Parallels may be drawn between Paul's justifications in v. 35 and Greek philosophical ethics, where these three themes appear in somewhat related forms. The Greek moral ideal put together the fine and the honorable (*to kalon*) with the good; the question of the relationship of morality to one's own advantage is of course a central theme of Plato's *Republic*, and the need for freedom from excessive material concerns in order to spend time in philosophical contemplation is recognized by Aristotle in the *Nicomachean Ethics*. I point this out, not to draw the herring of possible influences, but to attract attention to common forms of ethical argument that do not rest on theological authority.

It is clear, then, that there are nontheological strands in Paul's reasoning about the right thing to do. Just as it is too simple to characterize theological ethics in 1 Corinthians 7 as unquestioning obedience, so it is false to think of Paul's reasoning as concerned only with the intrinsic rightness of commands. There are nontheological and consequentialist elements in his thought. How they are to be related to the logic of authoritative commands is a complex question. It might well be the case that Paul would have foreseen no conflict between obedience to commands and desirable results; our duty might for him never be at odds with our happiness. Or perhaps it is more subtle: where the rule is "obey *unless*" (the third point in the previous section), consequences will determine the applicability of the rule. There are important issues to be followed up here, including the role of divine authority in relationship to values to be pursued as well as commands to be obeyed. But they would quickly lead us beyond our present interests, and we must return to the second feature of Paul's argument, his insistence on responsible choice.

This second issue is not strictly one of ethical justification, but instead concerns a necessary condition of moral action. It is generally agreed that actions are not worthy of praise or blame if their agents are not responsible for what they do; and indeed many philosophers regard responsible actions as ones in which the agent is significantly free to choose between right and wrong. It was precisely this perceived lack of responsible freedom in religious agents that brought about the charge of heteronomy and immaturity reported in section I above. According to the critic, believers must gain their autonomy by making choices for themselves.

But it need not take long to demonstrate that Paul's language in

1 Corinthians 7 reflects no shadow of the heteronomy by which religious morality is supposed by some to be haunted. Paul may not here employ the actual language of freedom, but there is nonetheless significant scope for its exercise at several levels. Socially there is the ability to choose between continuing and terminating a marriage under certain conditions, and the slave may take the opportunity for freedom in that most literal sense, should this be possible. On the level of personal relationships there is the freedom of equality within marriage, discussed in vv. 3–5, so that both partners share in responsibility. In one's relationship to the religious rite of circumcision there is freedom to live according to God's call, and with respect to singleness or marriage, the freedom to seek out one's own gift from God. With this last point we come to freedom at the level of individual choice, and I want to propose that there is not only room for this in 1 Corinthians 7 but also a fine description of what is involved in such choice.

The entire thrust of Paul's argument in his chapter 7 is in the direction of responsible decision. His aim is not to strangle his readers (*ouch hina brochon humin epibalô*, v. 35) with prescriptions, but to have them decide for themselves upon their own gift and call. It is because of this that he can say, as the conclusion to a delicate problem: let him do what he wishes (*ho thelei poieitô*, v. 36). Or again: she is free to be married to whom she wishes (*eleuthera estin hô thelei gamêthênai*, v. 39). It is especially significant that this notion of one's own free wish or will should be stressed in connection with choices that Paul himself would have considered second best. But perhaps that is because he saw that the conditions of choice are more significant that the choice itself, at least on the difficult matters under consideration in his chapter 7. Those conditions are admirably described in v. 37. The particular problem Paul addresses is secondary: what matters is the manner in which the decision is to be made. The agent in question cannot be under compulsion (*mê echôn anankên*), and one's decision must be in one's very own mind (*en tê kardia autou . . . en tê idia kardia*); moreover one must be in control of one's own will (*exousian de echei peri tou idou thelêmatos*).[26] Under such conditions, says Paul, one will do well. And we may add: one will fulfill an essential condition of morally responsible action. What more can the critic require?

VI. CONCLUSION

To sum up. The relationships between authority and justification in Paul's ethical reasoning in 1 Corinthians 7 are complex. An analysis of his argument reveals that Paul does not abdicate his own moral autonomy in his attitude to religious authority, nor does he expect his readers to follow in naive obedience. Instead, by offering both theological and nontheological justification for his ethical advice, he shows that for him at least theological ethics is not authoritarian. Further, he stresses the freedom of individuals to interpret the meaning of moral rules and principles, and to apply them to their own situation. Our paradigmatic case thus shows that for Paul faith does not think of morality simply in terms of unquestioning obedience to divine commands. The assumption of the philosophical critic cannot find support here; nor can the defenders of obedience easily continue to think they are defending the heart of theological ethics.

Or so it seems on the basis of this study. But we must not forget its limitations as only one piece of ethical reasoning. For perplexities remain. One is that the great advocate of freedom on such fundamental matters as the personal and social relationships discussed in 1 Corinthians 7 should become so dogmatic on less important things four chapters later in this same letter. And there is a deeper worry. It arises from the irony that some of Paul's later readers came to abdicate the freedom his chapter 7 gives them in order to turn Paul himself into their final authority. But a proper understanding of morality and faith should show that, where such attitudes persist, the reasons for them lie not in the nature of theological ethics but in the nature of the human heart.

CHAPTER FIVE

The Burden of the Weak:
1 Corinthians 8–10

Each should carry his own burden. Galatians 6:5

The strong should carry the weakness of the weak.
Romans 15:1

The weak are a burden. In spite of advice that all should bear their own weight, it is an ancient duty in Judeo-Christian morality that (as Paul puts it to the Galatians) we ought to bear one another's burdens. This means in practice that the weak end up being helped along by the strong; but it is not that kind of burden that the present chapter has in mind. Rather it is the heavy effect that the weak may have on the rights of others. I have in mind, not the trouble caused by those in need, claiming that they have a right to my resources because of my duty toward them; but the burden of having one's own rights diminished by the demands of those who can provide only weak grounds for their claims.

The burden seems preposterous. If something is truly one's right, it is just the sort of thing not to be surrendered on request; and if the request is ill founded, we can have no duty to consider it at all. Yet, according to many readers of Paul, it is something like this burden that he imposes upon the Corinthians in his discussion of the effects on the weak of eating food sacrificed to idols. The text is 1 Corinthians 8–10, well known for the power it grants to the conscience of the "weaker brother." We shall discover in this study the conditions under which this particular burden of the weak is legitimately assumed, and when it is not; and by the time we have finished we shall have questioned whether Paul's ancient advice about the weak has any practical application at all for us today.

I. THE QUESTIONABLE POWER OF THE WEAK

There is much in 1 Corinthians 8–10 for careful consideration, and I begin with broad strokes in order to locate our problem with the weak. The issue is the Christian permissibility of eating meat that had been offered to idols, and Paul's letter reflects a difference of opinion on the matter with which he deals in his chapters 8–10. His treatment uses the language of permission, but also of right and freedom (*exousia*, 8:9, and *eleutheria*, 10:29 — though the RSV uses "liberty" for both). The notion of conscience (*suneidêsis*) also plays an important role in his reasoning. Most commentators see Paul as defending in general the right to eat meat, but arguing that on certain occasions this right should be surrendered because eating would be wrong. The wrong-making characteristic is to be found in the effects of eating upon a certain kind of observer, rather than in the act or the meat itself. And this brings us to our problem, for the observer in question is described as weak and ignorant, with a defective conscience. So comes the objection, raised in our text at 10:29: Why is my freedom determined by someone else's conscience?

In order to feel the force of the objection, I shall not yet descend to the details of the case. The complaint is not merely that the observer is expressing an opinion about the conduct of the person freely eating meat: part of the nature of acting morally is a willingness to give account of one's behavior, as we saw at the beginning of my chapter 4. Instead the issue is that the observer's weak conscience determines the scope of the free agent's activity, so that the agent is not free to exercise one of his or her rights — a right against which no good argument has been brought. This affords considerable power to the weak, which if used repeatedly would erode freedom and empty the meaning of "having a right." For faced with conduct of which they disapproved, the weak would only have to point out that their consciences were offended; the free would then be obliged to curtail their activities. Although they might continue to hold that their actions were in other respects correct, the free would not be able to exercise their rights, and to "have" a right that cannot be exercised is to have no right at all. Such a state of affairs is of course preposterous: it ends up giving the power to decide on permissible action to the least rational members of a community. Worse, it is the short way to moral chaos. Though it begins by keeping separate the rightness of certain activities in themselves from the desirability of performing them on specific occasions, it quickly hands over the arbitration of all behavior to those who have the strongest feelings of disapproval. In that kind of society morality would degenerate into manipulation.

It is impossible to believe that Paul expected his counsel to result in chaos, and difficult to think that readers of Paul should interpret him in ways encouraging that result. Nevertheless one cannot be confident that expositions of his advice do not tend to grant questionable power to the weak. We might remind ourselves of the long influence his advice has had on ethical discussion within Christianity: it is significant, for instance, that the *Oxford English Dictionary* gives Paul prominent place in its definition of the adjective "weak." Definition A2(b) reads:

> In the translations of the Bible from Tindale onward, used to render Gr. *asthenês*, *asthenôn*, applied by St. Paul (esp. in Rom. xiv and I Cor. viii) to believers whose scruples, though unsound, should be treated with tenderness, lest they should be led by the example of the more enlightened into acts condemned by their conscience. Hence allusively in *weaker brethren* (often supposed to be a scriptural phrase), applied to the more timorous members of a party, who are in danger of being shocked by extreme statements of principle or policy.

Such a description means that Christians are more likely to call others weak than to use the term of themselves. But it does reflect the fact that the "weaker brother," even if himself absent from discussion, has continued to play a part to our own day in the limitation of liberty.

Moreover, it is widely assumed that the weakness of the "weaker brother" has to do with the kind and scope of his moral judments. C. S. Lewis bears witness to this in his discussion of the meaning of "conscience." In setting forth the way in which conscience came to be regarded as an internal lawgiver, Lewis writes of Paul's term *suneidêsis*:

> In I Cor. viii. 10, St Paul says that if a "weak brother," a scrupulous person, sees you eating meat which has been offered to idols — a thing, in St Paul's view, innocent in itself — his *suneidesis* will be emboldened or "built up" to do likewise. (This is a bad thing because, being scrupulous, he will probably be worried about it in retrospect.) What St Paul really meant is a question for theologians; we, busied about the history of a word, are concerned with what he would possibly, or probably, or almost inevitably, be taken to mean by succeeding generations. I believe this passage would have suggested to them (as to most of us) the idea that *suneidesis* here means . . ."judgement as to what is right and wrong." The weak brother's scale of values, or standard of good and evil, originally classified the eating of sacrificed flesh as a sin; under your influence, encouraged by your example, he alters his scale or standard, modifies his moral judgement.[1]

This of course reminds us of our difficulty with the power of the weak. It is the weak brother who has the wrong moral belief, so why should he *not* modify his judgment? What good moral reason is there for my appearing to adopt his mistaken view by emptying my rights? Does not Paul's advice reduce moral freedom to its lowest level in any Christian community?

It is time to investigate just what power Paul's counsel about eating meat does give to the weak. To do this we must engage in the task Lewis left to theology (though we shall require tools that are philosophical): the determination of what Paul "really meant." We shall have to understand something of the situation in Corinth that he addressed, but (as in our other studies in this book) our concerns are not primarily historical. Paul's meaning must be seen in the ways his arguments work, the conclusions that they do or do not entail. And so to the details of his text.

II. EATING MEAT IN CORINTH

In our own day moral questions about eating meat are not major issues in Christian ethics. There is a good case for a reduction in the amount of meat eaten by affluent Christians in the West, both on grounds of health and because the consumption of animal protein seems an inefficient and wasteful use of the earth's resources; so some Christians have argued for a modified diet. A few may practise vegetarianism for these reasons, or to avoid cruelty to animals (though perhaps because of their understanding of creation, Christians have not been prominent among advocates of vegetarianism based on animal rights).[2] In other respects, what one eats is not an issue for most Christians.

It was not always so. The first Christians were of course Jewish, brought up with divinely sanctioned laws about what to eat and with whom. Gentile converts did not share this tradition, but they lived in pagan cities where at least some of the available meat would have been offered to pagan deities in ritual sacrifice before being sold.[3] Diet thus raised religious questions of great importance, and these came quickly to the fore when Jewish Christians first ate at the same table with gentile Christians in Antioch. There Peter's volte-face on table fellowship (according to Paul in Gal. 2:11ff.) indicates the depth of the issue, and its complexities were many. Jewish Christians had to decide whether to continue to abide by the dietary laws of the Old Testament, and whether gentile Christians should adopt those laws. If the gentiles were free from Old Testament proscriptions, it was still possible that their meat purchased from a pagan source had been offered to idols, and neither Jew nor gentile Christian should be compromised by idolatry. Christians might attempt to be careful when doing their own shopping, but they would have problems over food when served by pagan friends or when they were invited to eat at temple feasts for social or business reasons. One's eating practices thus focused fundamental issues of religious commitment and identity in a way without parallel for us.

How these issues came to be resolved is a task for the historian and sociologist of early Christianity. It appears that there were Christian vegetarians in Rome, but the fact that Paul calls them weak (Rom. 14:2) suggests that this was not the preferred solution. We know that the Old Testament distinction between clean and unclean foods was dropped by some Jewish Christians like Peter: it must have been a significant step, but the account we have of Peter's vision in Acts 10 makes it more of a psychological than a theological problem (cf. the comment "thus declaring all foods clean," in Mark 7:19, entered as an aside). The sticking point came, it seems, over meat suspected of having been offered to idols. Whenever the Jerusalem Council was held, whoever was present, and whatever is made of its reporting in Acts 15, it reminds us that throughout the early period of Christianity there was a strong conviction against the eating of such meat. *Eidôlothuta* it is called, articles of food offered in sacrifice in idolatrous worship,[4] or for the sake of brevity here, idol meat: it is associated with idolatry and fornication in Revelation 2:14 and 20, proscribed in the *Didache* (6.3), and by the church for a long while thereafter.[5] The so-called Apostolic Decree of Acts 15:29 thus expresses an early and influential judgment that, if gentile Christians are not bound by circumcision or the dietary laws of Moses, they must nevertheless refrain from idol meat as uncompromisingly as they must keep themselves from fornication.[6]

It might reasonably enough have worked that way in the development of Christianity until, with the decline of paganism, meat was no longer associated with idolatry. But it did not happen like that, because of Paul and the Corinthians.

To offer a detailed reconstruction of the ways in which the issues of food and idols made themselves felt in Corinth, and how Paul handled them prior to the extant letter we have as 1 Corinthians, would require more skill (and imagination) than is available here. The questions are fascinating, for they deal not just with eating practices and Jewish-gentile relationships in Corinth, but also with Paul's authority in relation to the Jerusalem leadership of Jewish Christianity. On such matters scholarly opinions conflict. Our interest in Paul's discussion of the weak will not be seriously compromised by ignoring some of the complexities and by leaving some issues unresolved. Because the text does, however, require a setting, I offer a few observations.

The letter reflects a conflict between those who believe that it is permissible for all Christians to eat idol meat and others who do not; and as subsequent discussion will demonstrate, it is clear that, on theological or religious grounds, Paul sides with the permissive. His ethical concern is centered, not on the rights and wrongs of objects or activities in themselves, but solely on the consequences of engaging in a piece of permissible behavior. This means that I find it difficult to accept C. A. Pierce's account, in his *Conscience in the New Testament*. On his view Paul probably taught the Corinthians the Apostolic Decree about idol meat on his first visit to Corinth. He himself "really disapproved of the eating of sacrificial meats: were he to discover he had eaten them he would himself suffer conscience."[7] But after Paul's departure some of the Corinthians were carried to excess by their new freedom in Christ and, in the name of a liberated conscience, indulged in idol food to the distress of others. Paul then writes to correct the situation. He makes no reference to the Apostolic Decree, because a renewed appeal to authority would have been shrugged off by the libertarians.

Much more likely is the opposite opinion, that Paul first came to Corinth himself asking no questions about the food set before him.[8] After he left, new developments caused him to be in touch with the church by letter. Perhaps various liberties were taken too far by some Corinthians; perhaps visits were made by Jerusalem leaders or their representatives; perhaps (as John Hurd has it) Paul agreed to communicate the Apostolic Decree to his converts at this time. The cause is not germane to our study; the result is that Paul wrote the Corinthians not to have dealings with immoral people (1 Cor. 5:9). In return he received a letter from his church, and it is likely that it raised the issue of idol meat with him. Without being required to accept the whole of John Hurd's thesis, we may take as a helpful reconstruction his attempt to convey the substance of their concerns. In reconstruction, they write:

> We find nothing wrong with eating idol meat. After all, we all have knowledge. We know that an idol has no real existence. We know that there is no God but one. For those in Christ all things are lawful, and as far as food is concerned everyone knows that "food is meant for the stomach and the stomach for food." We fail to see what is to be gained by the avoidance of idol meat. You know yourself that when you were with us you never questioned what you ate and drank. Moreover, what of the markets? Are we to be required to inquire as to the history of each piece of meat we buy?

And what of our friends? Are we to decline their invitations to ban-
quets because of possible contamination by idol meat?[9]

The Corinthians thus reinforce their theological claims and moral
views by referring to Paul's own example, and they point up practical
difficulties in avoiding idol meat. It is in reply to these questions that
Paul writes 1 Corinthians 8–10.

III. THE STRUCTURE OF PAUL'S ADVICE

Paul deals directly with the Corinthians' questions in chapter 8 and
the last section of chapter 10, and it has been difficult for some of his
readers to understand how chapter 9 and the first twenty-two verses of
chapter 10 fit with this material. Paul defends his rights and behavior
in chapter 9, without mentioning idol meat; and in the first section of
chapter 10 he forbids eating that would be idolatrous, and in the second
section he permits eating without asking questions. So these three chapters
of the letter have provoked questions of consistency, literary as well as
ethical.
        Our interest here is confined to the nature of Paul's ethical advice.
The natural place of chapter 9 in the context of idol meat has been defended by John Hurd and C. K. Barrett;[10] and if we take 10:1–22 to forbid idolatry and association with demons (which it does) rather than the
eating of idol meat (which is nothing, because an idol is nothing, 10:19),
then we will be free to explore chapter 8 and 10:23–11:1 for consistency
within the structure of Paul's argument.
        The second passage contains advice about specific situations (cf.
the questions asked in the reconstructed letter above), and explicitly permits eating on some occasions, whereas chapter 8 does not grant positive
permission. Nevertheless, the specific advice rests on general theological
premises and ethical principles that have their counterparts in chapter
8; so it is wrong to think of the spatial distance between the two passages
in the letter as reflecting a logical distance. The two are readily unified
into one complex and coherent argument, as the following account will
demonstrate. It shows that Paul's reasoning can be set out under three
major headings. (1) First comes a statement with theological claims and
moral judgments that yield specific advice; (2) then comes Paul's qualification of this statement and its theological claims, and his introduction
of additional moral considerations yielding different advice; (3) finally
there is an appeal to Paul's own behavior in light of his argument.
        I take the RSV text verbatim, including its quotation marks for

passages from the Corinthians' letter to Paul. The headings (in upper-case type) are of course added, and the interrogative mood in 8:10 is changed to the indicative (E.ii.a). Some conjunctions are omitted, as are the repeated opening words of 8:1 in 8:4; and I have added the words "Some are worse off if they eat" in E.ii in order to relate Paul's reasoning to the judgment in B.ii that we are not worse off if we eat. But otherwise the entire text of the two passages is reproduced here — with the exception of the objection voiced in the two questions of 10:29b–30, which belongs nowhere in the argument. Because, however, it is the problem that generated our concerns about the weak in the first place, we will not forget to return to it.

THE RESTRUCTURED TEXT OF 1 CORINTHIANS 8 AND 10:23–11:1

Now concerning food offered to idols (8:1)

I. Basic Statement

We know that "all of us possess knowledge" (8:1).

A. THEOLOGICAL CLAIMS
  i. We know that "an idol has no real existence" (8:4).
  ii. [We know] that "there is no God but one" (8:4).
     EXPLANATION: For although there may be so-called gods in heaven and on earth — as indeed there are many "gods" and many "lords" — yet for us there is one God, the Father, from whom are all things and for whom we exist, and one Lord, Jesus Christ, through whom are all things and through whom we exist (8:5–6).
  iii. "The earth is the Lord's, and everything in it" (10:26).

B. MORAL JUDGMENTS
  i. "All things are lawful" (10:23).
  ii. Food will not commend us to God. We are no worse off if we do not eat, and no better off if we do (8:8).

C. SPECIFIC ADVICE
  i. Eat whatever is sold in the meat market without raising any question on the ground of conscience (10:25).
  ii. If one of the unbelievers invites you to dinner and you are disposed to go, eat whatever is set before you without raising any question on the ground of conscience (10:27).

II. Qualification on the Basic Statement

"Knowledge" puffs up, but love builds up. If anyone imagines that he knows something, he does not yet know as he ought to know. But if one loves God, one is known by him (8:1–3).

D. QUALIFICATIONS ON THE THEOLOGICAL CLAIMS IN A
   i. Not all possess this knowledge (8:7).
   ii. Some, through being hitherto accustomed to idols, eat food as really offered to an idol (8:7).
E. COMPETING MORAL JUDGMENTS
   i. [vs. B.i] Not all things are helpful; not all things build up (10:23).
   ii. [vs. B.ii] [Some are worse off if they eat.]
      a. If anyone sees you, a man of knowledge, at table in an idol's temple, he might be encouraged, if his conscience is weak, to eat food offered to idols (8:10).
      b. Their conscience, being weak, is defiled (8:7).
      c. By your knowledge this weak man is destroyed, the brother for whom Christ died (8:11).
      d. Sinning against your brethren and wounding their conscience when it is weak, you sin against Christ (8:12).
   [Additional Principles]
   iii. Let no one seek his own good, but the good of his neighbor (10:24).
   iv. Whether you eat or drink, or whatever you do, do all to the glory of God (10:31).
   v. Give no offense to Jews or Greeks or to the church of God (10:32).
F. SPECIFIC ADVICE
   i. Take care lest this liberty of yours somehow become a stumbling block to the weak (8:9).
   ii. If some one says to you, "This has been offered in sacrifice," then out of consideration for the man who informed you, and for conscience's sake—I mean his conscience, not yours—do not eat it (10:28).

III. PAUL'S OWN BEHAVIOR

   i. If food is a cause of my brother's falling, I will never eat meat, lest I cause my brother to fall (8:13).
   ii. I try to please all men in everything I do, not seeking my own advantage, but that of many, that they may be saved. Be imitators of me, as I am of Christ (10:33–11:1).

To lay out Paul's argument in this way is to reinforce my claims from chapter 4, above: theological ethics is a matter of reasoning to conclusions, not a simple question of obedience to authority. We saw in connection with the topics of 1 Corinthians 7 that Paul's example was not in itself determinative for others; if here in 11:1 he asks the Corinthians to imitate him, it is not because of his status but because the reasons offered for his own conduct will apply to them as well (see section III.i in chapter 4, above).

Further, we are in a position to see the force of Paul's argument and its conclusions in the first part. The quotation from Psalm 24:1, shown as a theological claim in A.iii, suggests in this context that the divine benediction in creation is sufficient to make all kinds of creatures permissible food. This would be a surprising conclusion, flying in the face of Jewish dietary laws, if we did not know on other grounds that the primitive church was willing to abandon the distinction between clean and unclean foods. Paul never qualifies this claim: it is reasonable, then, to take him to hold that food in itself is religiously and morally neutral. The judgment in B.ii is simply an expression of this point. What, however, of idol meat? It could be argued (and undoubtedly was) that, though meat in itself was neutral, its association with idols was sufficient to proscribe it. The association might be seen as a quasi-physical taint or pollution, infecting the meat; or the act of eating might be regarded as an acknowledgment of idols and therefore dangerously close to idolatry. Such arguments carry no weight for Paul, because of his strong theological conviction expressed in A.ii, which allows him to hold in A.i that an idol is nothing at all. Meat cannot be polluted if there are no idols; eating meat cannot be an acknowledgment of idols on the part of those who know there is but one God and one Lord, Jesus Christ. Given such understanding, then, Christians may eat all meat regardless of its source, both in private within their community and on public secular occasions.

This conclusion, though bold in the context of early Christianity, has a certain cogency once both idolatrous superstitions and Jewish dietary laws had been discarded. Notice, however, that this account has made no use of the judgment in B.i that all things are lawful (or better, *permissible*: there is no reference to the concept of law here). The judgment could be appealed to and would support the conclusion; but because it allows everything, it also prohibits nothing, and could be used to support a contradictory conclusion as well. The limitations imposed by its qualifying claims in E.i are thus extremely important, and it is likely that Paul is quoting a Corinthian maxim rather than setting out an ethical principle of his own.[11]

Before turning to the qualifications introduced in the second stage of the argument, it is useful to note that the specific advice of the first stage is entirely compatible with Paul's treatment of food issues in Romans 14. There he does not discuss idol meat as such, it is true; nevertheless he states clearly his conviction that nothing is profane or unclean in itself (v. 14), and stresses that all Christians should be allowed to decide for themselves on their eating habits, free from the judgment of others (vv. 1–13). The reasoning permits the eating of idol meat. If Paul had wanted to prohibit this in Rome, he would have had to introduce additional considerations about idolatry; and because they are not present, we may take his position to be consistently in favor of the Christian right to eat all foods.

It is, however, one thing to be permitted to do something, and another to decide that it is right at this time and in this place to do it. One's duties ought to be performed; but what is permissible does not always have to be done. I am permitted to park my car in this lot: but there is only one space left, and I know that you, nearing the same space from the opposite direction, are late for a lecture. I cannot claim it my duty to use the space, any more than you can claim it as your right. What, then, about actually exercising the Christian right to eat idol meat?

Paul argues in the second stage of the structuring set out above that additional considerations can make it wrong in certain cases to do what is permissible in general. That this is indeed the burden of his argument is demonstrated in the nature of his qualifications: he never takes back the basic claims and moral judgments he has reached in the first stage, but only introduces competing moral principles, which will sometimes override the ones already established. They all have to do with the consequences of actions upon others, and whether they will be strengthened, built up (the qualification on the basic statement; and E.i), on the one hand, or destroyed, on the other (E.ii and its sequence). A succinct statement of the qualification on the permissible of B.i comes in E.iii: one should seek the good of the other, not one's own advantage. Paul's personal claim in III.ii is only an instance of this general rule, which is far more than a rule of courtesy in that its ultimate object is the building up of other persons, not merely an attempt to make them feel at ease. In E.iv we do not alter this basic principle (which is really the principle of agapeic love, to be discussed in section III of chapter 7, below), but add a religious dimension to it: it is followed for the glory of God.

But all this is general. We might readily agree that, for the sake of someone else's good and therefore for God's glory, it is right on occasion to refrain from doing what is permissible and not obligatory. But we have a natural interest in the "occasion," for surely it must be right on other occasions to do what one is permitted to do. The earlier example was mere courtesy, but it will do: by coincidence the lot is almost full again, but if I have the lecture today and you do not, will you not feel it right to wave me into the last parking space? In the moral sphere, where something is my right or is permissible for me, then I may or may not do that thing; yet if it is sometimes wrong (as it may be) for me to do it, then there must always be a sufficient reason why this is so. It is this reason that distinguishes one occasion from another: only when it is present, is it proper to think of refraining from doing what I am permitted to do.

Some Christians may feel that self-denial is a sufficient reason to give up their rights on any or all occasions. That it may sometimes be a reason for not doing the permissible is clear; that it is a general reason sufficient in itself is not at all obvious. In any case Paul does not invoke it here. In III.ii he says he does not seek his own advantage, but this is not self-denial and is as different from it as a refusal to take interest on a loan is different from giving away your money. Not to seek one's own is, as we have seen, to seek the good of the other; but it needs to be spelled out how the good of the other is affected by my actions. What, then, are the reasons Paul invokes in the specific case of idol meat, reasons he thinks sufficient to justify the nonperformance of the permissible?

The answer is found principally in the explanatory section under E.ii above: some Christians are worse off if they eat, so obviously I cannot seek their good if my eating permissible food causes them to eat. But why would my action make them eat? And why are they worse off, if I am not? Paul explains that the Christians he has in mind are encouraged by the example of those with knowledge; they imitate, and their weak conscience is defiled; they end up being destroyed. Hence his advice not to become a stumbling block, following on the principle of not giving offense (F.i and E.v), and his own resolution not to eat meat in such circumstances (III.i).

IV. AN OBJECTION

Paul has therefore offered a series of related reasons for refraining from the permissible. The question is whether these are sufficient reasons, and he himself raises a problem we must now consider. It is the objection voiced in 10:29–30, which found no place in the structure of Paul's reasoning, but which relates to the questionable power of the weak. Paul counsels not eating for the sake of the conscience of an observer (F.ii), then continues by asking (RSV):

> For why should my liberty be determined by another man's scruples? If I partake with thankfulness, why am I denounced because of that for which I give thanks?

Exactly how these questions fit the flow of the chapter as we have it (rather than the logic of the argument I have set out) has been thought by some so problematic that they have considered them a gloss. Another view sees Paul as making a point following on v. 28, that eating meat is wrong because it will lead to slander. John Hurd notices the parallels between the questions and Paul's defense in 9:1 and 4, and offers this as evidence that Paul had actually been criticized for his eating habits. I take them as an objection to Paul's qualified counsel not to eat meat on some occasions: though there are some difficulties with this,[12] Paul's advice is susceptible of the kind of objection embodied in these words, and that is sufficient for our purposes.

We may put it this way, remembering the problem, considered earlier, of restrictions on liberty because of the weak. The weak have now been characterized as easily led to imitate behavior perfectly permissible in itself, but behavior that defiles their unenlightened conscience and causes them to stumble. It is a bad thing to cause them harm, of course. But Paul assumes that my freedom to do the permissible should be curtailed by their weak and inferior conscience. Why so? For one thing, if he is right, then every defective conscience could make claims on my rights, and I could be obliged to reduce the permissible to the level of the weakest in my community. For another, there is something fundamentally wrong with allowing the weak to persist in their mistaken views. What they need is education, not accommodation. If I am genuinely concerned about their good, I should be strengthening them by helping them toward a proper understanding of the permissible, not giving in to their improper demands.

Though Paul does not of course state these objections in this fashion, they lurk in the vocabulary of liberty and the weak conscience in our text. And though there is no answer to the question of 10:29, we can construct a plausible rejoinder that will demonstrate under what conditions Paul will have sufficient reason to curb his permissible behavior. The rejoinder requires a fuller understanding of the weak, their conscience, and their fate.

V. THREE KEY CONCEPTS

Recall the major justifying reason Paul may offer against eating permissible food; some are worse off if they eat (E.ii). These are the *weak*, who *stumble* through a defiled *conscience*. Each of these three concepts requires elucidation.

i. The Weak

Weakness is a recurrent theme in the Corinthian correspondence, from the opening chapters (discussed in section I of chap. 2 above) to

Paul's self-defense in 2 Corinthians 10–13. Although he willingly emphasizes his own weaknesses, Paul does not, however, belong to the category of the weak in 1 Corinthians 8, the class under discussion here. They form a special group, distinguished in three ways.

First, they are opposed, not directly to the strong (Paul does not talk of the strong in these chapters, in spite of our natural tendency to use the term in commentary), but to those who have knowledge (8:7, 10; cf. D.i, above). They thus lack full appreciation of Christian beliefs we should regard as fundamental — the beliefs set out in A.i and ii, above.

Secondly, their "conscience" may be defiled or contaminated (8:7; E.ii.b). The subject of contamination we shall consider shortly; what is important here is that the weak are those so accustomed to idols that they cannot bring themselves to feel that idol meat has been disinfected, so to speak, in Christ. The use of "being accustomed" (*sunêtheia*) in 8:7 suggests the force of habit: the weak are still caught in the associative feelings of paganism. Like children who cannot drink milk because they have just learned its association with cows, the weak cannot help but sense the presence of the idol in the meat, and they feel defiled.

Thirdly, the weak are weak not just in knowledge and feeling; they are weak too in conviction and resolve. Whereas others might learn to avoid situations with unpleasant associations, the weak are easily led to imitate the behavior of those with more secure knowledge (8:10; E.ii.a). Paul's example may or may not be hypothetical, but it illustrates the kind of persons he has in mind — those who have such shaky moral conviction that they look to others to determine their own conduct, even when the result is a painful and divided consciousness.

If we ask about the identity of the weak in Corinth, it will be clear that Paul cannot have Jewish Christians in mind: they neither lack knowledge nor are accustomed to idols. (It may be different in Romans 14, where the weak could be those scrupulous about Jewish dietary laws.)[13] Some think that Paul is not actually referring to an existing group of persons in the Corinthian church. John Hurd argues for a unified position in Corinth rather than a split between stronger and weaker parties, claiming that the existence of the weak in 1 Corinthians 8–10 is only hypothetical.[14] And others suggest that, because the pressure against idol meat has come from Jerusalem, Paul is being perverse: he accedes to the Apostolic Decree but manages the insulting suggestion that the "weak," for whose sake the Corinthians should abstain, are really the Jerusalem leadership.[15] But that seems far too forced: it assumes not only that Paul did endorse the decree, but also that he was so perverse as to characterize the Jerusalem leaders as weak in the sense we have just described. Moreover, it makes little difference for us whether the weak are only hypothetical, for this will not affect Paul's reasoning in the least; in fact, moral argument usually makes use of hypothetical rather than real situations for the sake of clarity and economy. So we will take Paul to intend by the "weak" Christians whom we may call "underconverted":[16] new to the faith, but not yet of sound Christian mind. C. H. Dodd captures this condition (though he writes of Paul's treatment in Romans) by saying that the weak are "haunted by a superstitious fear of some imaginary sanctity attaching to *things*, a fear inaccessible to reason"; or again, that they present for Paul "opinions and prejudices which, though sincerely held, have no rational ground, but are of the nature of *taboo*."[17]

ii. Stumbling

When the weak eat idol meat, they feel contaminated. But that is not all: Paul is anxious to stress just how bad the results of eating are for them. Their conscience is wounded as well as defiled — and worse, a brother for whom Christ has died is destroyed (8:11, 12; E.ii.c and d). This is strong language (it recalls the destruction of worldly wisdom in 1 Cor. 1:19), but because Paul uses it again in a similar situation with the same phrase, "the brother for whom Christ died," in Romans 14:15, he must intend it seriously. That this is so is strengthened by the other terms he uses for the fate of the weak: the noun *proskomma* in 8:9 (cf. *aproskopoi* in 10:32) and the verb *skandalidzô* twice in 8:13. Again we must think Paul's vocabulary deliberate, for both concepts reappear in the Romans passage (see 14:13 for *skandalon*, and 14:13, 20, 21 for *proskomma*, etc.). The intransitive verb *proskoptô* refers to tripping, stumbling over an obstacle such as a stone projecting from a path, falling, failing to reach one's destination; *skandalidzô* means to bring this upon someone else. Their close connection may be seen in Romans 9:33, "a stone on which to stumble and a rock on which to trip" (*lithon proskommatos kai petran skandalou*, quoting Isa. 8:14; cf. 1 Pet. 2:8). The literal use may be seen in "Anyone can walk in daytime without stumbling . . . but if he walks after nightfall he stumbles" (*proskoptei*, John 11:9, 10); but the most common New Testament usage refers to moral and religious stumbling. That this is a most serious matter may be seen particularly in *skandalon*. It is because the crucifixion is for the Jews an insurmountable barrier to faith in Christ that it is called a *skandalon* (1 Cor. 1:23; cf. Roman. 9, etc., noted just above). To become a *skandalon* for others, is not just to impede their progress but to block their way so that they do not arrive at their goal. The judgment on such blocking is harsh: the angels gather these "stumbling stones" and cast them into the blazing furnace (Matt. 13:42; cf. 18:6), and Jesus had strong words for Peter's attempt to keep him from his goal — he called him Satan and a *skandalon* (Matt. 16:23).

What happens, then, to the weak who eat idol meat is no trifling matter. The example of those with knowledge causes them to stumble and fall, so that they are destroyed; in the words of Romans 14:20, the work of God is brought to an end for the sake of food. Hence Paul's principle of action in 1 Corinthians 10:32 (cf. E.v): lay no stumbling block (do not be a *proskomma*) before Jews or Greeks or the church of God.

It is important to understand the principle in this sense, and not as the simple counsel of courtesy suggested in the RSV "give no offense." That translation might descend from the Latin *offendo*, close in some uses to *proskoptô*; but contemporary talk of "giving offense" quickly reduces the discussion to the level of upset feelings, and makes Paul's point about the weak the fact that they will be displeased by the behavior of the more liberated. They may well have bad feelings and be "offended" in that sense: but that is only a minor matter in the argument. For the emphasis is rather on wrong *actions*; as the KJV has it in 8:13, food will "make my brother to offend" — that is, to become an offender. But even that does not capture the full force of Paul's *brôma skandalidzei ton adelphon mou*: we need to add that, in committing what he considers an offense, my brother is so seriously damaged that his very identity in the faith is put at risk. He has not only done what he ought not to have done; he has been wounded and brought down.

iii. Conscience

The reason why the weak eat and are destroyed lies in their "conscience." The word is familiar enough to us, even if we find it difficult to be precise about its meaning. Conscience has something to do with our sense of right and wrong; and if it is a mistake to treat it as the ultimate source or justification for our moral beliefs (for my conscience may be misguided), still conscience seems to be regarded as a subjective apprehension of moral principles whereby we rule and judge our behavior. It has, or is, a "voice," sometimes the voice of disapproval coming from our "better self," sometimes the internal voice we ought to obey against other commanding voices such as that of the state. Whether we link it to a rational intuition of the good, regard it as a faculty of personality, or explain it in terms of social conditioning, conscience is a recognizable feature of our moral psychology.[18] Moreover, as commonly understood, conscience may well have different contents for different moral agents. We would not counsel others to follow the dictates of their own consciences unless we thought the dictates of other consciences (including perhaps our own) would differ from theirs.

It is this difference that may trouble those objecting to Paul's advice in F.ii to surrender the permissible for the sake of the conscience of the weak.[19] By definition the weak will have a conscience (in the sense just described) that is misguided and defective. Among its deliverances will be the mistaken moral judgment that eating idol meat is impermissible in itself. But (by now the refrain is anticipated) if I abstain for that reason, I shall go against *my* conscience; my right of action will shrink to the small sphere permitted by the weak.

It is, however, a mistake to construe the problem in these terms. The weak do of course regard eating idol meat as a wrong action. But it is not their truncated set of moral principles that determines my action; it is something else.

To appreciate this, we must reflect on Paul's use of *suneidêsis*.[20] He uses the term more often than any other New Testament writer (fifteen times: it also occurs twice in Paul's speeches in Acts, six times in the pastoral letters, five times in Hebrews, and three times in 1 Peter). Because twelve of Paul's uses are in the Corinthian correspondence, C. A. Pierce argues that the term must have been a catchword in Corinth, taken up by Paul in his ethical teaching. Pierce further claims that Paul does not fundamentally alter the meaning of *suneidêsis*, which has its setting in popular speech in the Hellenistic world (there is only one occurrence in the Septuagint, and no Hebrew equivalent for the concept).

The basic meaning of the word, according to Pierce, is much closer to its root sense of sharing in knowledge than to our developed notion of conscience. For *suneidêsis* is not an internal arbiter of right and wrong, a guide to future action with independence from external authority, concerned both with the self and with others. Rather it is directed to the past, as a painful reaction to one's own misdeeds. It has some ethical function in that one might learn from its pain. But because it can be deadened or supplanted by habits, it is not sufficient to teach any moral principles beyond the prudential avoidance of pain..

Some of Pierce's claims have been questioned, for example by Christian Maurer,[21] and his contrasts with the modern concept of conscience sometimes seem more polemical than analytic. Still, his major stress on the centrality of self-awareness in *suneidêsis* finds a good deal of agreement from others, and most importantly, from our text. In support there is C. S. Lewis who develops a special term, "consciring," to force away from *suneidêsis* modern senses of conscience as lawgiver.[22] To "conscire" is to bear witness with oneself about a secret, usually a guilty secret; in other words, it is to come to a kind of value-consciousness about the self, though not necessarily in developed moral categories. Christian Maurer also uses such terms as "self-awareness" and "self-consciousness" in his treatment of Paul's use of *suneidêsis*, and makes the helpful comment that in 1 Corinthians 8 Paul's language may be used either of *suneidêsis* or of the person in question.[23] In this way the text will support Pierce's emphasis. In 1 Corinthians 8:10 the weak "conscience," which is encouraged to eat, is simply the person lacking knowledge and sense of his or her own mind on the matter; in 8:7 the defiled "conscience" is just the person who feels contaminated; in 8:12 the wounded "conscience" is nothing other than the wounded brother or sister who is destroyed.

This understanding of *suneidêsis* fits well with the description of the weak offered a few pages back. There we spoke of a "painful and divided consciousness," resulting from the eating of idol meat, and it is that state of mind Paul intends by his reference to a wounded or defiled "conscience." Because the weak have no strong sense of identity, they are easily led to feel bad about themselves.

We may now apply our understanding of *suneidêsis* to the repeated phrase "for conscience's sake" in 1 Corinthians 10. Twice Paul says that it is permissible to eat without raising questions *dia tên suneidêsin* (vv. 25, 27); once he advises not to eat, using the same phrase, and explaining that it is because of the *suneidêsis* of the observer (vv. 28–29a). Note, however, that although the form of words is the same in all three instances, *suneidêsis* functions differently in the third case. For in the examples of permissible eating, it is not *suneidêsis* that is the ground of the rightness of eating idol meat; Paul does not argue that the Corinthians should consult their "consciences" and eat if they discover some kind of internal green light (though perhaps something like this is his point in Rom. 14:22 – 23, but without mention of *suneidêsis* there). The ground of permissibility is instead the theological judgment that the earth is the Lord's — and that by implication it does not belong to idols; in other words the claims set out in A. i, ii, and iii, above. In the third case, though, the *suneidêsis* of the observer does function as the ground for refraining from the permissible. This means, I think, that we best understand *suneidêsis* in these examples as bad feeling, a sense of defilement, and not as an internal codebook of morality. The Corinthians may eat idol meat without paying attention to the question raised by feelings of pollution, unless of course someone else is caused to experience those feelings and is ruined. I conclude that, though C. S. Lewis is correct in discerning a "great semantic shift" from "conscience" as internal accusing witness to "conscience" as internal moral lawgiver,[24] the shift belongs to the "succeeding generations" of Paul's readers. The older sense, as Pierce argues, works perfectly well in 1 Corinthians 8–10.[25]

Thus in refraining from the permissible I do not go against my moral conscience, nor do I allow the morally defective conscience of the weak to determine the scope of the permissible for me. Paul is careful to say in 10:29b that it is my freedom (*eleutheria*), not my right, that is determined. And it is the bad feeling caused by my behavior that is the operative factor: that is what "because of his *suneidêsis*" means.[26]

VI. THE OBJECTION ANSWERED

We are now better able to appreciate why the weak stumble and how bad their fate is; and we may therefore be more precise about the sufficiency of the conditions under which it is proper to surrender to them the right to do what is permissible in itself. Remember where we had left the objection. Although acknowledging that for the sake of someone else's good one might sometimes refrain from doing an action right in itself, the objector wanted to know why the defective conscience of the "weaker brother" should be a sufficient reason for this, and why seeking the good of the weak should not result in their being educated rather than accommodated. Should they not be brought (in C. S. Lewis's words) to modify their moral judgment?

Paul's answer may be constructed from our understanding of the fate of the weak. Contrary to the common view reflected in both the *Oxford English Dictionary* and Lewis's account (section I, above), the "weaker brother" of 1 Corinthians 8–10 is not simply scrupulous, in danger of being shocked. Nor is it his scale of values Paul has in mind. Instead he is still subject to the attack of bad feelings associated with the polluting presence of idols. His Christian understanding is not sufficiently developed to instruct him about the rights and wrongs of eating; and he is so weak that if he sees someone exercising the right to eat idol meat, he will not express shock or moral indignation: instead he will imitate this action in spite of himself. As a result he will feel polluted, and his very status as a Christian will be destroyed. The harm done, then, to the weak is not trivial. To seek his good in this case is to refrain from an act that, because of his weakness, will compromise his faith. Although he needs a better Christian understanding, his present situation is such that he is not able to appreciate education by example, because it leads only to imitative behavior without dealing with the irrational and destructive feelings associated with that behavior. So Paul might well turn around the point with which we began this study: it is not the weak who have the power to restrain the free; it is the free who, like it or not, have the power either to destroy the weak or to seek their greater good.

At the same time, our initial account is seen to be a misconstruction of Paul's treatment of the weak. Out of the language of offense, scruple, and shock that surrounds the "weaker brother" we built a problem not actually addressed by 1 Corinthians 8–10: the problem of having liberty limited because it will cause another person to experience feelings of disapproval. Nothing in the structure of Paul's ethical reasoning here speaks directly to that situation. A "brother" with a tender conscience, or a conscience he thinks more sensitive to the right than mine, is not "weak" in the Pauline sense unless he will be led to do the thing that he abhors; he will not "stumble" in the Pauline sense unless he is so upset that he trips and falls. To think otherwise is indeed to grant questionable power to the timid or narrow-minded, and to open oneself to their manipulation. In respect of such persons the objection against accommodation does have force: sometimes the strong ought not to take on the burden of restricted rights but ought instead to educate the weak. The burden should be shared.

VII. SHARING THE BURDEN

We have returned to our beginning. But when should we take on the burden of the weak, and when should the burden be shared? What is the applicability of Paul's ancient advice, now that idolatry and food have long ceased to be associated?

It is difficult to find any simple application to the questions about food we mentioned at the beginning of section II above. It cannot be claimed that Christians who argue for a modified or meatless diet are "weak" in the Pauline sense, even though Paul characterizes the vegetarians in Rome as weak in faith. Those we described have reasons for their convictions, which, though restrictive on the eating of meat, may well be right (for one's moral maturity does not increase necessarily with the sheer number of items on one's list of permissibles). Perhaps considerations of courtesy will suggest that I refrain from serving myself meat when I invite one of these Christians to dinner. But if this is so (and it may not be so, depending on our mutual understanding), my behavior is not governed by the belief that carnivorous acts will destroy my vegetarian brother.

It might be argued in such a case at least *part* of Paul's advice is followed: Is not the courtesy extended by my refraining from meat an instance of the general principle to seek the good of my neighbor and not my own (E.iii)? Perhaps so: but this principle is so general (it is an expression of the beneficence fundamental to morality) that by itself it does not tell me when I should refrain from some action and when I need not refrain. After all, it is not a Christian duty to do whatever my neighbor *thinks* is for his or her good. That is why the rest of Paul's reasoning is required: we must not be stones of stumbling, and the destruction of the faith of the weak is indeed a sufficient reason to limit my behavior.

If Paul's advice no longer applies to food, is there any other area of Christian behavior where it might be invoked? Given the way the argument of 1 Corinthians 8–10 actually proceeds, it seems to me difficult to construct a plausible situation in which a body of present-day Christians would be so weak as to be destroyed by the permissible actions of a stronger group. Certainly many of the issues on which Christians feel strong disagreement cannot be so construed: but those with more experience or imagination than I may find themselves faced with believers weak in the Corinthian sense. If so, they would be able to make use of Paul's "weaker brother" argument in its full force.

Nevertheless, in relying on Paul's characterization of the fate of the weak, my argument may be considered too strong. It could be maintained that a weaker version of Paul's advice still finds legitimate application in Christian ethics — perhaps in the counsel to refrain from actions whenever my neighbor will be seriously "offended" in the usual sense of that word, even if my neighbor does not copy my behavior. In this way the standard "weaker brother" argument may be rehabilitated to some extent.

To the more moderate version we may say yes — but also no. Certainly it is not morally insignificant to cause others distress by one's own behavior. Nevertheless this distress is not always wrong. It is clearly wrong when the offending action is itself wrong; then the distress it causes only adds to the wrongness. But sometimes the offending action is not wrong; and it may even be a duty. Then the distress the action causes in an observer, though not good in itself, must be regarded as a necessary evil. It is regrettable if the observer does not approve what the agent regards as a duty; but this disapproval is not a sufficient reason to defeat the agent's duty. Nothing in Paul's advice requires the Christian to refrain from the obligatory, even though others may suffer through misunderstanding or disagreement.

But what of actions I am not required by duty to perform? If I do not have to do something right in itself, does not love constrain me to refrain if it will upset my neighbor even though I am reasonably sure that he or she will not suffer the grave damage Paul describes? To this there is no general answer, and therefore no general applicability of Paul's advice about the "weaker brother" even in its diluted form. It all depends on what is at stake. Where it is more important to make my neighbor welcome than to exercise my right, it would be unloving to ride roughshod over his or her feelings in the name of Christian liberty. But sometimes important principles reside in the permissible. We may ask how Paul felt about Peter's refraining from permissible eating in Antioch for the sake of offense caused to James: and put that way, the issue of eating meat takes on a wholly different complexion.[27] Paul might well eat no meat in Corinth for the sake of the weak: but at other times and in other places, eating meat may be an affirmation of a fundamental liberty. If my brothers and sisters have not yet grasped this liberty, it may be right to do the permissible in spite of their feelings. They may learn. If they do not fully accept my reasons for themselves, they may nonetheless come to see that what they thought forbidden is at least permissible for me. And then it would not be incumbent on me to refrain; it would instead be incumbent on them to refrain from placing the burden of disapproval on me.

It is significant that when Paul came to write to the Romans on our topic, he laid responsibility squarely on the weak not to despise or judge those whose sphere of permissibility is greater than their own (14:3–13a). Significant, because whenever this happens, the "weak" are no longer weak in the Corinthian sense. They have made advances in Christian understanding and are learning to share the burden.[28]

Weakness remains an indelible feature of the human condition and our Christian experience. We each have found ourselves in need; not only apostles know the paradox of strength graciously given in weakness. And as we have been helped, so we must bear the infirmities of others. In some times and places — ancient Corinth, for one — this duty may mean a restriction, for the sake of our neighbor, on the exercise of our rights. This study of Paul's reasoning has shown the cogency of that advice for that situation. Nevertheless Corinth must be balanced by Rome. We have discovered no justification for the burden imposed by those who, in the name of a narrow sensibility, would limit Christian freedom. The weak are to grow stronger in the faith: and if there are dangers in offending them, there are also dangers in an easy accommodation, as we shall see in the next chapter.

CHAPTER SIX

For and Against Accommodation:
1 Corinthians 9:19–23

> If I pleased men I should not be Christ's slave.
> Galatians 1:10
>
> I also in all things please all men. 1 Corinthians 10:33

Among Paul's memorable dicta, "All things to all men" must have a chief place. It is, however, better remembered than understood. Innocuously it might be thought an apostolic version of "When in Rome . . . ", a simple counsel of courtesy. Less innocently it may be used to justify the dubious principle that questionable means are made acceptable by their ends. Commentators immune to such misunderstandings usually read the dictum as an expression of Paul's missionary strategy, thereby diverting attention from the moral perplexities raised by Paul's self-description. Our task is to attempt a sorting out of some of the puzzles surrounding what I call "accommodation" as it appears in 1 Corinthians 9:19–23.

There are four stages in our inquiry. Having first set out the issues from the text, we explore secondly the idea of accommodation; in the third stage these results are applied to Paul's theory and practice to see how he might justify being all things to all people; and we conclude with some observations on problems that still inhere in accommodation.

I. THE TEXT AND ITS PUZZLES

Though Paul did not use the language of freedom in discussing responsible choices in 1 Corinthians 7 (see my chap. 4, above), he now emphasizes the word as he begins his famous defense in chapter 9: Am I not free? It is clear that, whatever the charges against him, his reply invokes what we should call the rights of apostleship (Paul's own term is "authority," *exousia*), along with the claim that he has deliberately refrained from exercising his right to financial or material support. In fact, he has freely disregarded his rights in order to take on an absolute obligation to preach the gospel without charge. At v. 19 he summarizes his freedom and obligation, then moves to the accommodation statements that interest us (1 Cor. 9:19–23, RSV):

> [19]For though I am free from all men, I have made myself a slave to all, that I might win the more. [20]To the Jews I became as a Jew, in order to win Jews; to those under the law I became as one under the law—though not being myself under the law—that I might win those under the law. [21]To those outside the law I became as one outside the law—not being without law toward God but under the law of Christ—that I might win those outside the law. [22]To the weak I became weak, that I might win the weak. I have become all things to all men, that I might by all means save some. [23]I do it all for the sake of the gospel, that I might share in its blessings.

The passage begins and concludes with claims that are general, stressed in the sixfold repetition of "all."[1] Paul made himself a slave to all (v. 19) and to all those[2] he became all things (v. 22) for the purpose of winning as many as possible,[3] saving some in whatever way (vv. 19, 22). Between these general claims he gives a list of specific examples of his accommodation: there are four classes of people to whom he has become something, and all for the purpose of winning them (the word *kerdêsô* appears in vv. 19, 20 [twice], 21, and 22).[4] The structure is parallel: to the Jews,[5] to those under law, to those without law, to the weak, Paul became (*egenomên*, vv. 20, 22) as Jew, or as under law, or as without law, or weak,[6] in order that he might win each class. He closes the passage by pointing out that he does all (these) things for the sake of the gospel, so that he might be a fellow participant in it.[7]

That sets out the text, apart from three clauses: but those clauses are of central importance, for they tell us who is this Paul who accommodates himself in these ways. First, he is a free man, free from everyone else (or perhaps everything else:[8] *eleutheros gar ôn ek pantôn*, v. 19). Secondly, he is not himself under law (*mê ôn autos hupo nomon*, v. 20);[9] and finally, though he became as without law, he himself is not without law to God but within law to Christ (*mê ôn anomos theou all' ennomos christou*, v. 21).[10] These clauses will have to be analyzed more closely if we are to understand Paul's accommodation, but for now a more immediate matter attracts our attention: the puzzles that spring to mind upon reading Paul's words. Four present themselves.

1. Paul says that to certain Jews he became as a Jew, which suggests (in *egenomên* and *hôs*) that he was not a Jew. But surely he was. Do we not find him on many occasions willing to stress his Jewish heritage?[11]

2. The passage clearly deals with Paul's personal behavior, not simply his methodology in mission or instruction. The reader is meant to infer that Paul engaged in practices by which Jews or the weak or those without law would define their own lives. But the repeated *hôs* clauses are troubling: since Paul does not actually become weak or without law, he must have acted as though he were what he was not. Some commentators translate *hôs* "as if"; by acting "as if" he were something, Paul is only *pretending*, deliberately adopting a guise.[12] He may thus lay himself open to the charge of inconsistency and hypocrisy. For this reason we find ourselves asking about the morality of accommodation.

3. Perhaps the practice of accommodation could find some justification in Paul's stated aim: to win some of each class. Certainly there is a missionary context for the passage, and for the notion of "winning" within rabbinic Judaism. But there are other indications pointing away from a narrowly constructed missionary setting. The final clause of the passage widens Paul's purpose a little: he accommodates not only to win others but also to gain for himself in the gospel. More strongly, however, there is the presence of the weak in his list of examples. Accommodation is not simply for the sake of making converts, but also may be justified as a stance toward other Christians. These may be the "weaker brethren" who occupied us in the preceding chapter – but we are moved by this to wonder how the Corinthians might have connected to occasions and persons Paul's claims about Jews, those under law or without law, and the weak. Is there any light from Paul's actual practice to throw on his theory of accommodation?

4. Paul, we see, gives reasons for accommodating: to win some over, or to advance participation in the gospel. But are these *justifying* reasons? Are they clear enough, or good enough, by themselves? They are stronger than mere courtesy, and of greater force than considerations of self-interest, which might lie behind counsel to adapt one's behavior to one's environment. Paul was not concerned simply to make other people feel comfortable by fitting in with them. But his critics might not have accepted his stated purpose as a reason of sufficient weight to justify accommodation. They could have argued – and probably did – that he was destroying through his accommodation the work of God.[13] So our major puzzle arising from the passage comes to this: What underlies the Pauline practice of accommodation as its moral or theological justification?

Because these puzzles interlock with each other, we ought not to set about understanding Pauline accommodation by seeking to answer each of them in order. If answers come, it will be as we untangle a few major strands in the complexities of accommodation. In fact, it is best to begin the untangling not with Paul's practice or description, but with the notion of accommodation itself.

II. The Notion of Accommodation

We have called Paul's being all things to all people "accommodation." Paul himself provides no general term for this practice,[14] but our English word is not a bad label. It comes from the Latin *accommodare*, meaning "to suit" or "to fit"; and fitting is an activity requiring not only an object but also something to or for which the fitting is done. The basic activity of accommodating is thus relational as well as transitive: we accommodate x *to* y. Even bad hotels are supposed to suit their facilities, such as they are, to the basic needs of travelers.

There are no surprises in this elementary comment on the word "accommodation." If the term is used properly of Paul, it will be because it can be said that he adapts or suits something to a particular situation or set of people. Nevertheless this basic feature of the meaning of the term at least prompts us to ask not only *to whom* Paul accommodates, but also *what* it is that is accommodated. The text answers the first question by listing four groups, but it says nothing explicit about that which Paul suits or fits to these groups. It is Paul himself who is accommodated, to be sure, but in what respects?

We need to have some sense of the appropriate shape of an answer, so our first assignment is to break from the cluster of ideas associated with accommodation some specific ways of accommodating useful for this study. The break, though not clean, will allow us to see that the practices of accommodation are sufficiently complex to require separate assessment and justification. With that understanding we shall be better equipped to return to Paul.

i. Kinds of Accommodation

It is scarcely possible to advance by keeping only to generalities: our term must take its significance from the ways in which it may properly be employed. But in order to separate three pertinent usages, we begin from the counsel of courtesy referred to at the start of this chapter, "When in Rome do as the Romans do." Its generality is precisely what makes the principle disputable: it may cover manner of dress or speech, items of belief, moral behavior, and many a thing between or around them.

Nevertheless, by picking on speech we shall come to our first type of accommodation. Speak in ways familiar to the Romans, or you will not succeed in making yourself understood. This is an undeniable requirement of cross-cultural interaction, but the underlying principle remains in less striking situations. In fact, wherever there is any cognitive distance between speaker and hearer, communication is advanced by fitting the vocabulary of the one to the conceptual framework of the other. Since the epistemological conditions of people vary with time and place, misunderstanding is likely to occur where those differences are not accommodated. Or to put it less fussily, others won't get your meaning if you don't talk they way they talk. All teachers know this, or have at least been told it: start where the students are and move from the familiar to the unknown. So we might call this the principle of pedagogic accommodation, except that it is more general. We need this adaptation when we wish only to communicate beyond the customary boundaries of our vocabulary, even though we have nothing to "teach" in a stronger sense. I prefer therefore to label this adaptation *espistemological accommodation*. Accommodating in this way is like translating: the speaker has his or her own language, but adopts something new to meet the cognitive demands of an audience. Once that need is past, one's usual language is taken up again.

When the purpose is, however, pedagogic, hearers are unlike the speaker. They are expected to learn, to enlarge or revise their beliefs rather than to revert to their previous condition. How old terms can take on new meaning for them is an ancient puzzle;[15] but our interest here is in another direction. Is it ever appropriate to say, not that differing epistemological conditions have been taken into consideration, but that beliefs themselves have been accommodated from one context to another? It does not seem right to call the process of genuine learning "accommodation" if our term contains the idea of a temporary adaptation from which one can return to the familiar. But in other respects beliefs can properly be said to be accommodated. For instance, if the supposed difference between what you and I maintain is shown to evaporate on closer inspection, then it would be proper to say that your belief can accommodate mine. Agreement does not demand that we give up our respective positions.

But there is a less felicitous possibility. Our basic model of accommodation suggests that a belief might itself be changed to suit or fit in with another set of beliefs. Not that modification of belief is itself infelicitous: quite the contrary, when false beliefs are given up in order to embrace more adequate beliefs. The human species is nevertheless not always distinguished by rationality; and it may happen that I abandon a belief because I want to please you, or for some other end I value beyond the truth of that belief. An observer would have good grounds for accusing me of a compromising accommodation. For one thing, I have adapted something from my beliefs to suit yours (which shows the difference between this accommodation and a wholesale *conversion* to another belief system); and for another, my original belief remains to be returned to as in some important sense my "proper" belief, abandoned without rational justification (it is thus like the original language to be resumed after epistemological accommodation).

This type of adaptability of belief bears on our discussion of Paul, and although in other places it would take different shape,[16] here we may give it the label *theological accommodation*. It is not unknown. Nor is it found only in the blatant variety, as (say) the "con-man" evangelist of American literature. It also seems the appropriate label for the less spectacular process whereby (for example) believers in baptism for adults alone find themselves accepting without objection infant baptism for the sole reason that they have changed denominations. When in Rome, some profess to believe what the Romans believe.

This last example brings us to our third kind of accommodation. To worship for a time in a different Christian denomination does not require an adoption of every article of its belief; some practical compromise is both possible and desirable. You issue no public protest when infants are baptized in spite of your own conviction; you may join in the liturgy and perhaps act as godparent. Differences of belief remain, but you judge them unimportant in the situation, even if an observer silently attributes the wrong belief to you. Seeing the point for the Romans of some Roman customs, you participate. Later you return home to your customary behavior. This is an instance of what I shall call *practical accommodation*, in spite of the imprecision of the term. It covers many possibilities, from the trivial following of convention for the sake of courtesy to behavior that is morally significant — and thus covers what others may regard as sins (because they think you have compromised on important religious or ethical beliefs) or what indeed is a sin (if your action does in fact betray your values). There are thus differing degrees of practical accommodation: accepting the fish head at table in another culture as a token of hospitality; accepting meat known to have been offered to idols when one is a Corinthian Christian; accepting meat out of fear or embarrassment though one is a vegetarian.

These distinctions between epistemological, theological, and practical accommodation beg for more attention. That their breaking apart is not clean may be appreciated by thinking about the subtle connections that tie together theological and practical accommodation, a theme to which we shall have cause to return. Nevertheless our object is to understand and evaluate Paul's being all things to all people, so we must press on. But before returning to Pauline accommodation we should reflect a little on the justifiability of our three types of accommodation.

ii. The Morality of Accommodation

The bothersome aspect of all accommodation is its possible link with moral and intellectual vices such as inconsistency, insincerity, and hypocrisy. Its very nature requires that what is appropriate in one setting be changed for the sake of another setting, and although those who make changes may be praised as creative or ingenious, it is also possible for those who adapt too freely to be blamed as vacillating, weak, or devious. Of our types, theological accommodation seems blameworthy, whereas epistemological accommodation offers fewer moral perplexities.

This is because we have defined the theological accommodator as modifying beliefs for some reason other than their perceived truth or falsity. Although my thinking something does not make it so, and although I may come to believe for bad reasons something that is in fact true, still it is a vice to surrender or adopt beliefs without regard to their truth.[17] If we understand how a mild theological accommodation may come about under social pressure, nevertheless we do not endorse that way of acquiring beliefs — any more than we endorse indoctrination above proper education. And in severe cases our censure is strong: whoever puts on a set of theological beliefs in pretense, for personal gain, is a hypocrite and scoundrel, morally as well as intellectually reprehensible. Of course, if by accommodating theologically one means achieving a harmony of belief where supposed inconsistencies are evaporated by careful discussion, then respect for truth is maintained; and that is entirely laudable. But the process to which we attached the label cannot be commended.

Epistemological accommodation for its part requires little justification; it is a necessary means to bring about ends we value highly. It can be done poorly or well, and assessed accordingly. In itself it raises few moral problems, for it is not usually wrong to meet the epistemological conditions of your hearer. There is, however, the issue of sincerity, the consistency of belief with profession. It is possible only to pretend to meet others on their own ground, to mislead them in argument, to serve one's own interests by appearing to agree with them. The slick salesman or clever debater may be good at epistemological accommodation; but it is their technique, not their intellectual or moral virtue, that we admire.

The moral issues in these two kinds of accommodation thus have to do primarily with the ethics of belief, the rights and wrongs of holding, professing, and sharing convictions about what is the case. Practical accommodation falls more squarely into the sphere of morality proper in that it deals with actions as well as beliefs. Not that all accommodating actions have moral significance, of course; as we saw, some will belong to social convention and may be justified by the rules of hospitality. Nor is there necessarily any inconsistency in behaving differently in different social or even legal systems. When in Toronto, drive on the right side of the road; in London drive on the left. The rules are "opposite," if you like, and the two systems incompatible. But it is the *lack* of accommodation that is the dangerous inconsistency. Nevertheless, in other ways practical accommodation does require assessment and justification, and not solely over the matter of consistency. This is because of the close connection between action and belief.

Much of the behavior of interest to our study is belief-laden: it expresses theological convictions and moral values, because it takes place in a community that invests it with such meanings. Certain kinds of liturgical accommodation might be thought unacceptable, not simply because they raise questions about my sincerity, but also because they are tied up with a false theology. Likewise in the moral sphere. Although Western Christianity has been forced to rethink the ethics of marriage among polygamous recent converts, a missionary who became all things to all people in this sense might well be considered not just to be inconsistent but also to have committed a wrong. Practical accommodation may transgress the bounds of the acceptable, and so it must have moral and theological limits. Just as the theological accommodator is wrong to believe only because it pleases someone, so the practical accommodator may act wrongly in pleasing or winning others. It all depends. And that is why Paul's text is puzzling.

III. Pauline Accommodation

With this understanding of accommodation we may now return to Paul himself. He is not explicit about the ways in which he has adapted his message or behavior, nor does he offer detailed justification for his accommodation beyond the purpose expressed in winning some and sharing in the benefits of the gospel. But it is not difficult to come to some decisions about the ways in which he did or did not see himself practising accommodation.

Start with the obvious: Paul, we may be confident, did not view himself as making accommodations to others in his theological beliefs. To become as Jew or without law or weak was not for him to adopt the belief structures of these groups. That is the importance of the repeated *hôs* in our text. Paul became *as* these; he did not become one of them. The difference, though marked by a small word, is significant, for it allows him to act along with a group without sharing in the beliefs and reasons for action of that group. That he would reject any suggestion to modify an item of his belief for someone else's sake cannot be doubted: the Paul of Galatians is vehement about any attempt at all to change what he regards as the content of the gospel:[18]

> [6]I am astonished that you are so quickly deserting him who called you in the grace of Christ and turning to a different gospel — [7]not that there is another gospel, but there are some who trouble you and want to pervert the gospel of Christ. [8]But even if we, or an angel from heaven, should preach to you a gospel contrary to that which we preached to you, let him be accursed. . . .
>
> [10]Am I now seeking the favor of men, or of God? Or am I trying to please men? If I were still pleasing men, I should not be a servant of Christ. (Gal. 1:6–8, 10, RSV)

It is in the notion of "pleasing men" (*anthrôpois areskein*, v. 10) that Paul's language reflects the idea of theological accommodation. To "please" in this sense is to curry favor; Salome may be said to have pleased Herod in this way.[19] And the suggestion repudiated by Paul is that he was willing to dance theologically in order to gain the approval of some individual or group. No: he is Christ's slave, not held by anyone else — not even other apostles, as he goes on to explain in the first two chapters of Galatians.

This uncompromising commitment to the truth of the gospel he has received is an important feature of Paul's life, thought, and relationships with others. If it wins enemies for him, it makes him vigorous in his own defense, and jealous of his churches. It moves him to ridicule the Corinthians who may have sold themselves to compromise: "you bear it if a man makes slaves of you, or preys upon you, or takes advantage of you, or puts on airs, or strikes you in the face" (2 Cor. 11:20). So for Paul an essential part of being slave to no one is a freedom to maintain one's convictions without any adaptation to the demands or interests of others.

But are there no circumstances under which even a minor belief might be legitimately surrendered — say, for the sake of peace or unity? What about the matters discussed in my chapter 5, over which it is proper sometimes to surrender one's freedom? Paul did recognize that some items of faith were not worth debating on occasion: weak Christians such as vegetarians were to be accepted without critical argument (Rom. 14:1). Nevertheless this is not an accommodation of belief, with either the strong or the weak compromising on what they regard as right; it is instead a suspension of a critical attitude or (as in the Corinthian case) the freedom to exercise a right. It is hard to think of any theological accommodation of which Paul would have approved; and it is equally hard to think that he was wrong in this. If there is to be a rapprochement in beliefs, it should be the result of informed and reasonable discussion, not the product of accommodation as we have defined it.

What, then, is it for Paul to be all things to all people, if it is not at all to act the chameleon in his beliefs? The usual approach to our text answers that it is to adopt the language and thought patterns of this audience on this occasion, and that audience on another occasion, for apologetic or missionary purposes. A striking example of this kind of accommodation may be had in the Acts 17 speech to the Athenians, which starts from Athens rather than at Sinai or Jerusalem.[20] Because our text does refer to winning and saving, the standard commentary stresses Paul's accommodation as a missionary or evangelist.[21] We have already had reason to doubt this restricted construction of Pauline accommodation,[22] and to our earlier puzzles we may now add the observation that the Paul we know best is Paul the author of letters to churches. It is in these letters that we shall find instances of accommodation to which the commentators point — but this means that it will concern not so much evangelism in particular as methods of argument and instruction in general.

There is no reason to adduce detailed evidence of Paul's accommodating technique here; reference to two studies by others will suffice. The first is Henry Chadwick's oft-noted 1954 article "All Things to All Men"; the second, Richard Longenecker's chapter of the same title a decade later in his *Paul: Apostle of Liberty*.[23] Chadwick takes us through sections of 1 Corinthians and Colossians to demonstrate Paul's sensitivity to the situations with which he was dealing, and to argue that Paul does not directly challenge the beliefs of his readers; instead he "begins by accepting unhesitatingly their fundamental position. . . . he begins from where they are." Sometimes he employs the vocabulary of his opponents in a "different and disinfected sense." This is not to be wondered at: divine revelation itself is conditioned by "the capacities and situation of the recipient." Paul is no weathercock, Chadwick concludes, but instead an "uncommonly ingenious controversialist." He "had an astonishing elasticity of mind, and a flexibility in dealing with situations requiring delicate and ingenious treatment which appears greater than is usually supposed."

Longenecker's general approach overlaps considerably with Chadwick's position. Discussing various problems in 1 Corinthians, he sketches Paul's methodology as one that "begins on their own ground, at the point

where he finds agreement with them, and leads them on from there."
Or again: "Paul's approach to the question is that he begins in agreement with those he seeks to correct." Longenecker sums up:

> In every case he seeks to work from the one element of truth which
> they have grasped to a fuller understanding and expression of their
> liberty in Christ. . . . And by beginning with them at the point
> where there is common agreement and omitting such matters and
> arguments as will cause unnecessary offense, he is but manifesting
> his missionary and pastoral principle of being "all things to all men."

That Paul becomes to the Corinthians as the Corinthians or to the
Colossians as the Colossians we may grant. After all, it was an essential
part of my analysis of 1 Corinthians 8 and 10 that Paul first agrees with
basic theological and moral claims, and only then proceeds to instruct
by qualification and modification (chap. 5, section III). That is not the
whole of his method, to be sure: we must not forget the effective use
of the distancing technique of irony earlier in his letter to Corinth (discussed in chap. 2, section II). Nevertheless there are two things to be
said about the view that explains Pauline accommodation in this fashion.

First, it will be clear that this view reduces Paul's practice to
epistemological accommodation. That this characterization of his evan-
gelistic, apologetic, and pedagogic method is acceptable does not, however, mean that it adequately captures the meaning of our text. For Paul
does not give us in 1 Corinthians 9:19–23 a reflection on his polemical
strategy: nor does he claim to have adopted the vocabulary of those
without law, or to have begun from the basic premises of the weak. Instead his point is that he has himself taken on different ways of behaving, assumed different identities. His accommodation embraces more than
the epistemological; in fact it is primarily *practical* accommodation that
he describes.

This means, secondly, that the view that turns our text into a statement of accommodating pedagogic method cannot adequately take account of the troubling moral issues of hypocrisy and inconsistency we
expressed in the second puzzle of section I, above. It is true that pedagogic
techniques are not to be shuttered from moral scrutiny. As we have
already recognized, one can be devious in argument, insincerely agree-
ing to premises or riding on ambiguities to unwarranted conclusions. Paul
was himself aware of this when he came to Corinth. Whether in fact
he argued fairly is a legitimate question to ask: Chadwick shows this concern in his comment that Paul's "opportunism" "does not necessarily imply a complete lack of scruple"; and Longenecker, realizing that a charge
of devious technique is possible, is careful to assert Paul's sincerity.[24]

Socrates, we remember, got himself into trouble over his method because of suspicions on this count (Thrasymachus sneers about his reputation for dissimulation; *Rep.* 337a). Nevertheless, there is no hint that Paul's critics were upset simply for such reasons. It was his actions, attitudes, and claims that must have generated their charges. So even if Paul rejected theological accommodation, and even if his method can be defended, we are left with the question of the morality of his accommodative behavior. It seems that until we face squarely the issue of his *practical* accommodation, we have not settled what is involved in his being all things to all people.[25]

Yet it is just at this point that we feel the lack of specific information that would enable us to relate Paul's self-description to his actual practices. Our third opening puzzle asked whether light might fall on Pauline accommodation from the understanding of his behavior available to the Corinthians. The answer is partial. The extant correspondence provides no help on the matter of how the Corinthians would have taken his becoming as Jew or as under law — except that as a warning that in other places his behavior might be different from what it was in Corinth. Nevertheless his words need not have been utterly opaque to them. He has just pointed out at the close of chapter 8 that he would refrain from eating meat if his action were to have disastrous effect on the weak. On the reading of this issue that I developed in my chapter 5, his willingness would indeed be accommodative, for he would fit his practice to a particular circumstance without being bound to act similarly all the time. Given no weak for whose sake to suspend his right to eat, Paul's behavior would express his theological conviction that all meats are clean.[26]

Again, it is likely that Paul had not observed Jewish dietary laws on his first visit to Corinth (and had perhaps eaten idol meat); if so, this would provide an example of his becoming as one outside the law. Further, the Corinthians might reflect on other claims made in the letter. To the enthusiasts he can say that he speaks with tongues more than they all (14:18) — this in the course of an argument asking them to modify their own behavior. He identifies with the unmarried in that he has not invoked his right to a wife (9:5; 7:7), and with wage-earners in that he has refused the financial entitlement of the evangelist (9:15): if he has not exactly accommodated temporarily to these groups he has still adapted his behavior significantly for the sake of the gospel. So what we can glimpse of his practice bears out his principle of practical accommodation in these respects, and links up neatly with his general claim in 10:33: "I try to please all men in everything I do, not seeking my own advantage, but that of the many, that they may be saved."

Of more interest than Paul's actual attempts to adapt, however, is the question of the limits of practical accommodation. We have seen that, theologically, he is no "pleaser of men"; yet he seeks to please everybody in everything. It is possible to dismiss his language as emotional hyperbole, which carries him into contradiction: possible, but not necessary, for we may be able to reconcile his statements by working out those conditions under which accommodation is justifiable, and those where it is not. Although Paul does provide a reason for accommodating — to win some — nevertheless morally wrong means cannot be justified by this end. So we must go beyond it, to canvass a range of his comments on Christian behavior throughout 1 Corinthians. Three steps will take us to the place where his practice may find its justification.

First, Paul's contradictory desires to please everyone and yet to please no one but Christ should be related to the pervasive model of freedom and slavery in his letter. The theme of freedom is played off against the obligations and constraints others might impose on him. So in chapter 9 he stresses the rights of apostleship with his opening challenge: Am I not free? Apostolic freedom gives him a claim to material support and the right to "lead around" (not now a happy choice of verb) a Christian wife (9:1–18); it is a freedom from everyone else (9:19) and indeed from law itself (9:20). Four times he states that he is free to do anything whatever (twice in 6:12 and twice in 10:23; though he qualifies this freedom, he never negates it). And he regards himself as free from accountability to his converts or other human beings; he does not even pass judgment on himself (4:3).

Nevertheless this freedom is only one polarity. Paul is also the servant of Christ (4:1) and under his ultimate judgment (4:4). If outside law, he is still within law to Christ (9:22), and (the paradox is here restated) he has enslaved himself to all even though he is free from them (9:19).

Note, secondly, that this paradox is not true of Paul alone. Although he has certain apostolic privileges, he includes in the freedom of Christ all Christ's followers. So in the slogans that everything is permissible there is no appeal to privilege; Paul argues as though the principle holds for others as well. Christians are to refuse to become slaves to anyone (7:23), and even the household slave is the Lord's freedman (7:22). But again, such freedom exists only because Christians are not their own; they have been purchased (6:20) and are now slaves to Christ (7:22).

This means, thirdly, that, as the model of slavery and freedom is extended to all Christians, it will have implications for their behavior.[27] Free though they are, they must live in certain ways — and Paul does not shrink from making that clear. His letter is laced with imperatives, exhortations, advice, moral principles, and all manner of behavior-directing language. I cannot here analyze his ethical reasoning in the detail that his chapter 7 received earlier, but we may approach the matter by recognizing that for Paul there seem to be three ways of structuring freedom so that it does not become a carte blanche for whatever behavior one feels like indulging.

1. Freedom is structured most basically by a *Christ-regarding* limit, expressed in the idea of slavery to Christ. It makes idolatry utterly wrong (10:21), and is the basis for Paul's rejection of theological accommodation. But it also has a moral thrust: sins against one's body or brother are ultimately sins against Christ (6:15–20; 8:12). Interestingly, Paul does not invoke the teachings of Jesus as a code of behavior; slavery to Christ does not mean wearing the yoke of a new law. Whatever being "under the law of Christ" in 9:21 entails, it cannot be that.[28]

2. Another curb on completely unrestricted behavior is a *self-regarding* limit. All things may be permissible, but not everything is profitable for me; some actions will work against my own good, and end up enslaving me (6:12; 10:23; cf. 7:35).

3. There is also an *other-regarding* limit on freedom. In many ways this is the predominant ethical theme of Paul's letter. Paul himself does not regard his own good, but the good of the many (10:33), being willing for their sake to forego rights and privileges (8:13; chap. 9). His followers are to do likewise in imitation of him and of Christ (11:1). They must seek the interests of others above their own (10:23). The image of the church as body in chapter 12 stresses this regard for others, and that of course leads to the chapter 13 description of *agapê* as fundamentally concerned with the welfare of the other person. The exercise of freedom must not contradict the aim of love, which is to build up (8:1); and that aim must characterize the whole of the Christian life (16:14).

It is not inappropriate, therefore, to suggest that the complementary themes of freedom and love are dominant in Paul's understanding of Christian behavior. We may use again, as we did in chapter 4, above, his summary in 7:35: freedom, because there is no tight rein; and love, directed toward Christ, others, and the self.[29] This will tempt us to questions about the role of law, rules, and principles in Paul's ethics. But we must resist, in order to return finally after these steps to Paul's practice of accommodation—though it is worth noting that love for Christ and love for others are not identical types of love (see chap. 7, below, section III).

We want to know how Paul might justify his being all things to all people. In answer he might first employ his notion of freedom. By defining himself only as Christ's slave, Paul cuts himself free from other identities. This means, I think, that he no longer regards himself as a Jew.[30] That is crucial: by disclaiming his former life Paul may justify behavior that otherwise would indeed be inconsistent. To adopt the eating habits of gentiles is not playacting on the part of someone who is still underneath a Jew; to act as without law is not the unscrupulous behavior of someone who has temporarily contradicted his or her true manner of living. As slave to Christ alone, Paul freely wears the dress of Corinth, Rome, or Jerusalem. Since there are some Christians who are Jews, some who follow law and some who do not, and some weak, Paul legitimately identifies himself with each group as the occasion requires. In such a fashion he might settle some of our puzzles about his accommodation.

More positively, however, it is open to Paul to justify his being all things to all people in terms of love. Perhaps we can phrase his goal of winning many and sharing in the gospel by saying that his is an *agapeic* accommodation, designed to advance the welfare of others. It is not, as we remember from our third puzzle, a narrowly missionary — or even epistemological — accommodation. Wherever there are those whose interests he may serve, Paul will adapt himself to their needs. Nevertheless this very love also requires that Paul cannot literally be all things to everyone. That part of his dictum is indeed hyperbole. His love for Christ forbids (as we saw) not only theological accommodation but also any act — such as fellowship with demons (10:20f.) — that would betray that loyalty. His love for a brother in Christ demands that he not act out his freedom to the destruction of someone else (8:11). Nor could he legitimately accommodate where he himself would lose his freedom or his standing in Christ.[31]

We may conclude that Paul's practical accommodation, though a significant expression of his freedom in Christ, is guarded by theological and moral limits. Had he seen himself still subject to law, his behavior would have been unjustifiably insincere; or if in suiting his actions to a particular occasion he had compromised either truth or morality, his accommodation would have transgressed the permissible. But we have no reason to believe that Paul intended to adapt in these unacceptable ways, and so his slogan is defensible. He "pleases all men," not literally "in all things," but only in those things that lead to their welfare in Christ. He cannot please those who deny the very conditions of that welfare. The contradiction between his claims to please and yet never to please is thus generated by a difficulty in pleasing itself, a difficulty recognized by both children and parents. Wherever immediate desires (the demand of "Please!") conflict with long-term satisfaction or welfare ("You won't be happy"), that contradiction is part of human experience.

But it should be recognized that, whereas Pauline accommodation might be justified within these limits, and his pleasing others reconciled with his pleasing only Christ, the dictum "all things to all men" is not itself a justifying principle. It describes Paul's practice and his methodology in mission and instruction; it does not itself make any of his actions right. We saw at the end of chapter 5, above, that the general principle of beneficence expressed in 1 Corinthians 10:24 and 10:33, seeking the welfare of all types of people, is an insufficient guide to the exercise of Christian rights. Sometimes welfare is advanced by refraining from the permissible, and sometimes by enjoying one's freedoms. Likewise with accommodation. We are to serve the good of others, but whether this requires adapting or standing fast is another question. In fact, as we shall learn in the final section of this chapter, even when accommodation remains within its proper moral and theological bounds, it may still go wrong.

IV. AGAINST ACCOMMODATION

We have recognized that accommodation may be blameworthy where it is insincere or inconsistent, or where it violates moral and theological principles. This suggests that the good intentions of the accommodator are important: but we must now understand that accommodation may contain problems that even sincerity cannot eradicate.

A fundamental difficulty resides in the fact that accommodating behavior is (as we saw in section II.ii, above) belief-laden and consequently subject to misinterpretation. I may illustrate this by two incidents in Paul's life, not connected with Corinth but illuminating nonetheless. The first received brief mention at the end of chapter 5, above: the quarrel between Peter and Paul at Antioch. In Paul's eyes Peter had denied the truth of the gospel by withdrawing from table-fellowship with gentile Christians just because some Jerusalem Christians from James had arrived on the scene. Paul attributes Peter's action to fear and labels it hypocrisy (Gal. 2:12–13); he might maintain that it is a sad case of insincere theological accommodation. But, as Peter Richardson has argued,[32] Peter could reply that he was not compromising the gospel but rather accommodating the feelings of Jewish Christians. On gentile territory Peter could act as without law; given a Jewish presence, he, as the apostle to the circumcised, acts as a Jewish Christian. It is unfortunate that we do not have Peter's comment on Paul's charge, for it might teach us something of the ambiguities of accommodation.

The second incident is Paul's support of the men discharging their Nazirite vow, reported by Luke in Acts 21:17ff. Again we have only one perspective: but because my point is to illustrate a typical danger in practical accommodation, detailed historical questions may remain in the background. Suppose, as Bornkamm has suggested,[33] that Paul undertook to participate in what he regarded as a private ceremony in order to demonstrate that Jewish Christians may still observe parts of the law, and thus to affirm the unity of Jew and gentile in the church. Still his action was not private, and opened itself to misinterpretation on the part of others. The Jews from Asia may have thought him insincere, even mocking; and in stirring up the crowd they set in motion a chain of events leading from Paul's accommodation to his martyrdom. So whatever Paul's motive or justification in this act of becoming as Jew to the Jews, it is clear that the interpretive gap between his understanding and the significance attached by observers worked against his original reasons for accommodation.

Consider next another difficulty in the ability of practical accommodation to achieve its goals. Behavior might be adjusted to this group or that in order to bring about the benefits of the gospel, and it may be accepted as sincere. But it may also be thought *too* sincere: that is, the group may take the practice of the accommodator as a confirmation of its own ways, instead of an adaptation intended to move its members closer to Christian comprehension and freedom. For instance, the Corinthian weak who occupied our last chapter require practical accommodation if they are not to be destroyed. Nevertheless, as we came to appreciate in that study, their slender hold on the faith requires strengthening. Accommodation may be called for in the first instance: but by itself it will not achieve the goal of a robust faith. If we are indeed to please all men by seeking their good, we will fail to promote that good by actions that only endorse limited apprehensions of Christian liberty and truth.

Finally there is what may be called the danger of infection, where the position accommodated to works itself back into the accommodating mind. It may be only partial. The laudable effort to express beliefs in the language of the hearer may introduce into one's own vocabulary concepts that subtly alter the shape of those beliefs. The Greek concept of *psuchê*, useful to early Christian thinkers in relating their faith to philosophy, brought with it a dualistic view of persons then read back into the New Testament (see chap. 3, section II, above). Or think of Pope Gregory the Great's instructions in 601 A.D. to accommodate to the pagan English by leaving their temples standing but with idols replaced by altars and Christian relics. "For it is certainly impossible," he writes, "to eradicate all errors from obstinate minds at one stroke, and whoever wishes to climb to a mountaintop climbs gradually, step by step, and not in one leap." Gregory justifies this as similar to divine accommodation in revelation, and the counsel may have been both prudent and wise in that light. But who knows what infection of Christian belief by superstition it fostered in the early Anglo-Saxon church?[34]

The infection may reach further in prolonged practical accommodation. One may start by following out the customs of a group; but in time repeated behavior brings with it the perspectives and beliefs of the group. That was the insight in Pascal's famous recipe for those who could not believe, even though it was in their best interests:

> You would like to cure yourself of unbelief, and you ask for remedies. Learn of those who were once bound and gagged like you, and who now stake all that they possess. They are men who know the road that you desire to follow, and who have been cured of a sickness of which you desire to be cured. Follow the way by which they set out, acting as if they already believed, taking holy water, having masses said, etc. Even this will naturally cause you to believe and blunt your cleverness.[35]

This accommodation thus ends in conversion. That the result was cure for Pascal and not illness has nothing to do with the process he recommended; the procedure may work for any system of beliefs, regardless of its truth or falsity, and in spite of the original intentions of the accommodator.

So there are no easy answers about accommodation. We have perhaps settled some of our puzzles about Paul's being all things to all people, though we could wish for more light on Paul's actual practices in the early tensions between Jewish and gentile Christianity. In coming to appreciate differences in ways of accommodating and their moral or theological acceptability, we have seen how Paul might justify both his epistemological and his practical accommodation. Nevertheless, we have also recognized that there are limits to accommodation, imposed by the need for consistent belief and by the demands of morality. Even justifiable accommodation risks failure and may cause grave damage. If Paul's slogan has been more readily remembered than understood, we must confess that it may be more easily discussed than practised.

CHAPTER SEVEN

Partial Knowledge:
1 Corinthians 13

Now I know in part. 1 Cor. 13:12

We begin with a puzzle. It may not be difficult to solve, but we shall find that its solution generates something more for investigation. Not surprisingly: the objects of our inquiry often multiply spontaneously, as though they were Russian dolls with self-reproducing powers: no sooner is one inspected and taken apart than another is born from within.

Our perplexity arises from Paul's claims in the last part of 1 Corinthians 13. It is not what seems to have bothered some commentators, the closing statement that faith and hope "abide" along with love. They reason that if Paul means only that all three virtues persist throughout the present life, then this does not account for the endurance of love in the life to come; but if all three are to endure with that permanence, then Paul's claim seems inconsistent with what he says elsewhere about faith and hope. For those are only temporary virtues required by our present lack of seeing: we walk by faith because we do not now see (2 Cor. 5:7), and hope because we do not yet have (Rom. 8:24–25). The puzzle of inconsistency need not arise, however, if we understand faith as trust no matter what the present circumstances, and hope as trust for the future;[1] indeed love requires both of these wherever it is found, in this life or the next.

Nevertheless loving trust also requires knowledge, and it is here that our perplexity does arise. For Paul claims in 1 Corinthians 13:8 that knowledge will, in the future, vanish away. This is strong language, for which the context does not prepare us. Paul has been discussing only the superiority of love, a superiority that does not supplant the spiritual gifts he has listed in chapter 12 but is instead necessary for their worth. Tongues, prophesies, knowledge (the order begins at the bottom of the

142

lists in 12:8–11 and 28), even miracle-working faith and self-sacrificing deeds are worthless and unprofitable apart from love (13:2–3). Love itself will never come to an end. But the superiority of love turns out to be such that some of the things it makes worthwhile will in fact end. Whatever prophesies there are will be done away with; tongues will cease; and (then the crucial claim) knowledge itself will be abolished.

We take Paul to mean that the abolition of some activities will come in the eschaton, in the life with God awaiting believers beyond death. That love should persist in that life accords with Christian expectations: without it, as we saw at the close of our discussion of resurrection in chapter 3, above, no heaven could be heaven. That tongues should cease and prophesies end may trouble some who value certain religious experiences, but what is philosophically puzzling is Paul's claim that knowledge will itself be abolished. How so? When faith remains, why should knowledge vanish? How indeed *could* knowledge be destroyed without dissolving both faith and love into unrecognizable elements and making mockery of the hope that we as persons will persist in the resurrection?

We begin to answer by reminding ourselves that Paul preserves the intelligibility of his claim in asserting not that he will then know nothing but that he will then know fully and completely. Now he knows in part; then he will know as fully as he is now known. So what is to be abolished is the partiality of knowledge, its incompleteness.

Thus we arrive at the theme of our final study, partial knowledge. This is Paul's characterization of our present knowledge of God, and if we can explore its meaning, it may yield things of importance for the understanding that faith seeks.

The answer to our puzzle is only begun, however. The mere contrast between partial and full knowledge does not tell us how we move from one to the other, or why indeed Paul should use such strong language about the move. Why should he posit the destruction of the partial? Would it not be more natural to talk of filling in the pieces or rounding out the incomplete?

I. PARTIAL KNOWLEDGE: A KNOWLEDGE OF PARTS?

To understand Paul's claim, we need to work through his own words in 1 Corinthians 13:8–13. Love never ends, he says, but:

> [8]as for prophecy, it will pass away; as for tongues, they will cease; as for knowledge it will pass away. [9] For our knowledge is imperfect and our prophecy is imperfect; [10] but when the perfect comes, the imperfect will pass away. [11] When I was a child, I spoke like a child,

I thought like a child, I reasoned like a child; when I became a man, I gave up childish ways.[12] For now we see in a mirror dimly, but then face to face. Now I know in part; then I shall understand fully, even as I have been fully understood.[13] So faith, hope, love abide, these three; but the greatest of these is love. (RSV)

We note immediately that Paul's language is strongly reminiscent of his critique of worldly wisdom in his chapter 1. The verb translated "pass away" or "gave up" in vv. 8, 10, and 11 is in its active form *katargein*, "to abolish" or "to make completely useless"; it is the same verb Paul used in 1:28, where God is said to choose the lowly and despised to "bring to nothing" the somebodies of this world. They are those who (as we saw in chapter 2, above) think themselves wise, and whose wisdom God destroys (*apolô*, 1:19). In this judgment we can find no glimmer of a process of filling in the partial or rounding out the incomplete understanding of the conceited. Although it does not follow that in chapter 13 the abolition of knowledge is a judgment, as it is in chapter 1, that does not help our perplexity. The earlier judgment was (on our account) God's destruction of the inflated consciousness of the proud, not of human reason itself. But now it looks as though some form of legitimate knowledge is in fact destroyed by being brought to an end.

Perhaps the language of destruction can be explained by positing something special in the Corinthian situation to which Paul is alluding in his talk of knowledge. The word in 13:2 and 13:8 is *gnôsis*: perhaps he means, then, to speak about gnosticizing tendencies among certain of the Corinthians, not only to remind them again that having knowledge puffs up (8:1), but more especially to claim that this very knowledge on which they pride themselves will be destroyed. C.K. Barrett understands our puzzle in this way. *Gnôsis*, he says, is "secret information about God"; and "when God manifests himself at large no man can boast about his secret stock of knowledge." What is destroyed on this view is the restricted ownership of the knowledge, not its content.[2] Our puzzle would be solved in a move like that made by some to explain Paul's earlier critique of wisdom, by turning knowledge into something special.

But this does not seem the right way to approach the problem. It would be foolish to assert that Paul's language is not influenced by his evaluation of Corinthian pretense to knowledge, but it is almost as wrong to deny that his claim is unrestricted in scope. Paul is careful to include himself in his discussion: it is not that someone else's knowledge will be destroyed, but Paul's knowledge, and thus by implication the knowledge of all his readers. Criticism there may be of those who think they have attained wisdom, but it is a criticism that depends upon a fully inclusive statement about all knowledge of God in this present life by all categories of believers.[3] The puzzle therefore remains: Why is present partial knowledge destroyed rather than completed?

Will it help to look at v. 10, "when the perfect (*to teleion*) comes, the "in-part" (*to ek merous*) will be abolished"? If we think of destruction in terms of parts and wholes, the language makes little sense. Paul cannot mean that parts are literally destroyed or even made useless when all the pieces are assembled into a whole. Were the inner tube, tire, rim, and spokes all to vanish when I put my bicycle wheel back together, I should have difficulty riding to the library. Likewise, if the pieces of our knowledge of God vanished in the life to come, we would know then a good deal less than we know now. And yet the passage is often read as Paul's assertion that our present knowledge of God is *fragmentary*:[4] what is wrong with our condition is that none of us has the whole picture. That, of course, is profoundly true, and one of the reasons why we need to belong to a wider community, one that listens to the past as well as to the present. But if we leave the matter there, with partial knowledge as knowledge of bits and pieces, we cannot think that the fragments will pass away. This cannot be the best way to understand what Paul has to say about the partial nature of knowledge.

Perhaps we could try again. Does he mean that the fragments will lose their identity *as* fragments, but not their content, as thought the placing of the last piece in the jigsaw puzzle were to cause all the lines to disappear and the picture to be whole? That would express the completion in assembling a whole from its parts. Or does he mean by parts something like *ingredients*, where things change from being what they are to produce something new: eggs and cream and port are no longer eggs and cream and port but perfected into syllabub? But what is the epistemic perfection in which our present bits of knowing would act as ingredients? Fortunately we do not need to pursue the analogy: it has brought us to the place where we can recognize that if the partial knowledge now available is to be destroyed, it must be that another kind of knowledge will replace it. And rather than indulge in the fabrication of additional metaphors, we may turn to Paul's own illustrations. They show us that partial knowledge is not primarily a knowledge of parts, but instead knowledge that is imperfect.

III. PARTIAL KNOWLEDGE AS IMPERFECT

We must now devote attention to vv. 11 and 12, where Paul presents two comparisons of our present knowing in part: first the analogy of the child, and then the analogy of seeing "in a mirror dimly," as the RSV puts it. The second breaks into two, so we are given three descriptions of the nature of partial knowledge, to be examined in turn.

i. Partial Knowledge as Childish

The RSV of v. 11 may stand, with the reminder that to "give up" childish things is to destroy or make them completely useless. The contrast between infant and adult is familiar enough: Paul had used it in 3:1 to chide the Corinthians for their sorry condition (see chap. 2, section III.iv, above) and will use it again in 14:20 to ask for mature thinking on their part.[5] Here, however, its use is different. The child speaks, knows, and reasons in ways that, from adult perspective, are imperfect, and it is this epistemic imperfection rather than moral immaturity or innocence that Paul applies to our present knowledge of God. Even those who are mature in Christ will find their knowledge childish when the perfect comes.

In what sense is childish knowledge destroyed by maturity? Although it would be pointless to wring a great deal from Paul's illustration, its meaning is readily appreciated. To visit again as adult the places one knew only as a small child (if progress has not disturbed them) is to realize how much perspective may change. The house is in reality smaller, the museum more fascinating or less frightening, than memory had insisted. To look again at one's first letters (if parents have preserved them) is almost to meet the embryo of another author; to read again a book too rich for a childish palate, almost to read it for the first time. In experiences like these we find ourselves talking of perspective, recognition, and insight that were unavailable, although what is now known and appreciated was there all along. Not that we did not see *at all* what was there; rather, we saw and spoke imperfectly. The imperfect cannot persist in the face of fuller understanding; it is destroyed because earlier impressions are now useless and false. They do not even form a clear knowledge of parts: to say we had understood "bits" of some book is misleading if it suggests that full insight is simply a matter of filling in some more "bits." Once we have seen what an author is up to, our old way of reading the story is gone beyond recapture, except as an item in our biography. Child and adult can ever only play at being the other: the one because he does not know what he will be, and the other because he knows too well that he is not what he was.

Of course no one should claim that all knowing and reasoning in childhood is of this character. Were it utterly different from adult knowing, we could never make progress in learning. However, Paul's interest is illustration, not a contribution to cognitive psychology. What makes present knowledge partial, then, is its imperfection. We know, not parts and pieces, but partially; and not as a brick wall is partially built or a box of biscuits partially eaten, but as a story is partially understood or a roughed-in landscape partially painted. The imperfection of childish knowledge makes the jigsaw puzzle analogy inapt: what vanish in the life to come are not the fragments and isolated pieces, but the misapprehensions that burden our attempts to understand. Our knowledge will not simply be filled in: it will (to recall resurrection language from chap. 3, above) be changed.

ii. Partial Knowledge as Indirect Vision

We may solve our original puzzle about the abolition of knowledge on this understanding of Paul's first illustration. It is the imperfection of knowledge that requires its end. However, in v. 12 Paul adds another analogy to describe our present knowledge, and we must consider it now. Unfortunately the verse is difficult to translate: available offerings range from the deeply entrenched KJV "now we see through a glass darkly" through "we see in a mirror dimly" (RSV) to "we see puzzling reflections in a mirror" (NEB). In this section I consider the mirror image only, reserving the dark/dim puzzles for the next.

"For now we see *di' esoptrou.*" The preposition may mean "in" or "through" or "by means of"; it makes little difference how it is taken as long as we do not assume that Paul has us trying to peer right through a dark or smokey glass at objects on its further side. The glass is a *mirror*, and what we see is in the mirror, not available to sight apart from it. But what point is the metaphor meant to express?

There have been helpful studies of mirror imagery in the ancient world, needing no addition here. They point out that in Hellenistic literature mirrors are associated with three themes: clarity of vision, self-knowledge, and indirect knowledge.[6] Commentators generally agree that it is the third theme that Paul has in mind. Because God must be understood as the object of vision,[7] Paul's concern cannot be knowledge of the self; and because present sight is contrasted with face-to-face knowing, his emphasis must be on the indirect nature of our present knowledge of God.

This seems right. However, we should not pass over the use of mirrors for knowledge of the self so rapidly that we miss echoes of this theme in Paul. The basic purpose of a mirror is to reflect the image of the persons who use it, for only in this way can they ever come to see their own face. Paul's speaking of "seeing in a mirror" trades on this basic purpose: but he changes our expectations by putting into the mirror not the user but (in some sense) God, who is inaccessible by nature to human viewing. Paul also changes expectations by rejecting the notion of clear images, as we shall see in the next section. Moreover, he returns to an echo of knowledge of the self in his phrase "even as I am known" (*kathôs kai epegnôsthên*). But now the one who has full knowledge of Paul is not Paul himself; it is God. When the mirror drops away, Paul will see face to face and gain more than any mirror could give him; knowledge of God as complete as God's knowledge of Paul. The transfer is thus double: from the expected face in the mirror to God, and from an abandoned mirror (which does not give one's own face) to full knowledge of the self in God's face. Paul may have in mind a process in the reverse direction when he writes of faces and mirrors in 2 Corinthians 3:18, especially if we take the verb *katoptridzomai* to mean "reflecting in a mirror": human faces not only reflect the glory of God but are themselves changed from glory to glory.[8]

Still, the controlling theme of the image is indeed the indirectness of our present knowledge of God, and to work out some of the implications of the metaphor I consider this theme in three ways. I look first at the distinction between direct and indirect knowledge, then apply this to our knowledge of persons, and finally comment on the inferior status of images reflected in a mirror.

1. Since the metaphor expresses the belief that indirect knowledge is not as valuable as direct knowledge, we must ask ourselves in what sense this is so. If we classify as indirect anything not immediately evident to the mind, then all truths known by inference will be known indirectly. It seems strange, however, to deprecate as inferior something like the knowledge of an answer to a mathematical problem simply because it has to be worked out instead of being seen right off. So we are better advised to keep our present discussion centered on objects and events rather than truths. We may draw the difference between direct and indirect by saying that something is known directly when it is present in its own right, and indirectly when it is available only through a representative, perhaps in the form of a picture, description, or piece of testimony. Such a characterization does make indirect knowledge derivative: but that of course does not make it necessarily bad. Vast stretches of our knowledge must be indirect, for this is all we can ever hope to have of the past and all we need for most of the present as well; and there are many things we are thankful to know only vicariously. Further, it would be wrong to regard the indirect as always following in dependence upon the direct. The vehicles of indirect knowledge are often useful in promoting direct knowledge: we may become better acquainted with an event by attempting to describe it, even to ourselves.[9]

Nevertheless there remains an incompleteness to indirect knowledge when this is all we have of an object or event. For many purposes this will make little difference. Listening to Glenn Gould's recording of one of the Goldberg Variations may even be preferable to attending a concert or being present in a recording session. But in other cases direct experience will enlarge or heighten our awareness in profound ways. To read Elie Wiesel or William Styron on the Holocaust is to gain understanding of an unspeakable event;[10] to walk through an exhibit of photographs and documents from Auschwitz is to add other dimensions to understanding; in that exhibit to come upon a pile of empty suitcases bearing names of murdered people — suitcases not behind glass but available to touch — is to be confronted more directly with the edges of that event. And still one was not there.

2. The difference between direct and indirect, and the ways they work together to increase understanding, are important too in our knowledge of other people. But here the matter is more complex. It is not enough to say that knowing persons requires acquaintance beyond mere description, for that is true of many other things (cities and films, for example) where there is a difference between "knowing about" and getting to know for oneself. Nor is it right to argue that there is something so special about personal knowing that it may be separated completely from factual knowledge, as Martin Buber seemed to do with his distinction between "I-Thou" and "I-it" relationships.[11] In getting to know another person well, we find factual knowledge extremely important, and this means much useful knowledge will be indirect. Such indirect knowledge is by itself insufficient, as we have just noted; but it is also the case that direct experience alone may not yield everything we mean by knowing someone personally. This is because of the different senses we attach to "knowing personally." Sometimes to "know x personally" means only to know x for oneself as distinct from indirect knowing; but at other times it means to know, not an object or event, but a person, usually as a friend.

We can of course know other people "personally" in the first sense, as social workers or psychiatrists "know" people. But if we are to establish relationships, then any knowledge that remains detached or observational, whether direct or indirect, will be insufficient even though necessary. Exactly how the "more" that is required should be characterized is difficult to determine, partly because of the great variety of relationships that human beings share. If we think of friendship as the paradigmatic personal relationship (even though friendships themselves hardly form a simple type), then terms like "mutuality," "reciprocity," "trust," and the like, will be important. Perhaps they must be present in some measure whenever we claim to know someone personally. But for our purposes we need only stress the matter of reciprocal acknowledgment. It would be odd for A to claim to know B personally if B could not even recognize A. We expect mutual recognition and sharing between the two.

To put the matter in terms from 1 Corinthians 13:12, personal knowing is face to face. Photographs may give indirect knowledge of a face; a face may be directly present to an observer who can identify and describe it to others. But "personal knowing" in the sense of friendship requires two faces to be present to each other. And that is why a mirror image must remain inferior, not only because of its indirectness but also because in the image the other person is not available for mutual knowing.

Though indirect knowledge of other persons is inadequate for personal relationships, it does not follow that personal knowing in any particular case would be a valuable experience. All of us could construct lists of people better known indirectly than personally. For the believer, however, to know and love God is supremely good. Inevitably, then, knowledge of God that is indirect, at the level of report or representation, will be inadequate and inferior. Although knowledge *about* God is necessary for faith, it is only part of the story. The mirror image stresses that present knowledge is partial in this sense, that *even if* believers had a fairly full grasp of facts about God, they would nevertheless not yet know God himself. Their knowledge remains unconsummated.

3. So much then for some ways in which the partial nature of our present knowledge of God is appropriately expressed in the metaphor of indirect vision. Although the metaphor should not be asked for more than it gives,[12] there is another aspect of Paul's image that deserves a comment. In stressing the indirectness of mirror vision, commentators have been willing to allow that images may themselves be clear and distinct representatives of their realities. Perhaps, however, we should think not of their success in representation but of their status in the scheme of things. Mirror images are ontologically intriguing in that they are completely dependent upon the realities that they reflect; unlike photographs, paintings, or descriptions, they can have no existence apart from those realities. Further, their subjects determine all their characteristics as well as their existence. A poor mirror may distort its subject, but only a magic mirror shows what is not there — and then of course it is more than a mirror.

Although it may strain interpretation to read Paul's metaphor, as some have done, in a Platonic context, Paul's mirror images do bear comparison with the shadows in Plato's cave.[13] For Plato the character of our knowing is colored by the status of its objects: only opinion, not firm knowledge, may be had of fleeting shadows. But Paul would need neither the vocabulary nor the metaphysics of Plato to believe that mirror representations are themselves inferior because derivative and impermanent. In consequence the knowledge engendered by such images is inferior in spite of the question of its clarity. Such knowledge must be destroyed when the perfect comes; we will know face to face, not by adding more angles to our reflecting surfaces, but by turning away from them completely.

So our present knowledge is partial because childishly imperfect and because indirect and inferior. Both the analogy of the child and the metaphor of the mirror combine in this judgment. Without the second we might hope that the objects of our knowledge are more stable, our vision more direct, than is the case; without the first we might hope for clear correspondence between image and reality. Together they agree in the presentation of the imperfection of present knowledge, and this is sufficient to link these pictures without resorting to artificial parallels between Paul's language and magical practices in antiquity.[14] Nevertheless they do not tell all of Paul's mind: there is still the phrase *en ainigmati* in v. 12, by which Paul characterizes our seeing in a mirror. It confirms the lack of clear correspondence between what we now know and what there is to be known; but where the picture of the child could suggest that it is only from a later perspective that we will appreciate how imperfectly we once knew, this phrase describes the way in which we see right now. The "even if" supposition about clarity of vision two paragraphs back was indeed hypothetical.

iii. Partial Knowledge as Puzzling

Our first task in elucidating this third feature of our present knowledge is to find an adequate English expression of the phrase *en ainigmati*. Paul does not supply a direct object for our seeing; the phrase is adverbial, describing the manner of our seeing whatever it is that we glimpse in the mirror. His hesitation is natural enough if we remind ourselves of the status of mirror images: what we see is not really in the mirror, but what is there is not something other than what is reflected. By not completing his verb Paul may refrain from claiming that there in the mirror is God, and instead concentrate on our way of viewing images.

The three translations quoted at the opening of section ii, above, left us with dark/dim puzzles. The KJV and RSV retain the advantage of an adverbial translation in "darkly" or "dimly," but by concentrating their meaning on the amount of light available to the viewer, they miss something essential. For they suggest that what is imperfect is simply our perceptual environment: were someone else to turn up the light a little, our seeing would be improved without effort on our part. Paul's phrase contains a different suggestion, however.

An *ainigma* is a riddle, something that requires untying or loosening or solving. If we sometimes call riddles "dark" utterances, or transliterate from the Greek into our English "enigma," we must not lose the sense of *challenge to understanding* that remains in the idea. Just as not all contradictions are paradoxes, so not all sayings difficult to comprehend are riddles: paradoxes are apparent contradictions that demand resolution, and riddles are knots in understanding asking to be untied, hidden meanings inviting disclosure. There is a prize to be won in a riddle that makes it like a game (indeed children enjoy playing with riddles), though the game may be taxing, and losing or winning of great importance (as in the riddle of the Sphinx or even the "riddle of the universe"). Parables are in a way like riddles grown into stories — but that is enough for now; we may take it that riddles are puzzles about meaning that invite active participation rather than passive illumination.

So a satisfactory translation of Paul's phrase must capture the active ingredient in *en ainigmati*. Because we cannot speak idiomatically of doing something "riddlingly," we may need to resort to the more generic notion of "puzzle" for a good translation. And good English construction gives us minor trouble over Paul's adverbial phrase. But if we bear in mind how we get to it, the NEB translation, "puzzling reflections in a mirror," is about as close as we are likely to come. That an object, "reflections," is supplied where Paul has none will do little harm (the one supplied is present in the metaphor, after all), as long as we do not forget Paul's hesitation to tell us anything about the content of the reflections.

With this understanding of the phrase, then, we return to Paul's text. It has been suggested that there is some incongruity in Paul's characterization of vision in this way when riddles more naturally belong to language: words, not pictures, are riddling. This has led to various conjectures: perhaps the phrase is a gloss, or perhaps Paul intended to say that we *see* in a mirror but we *prophesy* in riddles.[15] But other commentators have pointed out that there are Hellenistic references, in Plutarch and Philo, where *ainigmata* are the objects of sight or associated with mirrors: Dupont says that mirrors and enigmas are connected notions, one emphasizing indirect vision and the other obscurity of image.[16] Hugedé, following S. E. Bassett, argues that *ainigma* may mean only an illustration or image, so that Paul's addition of *en ainigmati* does little more than restate the mirror metaphor: vision is indirect in a mirror, and to "see an enigma" is to see a (less than perfect) representation of the original.[17]

However, if Paul had only wanted to state that we see images in a mirror, he could have said nothing but that. It is better, I think, to preserve the demand to seek interpretation in the notion of *ainigma*, to insist that the obscurity is not simply a lack of definition but akin to a riddle. The Septuagint has the phrase in several places, so the idea of a riddle cannot have been foreign to Paul;[18] and if he associates it with an object of vision we must not bleed all the "riddle" out of the concept to make it a mere image for the sake of consistency. English does sometimes bring riddles closer to the visual in our expression "to read a riddle" (say, in someone's face). In fact there are visual perplexities that demand interpretation: puzzles may be visual problems about spatial relationships as well as verbal problems about meaning, and the NEB translation does catch this feature with its "puzzling reflections." (Indeed, the English "enigma" does the same: there are enigmatic looks as well as enigmatic utterances. But perhaps the word is too close to the Greek to make translators comfortable with it.)

So we end up with a third characteristic of partial knowledge. Our present knowledge of God is puzzling, like a riddle: it is partial because we sense that what we have been given invites us to investigation and interpretation. It is not complete in itself. We are not like children resting content in our way of viewing the world in spite of adult warnings about future changes of perspective. We are instead children given puzzles and riddles, stories we know are somehow parables, and we realize that our solutions or interpretations are temporary, incomplete, perhaps inconsistent. We know too that the riddles and puzzles are capable of solution, so we do not despair; but their final unloosing awaits the direct vision when we shall know as we are known. Our partial knowing now will be dissolved and destroyed: puzzles are no longer puzzles once they have been solved.

I conclude, then, that Paul's analogies may be worked out, without undue distortion of his text, to provide a characterization of our present knowledge of God as partial because imperfect. It suffers the imperfections of childish experience, of indirect vision, and of puzzles requiring solution; and in each of these characterizations Paul can make sense of his claim that the partial will be made useless when full face-to-face knowledge of God is enjoyed in the life to come.

But notice where we are. Our initial puzzle was one about Paul's meaning: What could he intend by the destruction of knowledge? That is solved by attempting to interpret Paul's text: but that exercise leaves us with his claim that our present knowledge of God is itself partial and puzzling. What are we to make of that? A minor puzzle of interpretation, laid to rest, generates major questions to be addressed in their own right.

One group of questions must itself be laid to one side, to be picked up by others for their scrutiny. I have in mind matters of direct concern to the theologian or intellectual historian who wishes to assess Paul's thought for coherence or consistency, if not in details at least in general tenor. For one kind of assessment of Paul's claim is internal to his thought: it asks how well this particular view accords with Paul's other statements on the subject, or (perhaps more revealingly) whether it is consistent with his other assumptions and behavior, not only his explicit writing. Is Paul's characterization of the believer's present knowledge of God an accurate or even adequate summary of Paul's more general theological stance?[19] This question I am content to leave to the New Testament specialist, partly because it is proper to that territory and partly because the answer does not impinge with any weight upon the other major question awaiting our exploration. For even when issues of Paul's meaning are settled, we may still ask where his account ought to fit in any contemporary reflection upon the believer's present experience of God.

To that question there will be answer upon answer. In what follows I sketch one proposal. It will not be taken for the whole story: too little is said of the things the Christian knows, and much is made of the puzzles of Christian experience. Nevertheless by taking Paul's images seriously, this approach is able to bring together the text of 1 Corinthians 13 and some reflections upon contemporary philosophical discussions of the problem of evil. I begin by asking about the relationship between partial knowledge and our love for God.

III. PARTIAL KNOWLEDGE AND LOVE

Although we have discussed in some detail the closing verses of 1 Corinthians 13, our investigation as yet has not returned to the general theme of Paul's chapter. Where does love belong in this discussion? Presumably our loving as well as our knowing will be perfected in the life to come. But how do things stand here and now?

In some ways Paul's text is not particularly helpful on this question. As we saw earlier, in 1 Corinthians 8:1 and 13:2 he contrasts knowledge and love: whereas love builds up, knowledge (*gnôsis*) may turn out to puff up its holder. So love does not require this kind of knowledge but instead must work against some of its negative results. Again, we earlier remarked on the need for some knowledge of God if we are to love God, but if we ask Paul about this, we will find disappointingly little. Though there is much in his letters about God's love for us, he scarcely refers to our love for God at all. He mentions those who love God in Romans 8:28; in 1 Corinthians 8:3 he draws the contrast between having knowledge and loving God; but that is about all.

Nevertheless Paul cannot ignore the fact that in loving someone there must be knowledge: he confesses his hope in 13:12 that the vision of God will bring complete mutual knowledge between himself and God. Nor should we expect that he would ignore the essential place of knowledge in love were he to write to other readers on that topic rather than to the conceitedly wise Corinthians. His linking of perfected knowledge and enduring love suggests that in the life to come we may love God more because we know God clearly, without the imperfections of our present epistemic condition. But if that is so, does our present partial knowledge limit our present love? Are love and knowledge so related in this life that love is conditioned by knowledge?

Think back to our discussion of knowing others personally (section II.ii, above). We acknowledged there that getting to know some particular people might not be a worthwhile experience, though it could be beneficial to have a good deal of knowledge, even direct knowledge, about them. Although it is true that whenever we love, our love requires knowledge, it does not follow that whenever we know much about people we find ourselves loving them in the same proportion. Were that so, psychologically shrewd tempters would lose the will to have their victims go wrong, and families could no longer be such fertile breeding places of strife. As things are, effective hatred can use as much knowledge about its object as can benevolent love.

But (someone will rightly protest) talk of quantities of love or knowledge does not take us very far. Surely *what* we know of another person is important to our loving. And, we add, the *kind* of loving is also important. For sometimes by love we mean an appreciation of the good or the beautiful, an admiration that (in the language of Plato's *Symposium*) is a desire or yearning to possess what we lack in ourselves. If I call this eros-love, it will be on the understanding that it is far greater than sexual love; indeed it finds only one of its expressions in the desire for sexual completion and the overcoming of death through procreation. We should understand too that eros-love is not only acquisitive, for it may find creative expression in producing the goodness and beauty after which it seeks.[20] Nevertheless it is fundamental to this love that it is conditioned and fed by what it finds of positive value in its object. In this way, then, eros-love depends upon what it knows of good in its object. It is impossible, on this understanding of love, to see something you value without loving it, and equally impossible to accept the ugly and the bad.

At this point Paul returns to our discussion. For if he does not explicitly discuss the role of knowledge in love, he nevertheless has much to say about love, especially God's love for us and the love we ought to manifest to each other. Following well-worn distinctions, we may call this agape-love. In spite of Paul's literary hypostatization in 1 Corinthians 13, this love is not an abstract entity; nor is it primarily a psychological feeling or response. Agape-love is exhibited in relationships. It "suffers long," not as a pain stretches over time, but when people continue to maintain certain kinds of relationships in adverse circumstances. It "thinks no evil," not in general terms but in one person's refusal to think evilly of another. Its paradigm is of course God's love for us: while we were sinners Christ died for us.

In his characterization of agape-love Paul stresses that the intrinsic value of its object does not determine the presence or extent of love, making this different from eros-love. Not that agape-love *approves* of the ugly or the sinful: that would sever love from moral values and make it an irrational interest in whatever happens to catch the attention of the lover. When we term this love "unconditional," we do not mean that it is mindless or groundless, that it approves of anything whatever. It is an unconditioned *acceptance* of the other, a refusal under any conditions to will or to do anything but good toward its object. Put in language from an Old Testament context, it is unconditional covenant, a promise never to break off relations or exclude from membership, no matter what the circumstances. To love one's enemies is the supreme expression of such love: presumably an enemy is just the person who does not share this attitude but instead takes up the opposite stance of intending harm and destruction.

Because agape-love will not approve of what is evil, rejoicing rather in the true and good, it is not as different from eros-love as some have made it out to be. In accepting sinners God has in mind their redemptive good, though sinners may be incapable of producing that good on their own. Even divine love cannot be so graciously free that it bears no relationship to goodness; otherwise it will degenerate into mere whim.[21] What marks agape-love is its willingness to give itself for the sake of those whom eros-love would reject, in order to promise their good even at its own expense. But this difference suggests that knowledge may play a different role in the case of agape-love. To put it rather too simply: eros-love is conditioned by what it knows of good and beauty, whereas agape-love continues in spite of what it knows. It is not blind: it must know its object, and it must have some idea of what constitutes that object's good rather than harm. But it is resolute in its refusal to be put off by what it knows of its object's lack of worth. Love never fails.

Or so it is with God's love for us. But because God has taken up this attitude toward us with all that God knows of our condition, we ought to love each other in this way in spite of what we know, or do not know, of one another. Perhaps this is why Paul is anxious to promote love beyond knowledge, simply because it should not be decisive in loving. Love does not count up wrongs.

But we have not yet come back to the question that opened up this discussion of partial knowledge and love. God's knowledge of us may be complete and God's love remain unconditional, but from our side the relationship is rather different. It is often pointed out that our love for God must be of a different character from God's love for us. We may hardly hope to refrain from harming God or to seek the promotion of God's good: Who can damage divine omnipotence or contribute to divine goodness? No; our love for God is more like adoration, akin to eros-love in that it rejoices in what it recognizes as supremely good and beautiful, and desires to be made complete by possessing that enjoyment forever. Yet if that is the whole story, the imperfections of our present love for God will not simply be the result of fallen wills but also the product of our imperfect and partial knowledge. If we take Paul's images seriously, we will be faced with puzzles and ambiguities that can only frustrate eros-love, not call it forth.

Perhaps believers must hope for no other love than this in the present. Or perhaps their love for God is a matter of reflex action produced not by their own partial grasp but by God's own activity: E. Stauffer says of Romans 8:28 that believers return to God "nothing but the direct flowing back of the heavenly love which has poured out" upon them.[22] Nevertheless another possibility remains. It finds in Paul's characterization of our present knowledge of God a fairly accurate reflection of the ambiguities of Christian experience. But it asks whether this does not require that the believer adopt something more like agape-love than eros-love toward God. Just as there are elements in common between these kinds of love, so there may be analogous features in God's love for us and our loving God within the constraints of partial knowledge.

The question of the aptness for Christian experience of Paul's images of our present knowledge of God may be pursued through different terrains. There are psychological problems in trying to picture the face of the God we do not see; historical perplexities about revelatory events; logical riddles about concepts like omnipotence. Here, however, I want to settle our attention on the ambiguities of our experience of God's love and goodness in a fallen world. For (the problem is so familar as to need no restatement) the amount of evil and suffering in the world seems out of all proportion to God's love and power. Believers are like small children struggling with the demands as well as the benefits of parental love, encountering puzzles about the behavior of their heavenly Father and riddles they cannot solve. How, in the face of inconsistent evidence, shall we love God? The *how* is not simply a matter of inadequate perception of divine goodness or a flagging desire: it is a *how* of the mind that feels poignant contradiction between the claims of omnipotent love and all that is wrong with the world. If our love were only an eros-response, it would have to be blind or baffled.

So the believer may well agree with Paul that our knowledge of God's activity in the world is childish and imperfect. To use such language may suggest that the riddle of evil is to be resolved by unquestioning submission to parental authority, a submission that too easily ignores the evidence that counts so heavily against the rational goodness of that authority. This we must not do. Whom the Lord loves he chastens, perhaps: yet we know that for deliberately inflicted suffering to be chastening it must be deserved, proportional to merit, with remedial and not destructive intent. We who do not give our own children serpents for fish do not stone them when they refuse to eat their crusts. If it is true that we cannot claim to need no chastening ourselves, it is also true that the amount of suffering in the world and particularly among the faithful seems beyond all moral comprehension. Sometimes the notion of desert seems brutally ludicrous: Emil Fackenheim reminds us that the "crime" for which Jews were made to bear the unbearable Holocaust was their great-grandparents' keeping of the covenant.[23] And should our mind have no capacity to embrace suffering of that magnitude, we look, if we can, at the weight of evil on the fragile innocence of a little child — through the eyes of Wiesel or Dostoevsky, if our own have been spared the sight. Why, when the Christ has come, should the innocent still be slaughtered?

To ask how we may love God in the face of suffering is to pose the problem of evil in the believer's terms. The philosophy of religion these days does not generally discuss problems from the perspective of faith; it prefers to deal with evil as a challenge to the consistency of theistic belief. Philosophers rightly attempt to distinguish among questions posed by suffering: Alvin Plantinga, for instance, points out that there is a difference between defending the consistency of theistic claims and providing a developed theodicy that will give particular reasons why God permits suffering.[24] Even a theodicy will not solve what he calls the pastoral problem, the need to locate one's own suffering in the wider purposes of God. Our understanding is advanced by getting some of these distinctions clear, but one consequence has been that philosophers tend to pay more attention to the rational consistency of beliefs than to the philosophical issues involved in an adequate theodicy. So there has been much written on what is an important answer to the skeptical challenge, the "free-will defense," and too little on the charges against the justice and goodness of God, which remain even when that defense is success-fully conducted.

This is not the place to work out in detail all that is involved in philosophical theodicy, but because it bears directly on our partial knowledge of God and the nature of our love for God, I must say a little more. Put too simply, the free-will defense generally attempts to absolve God of responsibility for the world's evil by attributing that evil, or at least a major part of it, to agents other than God. When the challenger invokes God's omnipotence, arguing that God must, on the believer's own grounds, be powerful enough to prevent the evil actions of other agents, defenders reply as follows. It is not possible, they say, to control the ac-tions of free agents while leaving them free. Because omnipotence can-not intelligibly require God to do the logically impossible, it is not open to God to control actions that are free. So God's choice in creating might not have been between our world and a better one. God could have de-cided to create no free agents, or else a world with free agents; but once given their freedom, those agents themselves determine how much good or evil there will be in the world. Further, in Plantinga's version, it re-mains possible that in any conceivable world of free agents that God might have chosen to create, those agents would have caused as much evil as there is in our own world. Under Plantinga's possibilities the charge of the skeptic fails, for it does not follow from the omnipotence and goodness of God that there must be less evil in the world than there in fact is.

Nevertheless there is more to be said. Even if we accept the de-fenders' treatment of omnipotence, both the skeptic and the believer may doubt that it has adequately considered charges against God's goodness and justice. For it takes insufficient account of what we may too crudely call *the way things will turn out with the world.* Granted that God is not responsible for the actual choices of other free agents: God is, how-ever, ultimately responsible for their very existence. As creator God brings about the conditions necessary for their choices. And if God knows, or even has good reason to predict, that evil will triumph in the world, the choice to bring the world into existence will be inconsistent with moral goodness. If in this world there is undeserved suffering that is not re-deemable in some significant way, and that God could have prevented without bringing about more evil or less good, then divine justice and goodness are impugned. The elaboration of what is involved in the con-cept of the "triumph of the good," and the specification of conditions under which God's justice could be preserved, are philosophical tasks that ought to be pursued in the philosophy of religion. Although it cannot provide a theological reason for God's permitting evil, philosophy may nonetheless attempt its own work in theodicy by showing what an adequate theodicy would look like. Indeed, it is debatable that any more than this can be done at all: to put it in both legal and theological language, not all the evidence is in; the end is not yet. We do not know if there will be more good than evil at the end of the day; we cannot assign, with confidence, blame for wrongdoing; we do not know what might come from the ashes of our suffering. One of the extraphilosophical strengths of the free-will defense is that it can remind us that the outcome of the world is at least in part up to us: we may not now know how it will be, but we must not despair. At the same time, the riddle remains far beyond our individual efforts, and we must love without answers. So the wag had best leave his limerick unfinished:[25]

> God's plan made a hopeful beginning,
> But man ruined his chances by sinning.
> We trust that the story
> Will end in God's glory

To say that "at present the other side's winning" is to have more certainty than we are permitted. Of course we want the rhyme to work out, but neither fear nor rash hope should write as done what is not yet completed.

The upshot is that neither the skeptic nor the believer is able to pronounce with finality upon the goodness and justice of God. This means that the skeptic must not yet write off the believer as irrational; but the believer cannot claim that faith has received its final vindication. In the problem of suffering, believers recognize the aptness of Paul's characterization of their present knowledge of God. There are puzzles beyond their comprehension, snatches of story that they only partially grasp, imperfect reflections that do not yield up their full meaning. They must wait with patient endurance, in the hope that, when they see face to face, they will know as they are now known. If their hope is not groundless (it rests, they affirm, on the resurrection and God's promise), it is nevertheless not fulfilled. And if their hope is not to be irrational, they must confess that there is no philosophical guarantee either of resurrection or that the face of God will be the one for which they have longed.

How, then, will we love the God we know so imperfectly? If on occasion we are moved to love in adoration, there are other times and places in which we cannot find anything of God's goodness to call forth that love. Our apprehension is so partial and imperfect that we may be tempted in particularly grim circumstances to believe that God is not for us but against us. And in such trial, it seems that love for God is after all analogous to God's love for us. For believers are called upon to accept God unconditionally, when they cannot understand what good God may intend, or even approve of what they now seem to see.

In pointing to the need for an agape-love for God in this life, I do not ignore those differences between God's love for us and our love for God that we earlier noted. We cannot seek God's good as God seeks ours. But we can refuse to let God go. We can hang onto the promise of glory and, as it were, hold God to account for that which we do not understand. Such love is hardly a reflex action, a flowing back of divine love through passive human channels. It is hard work, harder than loving one's brother. In great trial it finds its parallel to "love your enemies" in Job's determination: "though he slay me yet will I trust him." Such love for God must be patient, bearing all things, believing all things, hoping and enduring all things.

But it must also, in a sense, have an End. Since we must love in this way because of our imperfect knowledge, our present unconditional acceptance must look forward to the good that is promised. If divine love seeks good for its objects, there must be good to be found, and our love for God cannot be irrational when God's for us is not. Our love and trust await resurrection and direct vision. We remember from chapter 3, above, how little we can say of the glory to be ours. Although philosophical theodicy forces us to think of what must be true of that glory for our love to find its true object, it cannot yield that glory. Only when we arrive will faith find its vindication and love be complete. Right now we are still a long way from home.

Notes

1. INTRODUCTION: PAUL AND PHILOSOPHY

1. That the letter is the product not of Paul's hand but of a follower in a Pauline school is Eduard Lohse's opinion, based on the theology in the letter (Lohse, *Colossians and Philemon*, 177–83). Ralph Martin surveys the issues and decides in favor of Paul's authorship (Martin, *Colossians and Philemon*, 32–40).

2. This is the only occurrence of the word in the Bible, though Acts 17:18 refers to philosophers—Stoics and Epicureans in particular. Paul's critique of the "wisdom of the world" in 1 Cor. 1–2 has sometimes been taken as a critique of philosophy; this is discussed fully in chapter 2, below.

3. Chap. 6, below, has some discussion of changing beliefs in the context of theological accommodation: see especially sections II and IV. Plato recognizes several causes for the surrender of beliefs considered true: persuasion, forgetfulness, the spells of terror or pleasure. The only change through force he recognizes is the force of pain (*Rep.* 413).

4. *Pithanologia* is here clearly negative in that it results in being misled. The term may mean only "persuasiveness," but both Plato (*Theaetetus* 162e) and Epictetus (*Discourses* I.8.7) recognize its dangers.

5. For discussions of the Colossian "heresy" or "philosophy" see Francis W. Beare's introduction to Colossians in the *Interpreter's Bible*, vol. 11; Lohse, on Col. 2 (especially his excursus on pp. 125–31 with additional references in n. 113); and Martin, 9–19. I take the translation "self-made religion" (for *ethelothrêskia*, 2:23) from Martin, 98.

6. Lohse, on Col. 2:8.

7. Martin, on Col. 2:8. Both Martin and Lohse use quotation marks around "philosophy" to mark it off.

8. Beare, on Col. 2:8.

9. See the RSV and the NEB on 1 Cor. 6:12, 13, and 8:1, 4; and the NEB alternate reading for 7:1; and below, chap. 5, section V.ii.

10. See Henry Chadwick, "All Things to All Men," 261–75, and my notion of epistemological accommodation in chap. 6, section II.i, below.

11. Hooker, "Were There False Teachers in Colossae?" 315–31. Professor Hooker retains the quotation marks for our term, but suggests that the warning is against *any* "philosophy" that "looks for salvation anywhere outside Christ" (326).

12. Cf. 2 Cor. 10:5, 6. Though these words need not be directed against philosophy itself, someone pushing for the possibility I am here considering may so take them.

13. The commentary referred to is that of Hans Dieter Betz, *Galatians*. For reviews see Davies, Meyer, and Aune, "Galatians," 310–28. The comparison of Paul's style to Cynic-Stoic diatribe has been developed chiefly by Rudolf Bultmann in *Der Stil der paulinischen Predigt und die kynisch-stoische Diatribe*; but see Stanley Kent Stowers, *The Diatribe and Paul's Letter to the Romans*.

14. Beare finds it tempting to think that Epictetus could have encountered Pauline teaching through Epaphras in Hierapolis, near Colossae, because of parallels between Paul's epistles and the Stoic's teaching (Beare, 134). J. N. Sevenster has a careful discussion of parallels between Seneca's philosophy and Paul's writing, concluding that the similarities are only superficial, in *Paul and Seneca*. For the view that Paul was strongly influenced by Epicurean rather than Stoic teaching, see Norman Wentworth DeWitt, *St. Paul and Epicurus*.

15. See Victor C. Pfitzner, *Paul and the Agon Motif*. The argument traces the source of Paul's metaphors to popular Stoic diatribe, without claiming that Paul had a detailed knowledge of Stoicism.

16. See C. A. Pierce, *Conscience in the New Testament*, who also concludes the Paul most probably took the term from popular usage. On *suneidêsis*, see chap. 5, section V.iii, below.

17. I may put this argument more graphically by supposing Paul to have been recently reanimated (why I do not say "resurrected" is explained in chap. 3, below). After some period of linguistic and cultural adjustment, he is able to receive visitors, and scholars are ready with their questions. "Why did you not quote more of Jesus' sayings?" "How did your expectations about the parousia develop?" "Are you sure you remember correctly when you claim you wrote to the church in Ephesus?" The philosopher is content to be last in line. After all the facts are sorted out it is the philosopher who will want to discuss with Paul whether supposed conclusions from his text indeed follow from that text. "What we, or you, *thought* you were saying isn't quite decisive," it will be pointed out. "This seems to follow from what you said, and if the consequences of that aren't entirely acceptable, how would you rephrase it? Does that rephrasing capture all your meaning? Because it still allows one to believe this other thing." And so on.

18. G. H. Trevor, "The Apostle Paul's Contribution to the Philosophy of Religion," 207.

19. As one example of this general movement, see the 1963, 1973, and 1983 editions of John Hick's *Philosophy of Religion*.

20. It takes only a glance at the index of almost any text in the philosophy of religion to see that Paul receives only passing mention, when mentioned at all; indeed Plato is often referred to more frequently than Paul.

21. On the genesis of the letter, see John C. Hurd, *The Origin of I Corinthians*, and section I of chapter 2, below. (In 1 Cor. 5:9 Paul refers to an earlier letter he sent, which is why my opening sentence in this Introduction speaks of the letter *known* as 1 Corinthians. The extant letter is not in fact the first.) My

comments on unity do not mean that I think the extant letter a composite of different layers: it is *one* letter on a series of loosely related topics.

22. I *do* mean the Judeo-Christian tradition. Although my philosophical reflections are on a Christian author, and my language often reflects Christian faith, the philosophical concerns belong to a common religious tradition.

2. FAITH, WISDOM, AND PHILOSOPHY: 1 CORINTHIANS 1-4

1. See Günther Bornkamm's emphasized conclusion to his study of this issue in Romans: *"the intention of the Apostle is not to infer God's being from the world, but to uncover the being of the world from God's revelation"* (*Early Christian Experience*, 59).

2. See Calvin, *First Corinthians*, on 1:21.

3. "The monks never finished telling the history of the world because they always began with the creation; if in dealing with the relations between Philosophy and Christianity we begin first by recounting what has previously been said, how will it ever be possible – not to finish but to begin; for history continues to grow" (Sören Kierkegaard, *Philosophical Fragments* [Oxford University Press, 1936], 92).

4. See John Hurd, *The Origin of I Corinthians*, 45–47.

5. For example, in his anxiety to stress that the identity of the baptizer is unimportant, Paul at first misremembers his facts (1:14–16). The RSV tidies this up by placing v. 16 in parentheses, suggesting that Paul was adding a foot-note rather than interrupting the flow of his dictation with a correction.

6. Conzelmann, *I Corinthians*, 30.

7. Hurd, 74.

8. Ibid., 82.

9. Ibid., 76.

10. Barrett, *First Corinthians*, 49.

11. Thackeray, *The Septuagint and Jewish Worship*, 97; Wuellner, "Haggadic Homily Genre in I Corinthians 1-3." Barrett approves 'of this approach (*First Corinthians*, 51), as does Ellis (" 'Wisdom' and 'Knowledge' in I Corinthians," 87). However, not only does Wuellner find a bridge between chap. 1–2 and 3–4 without including chap. 4, he also does not explain Paul's positive treatment of Christian wisdom: Wuellner's approach makes Paul's theme the prophetic one of divine judgment on human wisdom. Conzelmann's comment is apt: we can say only that Paul works here with the concepts and style of Jewish wisdom theology (*I Corinthians*, 44).

12. Much Pauline scholarship on 1 Corinthians seems not to move in the direction of Paul's own concern. It stays with the question of division, trying to discuss the identities of factions or the lack of factions, and their possible relationship to Paul's possible opposition in Corinth. These are historically interesting, if difficult, issues. If capable of solution, they could help understanding of the text; but they can also become so absorbing that they distort more central concerns.

13. For a basic research tool see Morton, Michaelson, and Thompson, *A Critical Concordance to I and II Corinthians.* Fischer makes helpful suggestions about the analysis of verbal patterns in Paul's letters ("Pauline Literary Forms and Thought Patterns"), though my approach here is rather different. I look for clusters of concepts rather than the pattern of a particular word, and do not link the verbal forms to paradoxical thought patterns as does Fischer.

14. Conzelmann's comment that the pattern is "circular," with 3:18–23 leading back to 1:18ff., is one such simplification (Conzelmann, 39, 79). The cluster of concepts in those two sections is strongly present in chapter 4 as well.

15. The grammer and interpretation of v. 6 are problematic. The RSV translation — "so you may learn by us to live according to scripture" — misses what may be a significant reference to going beyond proper bounds; Paul says he wants them to learn "the not beyond what is written." For discussions, see M. Hooker, "Beyond the Things Which Are Written," and Barrett on 4:6. Hooker thinks that the Corinthians add to scripture philosophy and rhetoric, the "rubbish" of 3:13–15, and Paul calls the Corinthians from this back to the scriptures he has quoted in chap. 1–3.

16. For references to the image of the theater in Roman philosophy and literature, see Conzelmann on 4:9; see also Paul's use of the metaphor of the games in 1 Cor. 9:24–27.

17. Conzelmann reminds us of the eschatological reversal of first and last in this image of the spectacle (Conzelmann, p. 88, n. 37).

18. Barrett (on 4:10) thinks the irony of v. 10 more subtle than that of v. 8 or v. 9, but this is difficult to understand. Perhaps this is because he takes *phronimoi* to refer to Corinthian "commonsense" instead of the more pejorative "wisdom"; but there is no reason to think that Paul meant any difference between *sophoi* and *phronimoi.*

19. Barrett is attracted to the notion of sacrificial cleansing in *perikatharmata* and perhaps *peripsêma*, translating the phrase with the former: "we have become the world's scapegoats" (on 4:13). Although I cannot judge the complexities of the issue, it seems clear that the more basic meaning of "filth cast out in the process of cleansing" is both adequate to the meaning of the verse and easily related to *ta mê onta* of 1:28.

20. If not Paul's first readers then his later ones cannot fail to be reminded of the sayings of Jesus about persecution (Matt. 5:10–12), blessing one's enemy (Matt. 5:44), and the hunger, thirst, and nakedness of the least of the brethren (Matt. 25:31–46).

21. This is why the notion of measurement is naturally associated with boasting: see 2 Cor. 10:13, though the meaning is very difficult to determine (see Barrett, *Second Corinthians*, on 10:13).

22. For a discussion of the biblical concept of boasting, see R. Bultmann, *Theological Dictionary of the New Testament* (G. Kittel, ed.; hereafter cited as *TDNT*), under *kauchaomai.* Bultmann thinks that the good sense of "boasting" — i.e., rejoicing in God — is paradoxical because the object of confidence is turned from self to God. I have preferred to describe this as an extended sense, reserving the notion of paradox for the apostolic boasting in one's own weakness.

23. John Hurd's approach to the Corinthian correspondence allows the possibility that Paul is a little too defensive at times, because it is he who has changed his perspective from the time of his first visit to them. The Corinthians' argumentative spirit is partly an expression of their desire not to go back on the freedom they first enjoyed, but now challenged by Paul's attempt to impose on them the apostolic decree from the Jerusalem church.

24. Although Paul says he writes to admonish rather than shame them (4:14), it is hard to believe that the Corinthians could have escaped shame. In 1:27 Paul had pointed out that God shames the wise; and in 6:5 he will speak of their lawsuits to their shame.

25. See Harold F. Brooks: 'The memory of it comes back to him in a sort of luminous mist, with clouds of glory trailing from the experience, the 'dream' he has had. . . . The ballad as he conceives it will have all the pathos and poetry appropriate to the man who has had the love of a high and noble lady, and lost her" (*A Midsummer Night's Dream*. The Arden Edition of the Works of William Shakespeare. [London: University Paperbacks, Methuen & Co., 1979], p. cxvii).

26. The evidence we might look for in 2 Cor. is the subject of much debate. But in any case Paul continued to have trouble with the Corinthians: see Barrett, *Second Corinthians*, 5–21.

27. Words like *nous* or *logos* can be translated "reason" in certain contexts. But here *nous* is used of the "mind" of the Lord or of Christ in 2:16, not of human reason; and the occurrences of *logos* have to do with word or speech more than reason (see my Appendix A). However, the chapters say much of knowledge and wisdom, central issues for *philosophia*.

28. For some examples of the view that revelation provides truths that a properly used intellect might discover, consider these. Augustine, *Confessions*, 6.5 (trans. Vernon J. Bourke): ". . . since we were too weak to discover the truth by clear reasoning, and because as a result, we had need of the authority of holy Scripture" (The Fathers of the Church, vol. 21 [Washington, D.C.: Catholic University America Press, 1953]). Thomas Aquinas, *Summa Theologica*, 1a, 1, (trans. Thomas Gilbey): "We also stood in need of being instructed by divine revelation even in religious matters the human reason is able to investigate. For the rational truth about God would have appeared only to a few, and even so after a long time and mixed with many mistakes; whereas on knowing this depends our whole welfare, which is in God" (Eyre & Spottiswade, 1964). A general discussion of views of revelation may be found in John Baillie, *The Idea of Revelation in Recent Thought*.

29. Plantinga's approach may be seen from his *God, Freedom and Evil*.

30. This work in religious epistemology argues that, just as belief in other minds or the reality of the past is within our epistemic rights, though not grounded in other more basic beliefs, so belief in God is properly considered as basic, not the result of inference from other beliefs. See Plantinga, "Is Belief in God Properly Basic?" 41–52. The discussion is continued in *Faith and Rationality*, edited by Plantinga and Wolterstorff; see also Penelhum, *God and Skepticism*, 147–58.

31. Richard Popkin, *The Encyclopedia of Philosophy*, under "Fideism."

32. See Hooker, *Pauline Pieces*, 27, and "Beyond the Things Which Are Written," 129–30. Margaret Thrall comments: "The philosophers and men of learning, for all their cleverness, were not able by means of their own wisdom to discover what God is like" (*First and Second Letters of Paul to the Corinthians*, on 1:21). J. Munck refers to "a more popular brand of mixture of philosophy, religion and rhetoric" (*Paul and the Salvation of Mankind*, 153).

33. To generalize, this has been the conviction of much German scholarship on Paul. Bultmann's views on gnostic pneumatics in Corinth may be seen in *TDNT*, under *gignoskô*, and in his *Theology of the New Testament*, vol. 1, section 15. Major studies have been done by Wilckens, *Weisheit und Torheit*, and Schmithals, *Gnosticism in Corinth*.

34. Again to generalize, this is the approach of many English commentators. W. D. Davies's study, *Paul and Rabbinic Judaism*, is a landmark. See also E. E. Ellis, " 'Wisdom' and 'Knowledge,' " for general comments; and Robin Scroggs, "Paul: *Sophos* and *Pneumatikos*," for a specific illustration of the conviction that the Corinthians did not hold a gnostic, revelatory *sophia* and that Paul is best explained from the context of Jewish and Christian apocalyptic-wisdom theology. But not all English scholars agree: see John W. Drane (*Paul: Libertine or Legalist?*) for the belief that there were "gnostic" elements in Corinth.

35. In vv. 22–23 the emphasis is upon wisdom/folly for the gentiles, for the seeking of wisdom is a particularly Greek interest. The Jews ask for signs and find only a stumbling block in the cross (on the notion of *skandalon*, see chap. 5, V.ii, below). Nevertheless, Paul cannot mean to draw a distinction between a *skandalon* and folly; the *skandalon* is rather an instance of folly. In support of this there are four considerations. (1) The folly of vv. 18 and 21 is general; (2) v. 22 is offered as an explanation for the folly in v. 21; (3) v. 24 brings together both Jews and Greeks in the opposite of folly, Christ's wisdom; (4) in demonstrating that worldly wisdom has been made folly, Paul quotes the Old Testament — a tactic for a Jewish, not a gentile, target.

36. On the rather problematic use of the Old Testament in these chapters, consult Hooker ("Beyond the Things Which Are Written") and Wuellner ("Haggadic Homily Genre").

37. "Rulers" probably refers to the historical rulers of Jesus' day and to the angelic forces behind them (see Scroggs, "Paul: *Sophos* and *Pneumatikos*," 43).

38. The doctrine is that human minds are separate from behavior in such a way that complete access to their contents is restricted to their owners. The development of the behavioral sciences has lessened the currency of the doctrine. On occasion the truth seems to be represented as the reverse, that the privilege of access belongs to observers, especially those with appropriate certificates and credentials.

The RSV translation, "what person knows a man's thoughts," suggests that Paul's purpose is the analogy of individual private thoughts, applied from individual people to God; Bultmann takes the verse this way (*Theology of the New Testament* I:205), as do Barrett and many others. Orr and Walther (*I Corinthians*) see the desirability of stressing a general content rather than the individual sense.

39. The RSV translation, "does not receive the gifts of the Spirit of God," adds the notion of "gifts," presumably picking up the language of v. 12, "so that we might understand the things freely given (*charisthenta*) to us by God." But gifts, especially in light of 1 Cor. 12–14, may be thought of as experiences and activities, whereas the context here in chapter 2 is more naturally epistemological. I have accordingly opted for the wording "the things of God," so that objects of knowledge are readily included.

40. So Scroggs, "Paul: *Sophos* and *Pneumatikos*," p. 52 n. 4; and Barrett on 2:14: the natural person is not bad or foolish or irreligious, but simply someone who has not received the Spirit.

41. Even Bottom's dream is not, strictly speaking, ineffable: for an exploration of this issue, see my "Margaret, Bottom, Paul and the Inexpressible."

42. The translation of these verses is notoriously difficult. On *sunkrinontes* (v. 13) as interpretation and *anakrinetai* (v. 14) as investigation, see Barrett, *First Corinthians*, and Ellis, " 'Wisdom' and 'Knowledge.' "

The whole context of chapter 2 supports the view that the language of revelation is intelligible, but if further evidence is required it might be discovered in chap. 12, vv. 8–10, where the top-ranking gifts of the Spirit are *logos sophias* and *logos gnôseôs*, whereas tongues and interpretation rank at the bottom.

43. Richard Popkin classifies Paul as an extreme fideist, referring to 1 Corinthians, in his phrase "St. Paul's contention that the central doctrine of Christianity was nonsensical by Greek philosophical standards" (*Encyclopedia of Philosophy*, under "Fideism").

44. Paul calls the Corinthians "fleshly" (*sarkinos*, 3:1; *sarkikos*, 3:3), not "natural" (*psuchikos*, 2:14). But it is hard to imagine a difference between these terms in our passage, as W. D. Stacey points out in *The Pauline View of Man*, 147-48. Both are opposed to *pneumatikos*.

45. See *Sophist* (227c-230e) for Plato's characterization of the Socratic method as it ought to work: where conceit is exposed, those guilty of it should grow angry with themselves. Bultmann draws attention to the condition of pride against which "shaming" is directed in the Greek Old Testament: "Since the reference is mostly to the *aischunthênai* of those who are full of proud confidence and expectancy, or to the fact that those who trust in Yahweh will not be confounded, *aischunthênai* often has almost the meaning of 'being disillusioned' (e.g., Jer. 2:36)" (*TDNT*, under *aischunô*).

46. This from H. Sasse, *TDNT*, under *kosmos*.

47. The view sketched here bears little likeness to John Bunyan's "Mr. Worldly Wiseman" (*Pilgrim's Progress*, second edition, 1678). Though Bunyan's personification of worldly wisdom is opposed to the way of the cross, his fault is not conceit; it is that he counsels Christian to go to Legality, in the town of Morality, to be rid of his burden. As Evangelist explains, Legality is the Law of the Old Testament, which can never save but only condemn. Bunyan seems to mean by "worldly" what most persons would advise, and by "wisdom" the prudence of living a moral life.

For yet another meaning of the expression, see *The Guardian* for Friday, January 14, 1983. Mr. Alistair Hill, QC, defending a young woman against a smuggling charge, explained the influence of her recruiter: "Here was the much older man, full of knowledge and worldly wisdom. He held some fateful fascination for her, and she fell under his spell" (p. 20).

48. And elsewhere in his letters. "Paul does not disclose a single example of his wisdom. Despite the carefulness and consistency of the section it surprises because Paul nowhere else in his extant correspondence suggests he has such a teaching, nor are several words and phrases that appear here repeated elsewhere by Paul" (Scroggs, "Paul: *Sophos* and *Pneumatikos*," 37).

49. Barrett puts it this way: "The wisdom Paul spoke with the mature must be further defined. It rests on the word of the cross, but is a development of this, of such a kind that in it the essential message of the simple preaching of the cross might be missed, or perverted, by the inexperienced. Essentially it differs in form rather than content, as meat and milk are both food, though differently constituted" (on 3:2). Scroggs cites others who hold this view (ibid., p. 37 n. 1) but disagrees with it.

50. This is a central point of Scroggs's study.

51. See Hooker, *Pauline Pieces*, 25–28.

52. One of the most influential is E. P. Sanders, *Paul and Palestinian Judaism*.

53. This point is clearly developed by Morna Hooker in her discussion of Sanders's *Paul and Palestinian Judaism*, "Paul and Covenantal Nomism."

54. For this reason I must take issue with Scroggs's conclusion to "Paul: *Sophos* and *Pneumatikos*": "The ultimate issue of this passage may thus prove to be that of the legitimacy of theology itself (as distinct from kerygma) and whether it is to be grounded in human wisdom (we would say today, 'natural theology') or in a listening to that Word which Paul called the wisdom of God" (p. 55). Scroggs's antithesis cannot be derived from the passage.

55. Sometimes "philosophical theology" is a synonym for "philosophy of religion," as in the well-known title of Flew and MacIntyre's *New Essays in Philosophical Theology*. I have in mind, however, not the analysis of religious concepts in general but more systematic works of theology, which address major philosophical issues and attempt to order them within a theological framework.

56. See Appendix B for a discussion of his contrary view.

3. DISEMBODIED PERSONS AND PAULINE RESURRECTION: 1 CORINTHIANS 15

1. Sometimes it is said that the OT view of the human being as psychophysical unity is compatible only with a doctrine of resurrection, not immortality, because there is no soul to be immortal. Recently Robert Gundry has challenged this monistic anthropology: see his *Sôma in Biblical Theology*, chap. 11, where he concludes that the OT sees a shadowy existence in Sheol "remarkably close to the Homeric view of the dead as souls existing in the underworld but not enjoying a full life" (133–34).

2. A. Oepke calls these "resurrections" (*TDNT*, under *anistêmi*), but it

is better to use "reanimation" because the stories present the revivification of corpses rather than the eschatological change to life beyond death that is now part of the general understanding of the term "resurrection." Sometimes "resuscitation" is used in these discussions, but we may prefer to leave that term to describe what happens to persons who are only apparently or clinically dead (one is "resuscitated" after drowning or heart failure).

3. "Immortality of the Soul or Resurrection of the Dead?" 47. Cullman stresses "teaching" to distinguish this from the characters and behavior of Plato and Socrates, which may accord with some NT values.

4. Wolfson, "Immortality and Resurrection in the Philosophy of the Church Fathers," 54–96.

5. For these views see: Flew's article, "Can a Man Witness His Own Funeral?" (where Flew presents the claim, reported at the beginning of this chapter, that survival is self-contradictory); Phillips, *Death and Immortality*; Penelhum, *Survival and Disembodied Existence*; Geach, *God and the Soul*, chap. 2, "Immortality."

6. This is part of the earliest baptismal formulae and of the Apostles' Creed, though the Nicene Creed refers only to Jesus' resurrection and the final judgment. See Philip Schaff, *The Creeds of Christendom*.

7. See Robert Jewett, *Paul's Anthropological Terms*, 206–7, for references, as well as Gundry, *Sôma in Biblical Theology*, 161–63. The first part of Jewett's chapter on *sôma* contains much useful material on the history of interpretation of this concept in Paul.

8. Robinson says that when 1 Cor. 15 is "set in its proper context of the whole Pauline theology, it becomes quite impossible to think of the resurrection hope in terms of the individual unit" (*The Body*, 81).

9. For instance, Bultmann, *Theology of the New Testament* I, section 17. Scroggs claims that "the spiritual body denotes a non-corporeal existence with its source in the power of God's gift" (*The Last Adam*, 66). "Since angelic nature is non-corporeal, spiritual, Paul must imply by his statement [1 Cor. 6:3] an acceptance of the Jewish view that the nature of eschatological man is to be equal or superior to the nature of the angels" (ibid., 68).

10. For instance, Oscar Cullmann and Robert Gundry. They agree on this, though Gundry is a full-fledged dualist; Cullmann is not.

11. "On Disembodied Resurrected Persons," 200–4.

12. This statement is too blunt as it stands: I mean, not that there must be as much suffering or evil or ignorance in a resurrection world as there is in this; but rather that in their basic structures and relationships, resurrected people should be as close as possible to people like us. Nor does this necessarily mean that resurrected people are revivified corpses; they might be bodily replicas, as discussed in n. 31, below.

13. Gundry's quarrel with Bultmann's dematerialization of resurrection causes him to set theological limits on philosophical activity: "It is to be feared that in both the idealistic and the existentialist treatments of *sôma*, laudable pastoral concern. . . [has] sacrificed theology to a current, and perhaps past, fashion in philosophy. Put otherwise, the attempt to use current philosophical

categories for making the Christian gospel intelligible—an attempt necessary so
far as it is possible—has gone so far as to transmute the gospel at this point. . . .
This is not to pass sweeping judgements on either of these philosophical approaches. But it is to say that the meaning of *sôma* intended by Paul in connection with the resurrection produces a piece of *môria* as scandalous to twentieth
century men as to the ancient Greeks and proto-gnostics (cf. Acts 17:12, 32; I
Cor. 1:23). The scandal is difficult—impossible—to avoid" (*Sôma in Biblical
Theology*, 168).

    14. This is from C. F. D. Moule, "St. Paul and Dualism: The Pauline Con-
ception of Resurrection," 113.

    15. For an open example of this, see Moule's general thesis in "St. Paul
and Dualism." He recognizes that he is using modern terms (p. 108) but thinks
that this can be validated as he moves to discuss Paul's own language. In the
end the language of "using up" matter as energy to produce new life is his preferred way to understand how Paul moves from "transformed" matter in 1 Cor.
15 to matter that is "exchanged" in 2 Cor. 5. Moule finds those concepts illuminating for Paul's thought although they are not Pauline.

    16. Someone who thinks that option 2 is more nearly Paul's own view will
be interested in fleshing it out and commenting on problems in option 3, as does
Bruce Reichenbach in "On Disembodied Resurrected Persons: A Reply." I am
grateful for his comments, to which I could respond only briefly in my "Reply
to Professor Reichenbach." In their light I have rephrased my options from their
earlier expression in "On Disembodied Resurrected Persons," 205–6, although
I have not here repented the categories themselves.

    17. Penelhum's name might also be invoked, though not loudly: in chap.
2 and 3 of *Survival and Disembodied Existence* he discusses the possibility of
perception and agency in disembodied persons.

    18. See Appendix C.

    19. Moule, 109. Moule gives several references for a range of eschatological
beliefs, including notions of transfigured bodies and beliefs that the resurrected
would be like angels.

    20. For references, see Ellis, "The Structure of Pauline Eschatology," 35.
For comments on the development of Paul's eschatology, see D. E. H. Whiteley,
The Theology of Paul, 244–48. Whiteley thinks that, although there is develop-
ment in Paul, there is no reason to see change in his thought on resurrection.

    21. I offered this short form of argument in "On Disembodied Resurrected
Persons," 206.

    22. There are differences of opinion over why some (but only some) of
the Corinthians denied the resurrection of the dead. Were they skeptics of a
Greek mold of mind? Were they gnostic-like enthusiasts (or proto-realized-
eschatologists?) believing themselves already to have been raised with Christ in
the only meaningful sense of resurrection? Did they believe that salvation be-
longed only to those alive at the parousia? See Conzelmann, *I Corinthians*,
261–63.

    23. The nature of and reason for baptism "for the dead" are much disputed
questions, fortunately not in need of answer for our study. Héring discusses some

opinions in *The First Epistle of Saint Paul to the Corinthians*, on 15:29. He reports that a century ago Frederic Godet had counted thirty interpretations; now Conzelmann tells us that "many count up over 200 different explanations" (I Corinthians, p. 276 n. 120).

24. The glory is not only peculiar to each *kind* of thing; it belongs to each *individual* thing within the kind: star differs from star in glory.

My reading takes the phrase *ho de theos didôsin autô(i) sôma kathôs êthelêsen* (v. 38) to mean that God gives not merely to each *kernel* a body as God has wished, but also to each particular thing of whatever kind. Paul goes on to say that this is true of each *seed*, but there is no reason why he would not extend it further. There is a linguistic difficulty here, of course; one does not speak of animals, fish, stars, and the like, as changing into something; hence to say that God gives "it" a (new) body is inappropriate. Nevertheless God is responsible for the infinite variety of bodies in existence.

As for *sarx*: when Paul says that there is one kind of flesh for humankind, another for animals, another for. . . , he need not be taken as making biological or taxonomic claims. Dahl (*Resurrection of the Body*, 32) thinks differently, that Paul is somehow separating human flesh from that of other species. But *sarx* as one general kind of *sôma* is separate only from seeds and stars and the like. *Within* the category Paul is merely pointing to diversity, not making claims about "substantial" or "qualitative" differences (contrary to R. Sider, "The Pauline Conception of the Resurrection Body," 430). Paul is saying, then, that human beings are not birds or cows or fish, that each *sôma* as *sarx* is different.

25. A reason for holding on to option 2 was the nature of Christ's resurrection, but this will be considered in the next section.

26. I have in mind Gundry's challenge to the accepted meaning of *sôma* as entire personality (n. 1, above). My earlier line of argument ("Disembodied," 206–7) took the shortcut of using *sôma* in that sense.

27. For the NT use of *sôma*, see E. Schweitzer, *TDNT*, under *sôma*. Gundry rests his case for the physicality of resurrection on his general analysis of *sôma* rather than on a detailed study of the ways in which the term actually functions in Paul's argument in these verses. In fact Gundry sometimes translates the term in ways that suit my argument: he calls it (albeit in a polemical context) "substantival entity" (Gundry, 162), and I claim that in·1 Cor. 15 *sôma* is an entity, a "substantival" entity, as long as we do not build physicality into the very meaning of "substantival."

28. Stacey, *The Pauline View of Man*, 149, 185; Gundry, 165ff.

29. I have said nothing about Paul's phrase in 1 Cor. 15:50 that "flesh and blood" (*sarx kai haima*) cannot enter the kingdom. In spite of the ontological ring of these words in English, it is unlikely that Paul means to assert by it that embodied persons cannot make it into the next world. The best understanding of the phrase is "weak mortals" or "frail human beings." J. Jeremias has an interesting discussion of the verse in " 'Flesh and Blood Cannot Inherit the Kingdom of God' (I Cor. XV. 50)," 151–59, debated by Conzelmann (I Corinthians, on 15:50), but supported by Whiteley (252-53).

30. Dahl: "It is vital to insist on the word *identity* as describing this rela-

tionship, because the whole idea has no meaning unless it is the *same* personality that is to be raised that exists now" (*Resurrection of the Body*, 94).

31. Hick's fullest account is to be found in chap. 15 of *Death and Eternal Life* (though by the end of the book he has moved away from "replicas" to other possibilities). Bruce Reichenbach also works with this idea of discontinuous replica bodies in his "Reply," 225–29, and in *Is Man the Phoenix?* 84–97 and 181–82.

32. Many commentators insist on the firmness of the link between Christ's resurrection and Pauline resurrection. This is the burden of W. L. Craig, "Bodily Resurrection of Jesus." F. Gerald Downing writes that the resurrection of Christ is "strictly analogous" to Paul's description of resurrection in 1 Cor. 15 (*The Church and Jesus*, 29). For a spiritualizing view, see Scroggs on 1 Cor. 15:47–50: the arguments for "the identity between Christ's body and the spiritual body of the resurrection indicate that for the Apostle his Lord rose from the dead in a spiritual body" (*The Last Adam*, 93).

33. See Craig, "Bodily Resurrection of Jesus," 52, who simply asserts that his "Premiss (1), *Paul equated Jesus' resurrection body with our future resurrection bodies*, is surely correct (Phil. 3:21; I Cor. 15:20; Col. 1:18)."

34. Güttgemanns (*Der leidende Apostel*) does this, but Gundry's comments seem apt (*Sôma*, 177–82). Whiteley regards the passage as referring only to survivors at the parousia, not the deceased (*Theology of Paul*, 249), but that makes little difference for our purposes—especially because he adds, "at the end all will be in the same condition, both the survivors and the deceased" (ibid., 254).

35. Cf. F. Gerald Downing: "The attempt (still made) to 'spiritualize' the Resurrection of Jesus is an attempt to by-pass the scandal of miracle (if scandal it be). In modern jargon (if it is to meet modern opinion that the attempt is being made), it would have to have been a 'physical' event of some order to have been an event at all. A human 'mental' change is as physical as resurrection; and if it is produced by 'God,' is just as miraculous a divine 'intervention.' This is so even if you multiply your entities and invent a concept of 'mind' as distinct from 'brain.' If the resurrection, bodily or mental, is in any sense an act of God, it is a miracle" (*Has Christianity a Revelation?* p. 81, n. 1).

36. Reichenbach so argues, thinking I should be embarrassed by the inconsistency of my thesis with Paul's wider theology, and its implication that God's resurrective activity is unnecessary ("Reply," 229).

37. On the "literalness" of the passage, see Whiteley: "This belief was part of the poetic background [Paul] shared with contemporary Judaism" (*Theology of Paul*, 283). The idea of more than one stage in resurrection is not, of course, new; it may be connected with beliefs about purgatory (ibid., 290), and it appears—in very different ways—in the eschatological speculations of John Hick (*Death and Eternal Life*) and Keith Ward (*Holding Fast to God*, chap. 10).

38. For a sustained defense of the possibility of disembodied persons who survive death, see the work of H. D. Lewis, most recently *The Self and Immortality* and *Persons and Life After Death*. H. H. Price's suggestion that the next world may consist of mental images is an intriguing one ("Survival and the Idea of 'Another World' "). However, one must have theological doubts about a resur-

rection world that is just like this one except that it has no "matter": Pauline radical change does not mean only this.

39. Not *all* the worries of the first type are solved: Augustine might still ask his question about aborted fetuses.

40. Talk of angels in such a context will be provocative, and I wish to make only two points here. (1) Historically angels have been associated with resurrection states: see 2 Baruch 51:10; and references to the relationship of the exalted Adam to angels in Scroggs, *The Last Adam*, 27–28. They seem like good candidates for bodiless beings, though I am not sure how the tradition treats that issue. (Gundry's argument, that the resurrected are like angels only because angels do not marry [*Sôma*, 153] does not account for the reason why marriage is inappropriate: and the most natural explanation is that bodiless spirits lack the obvious requirements for marital relationships.) (2) To talk of angels is to talk of possible rational beings who are not human; to say that the resurrected will be "like angels" is to raise the question of how human a resurrected "human" being could remain. The introduction of angels thus serves to focus what is the central concern of this study: the need for an account of resurrection change that is both theologically and philosophically satisfying.

41. Cullmann was right to draw attention to the importance of artistic expressions of resurrection light in "Immortality of the Soul." Although mention of specific works of art or music is inevitably personal, I was interested to note Ulrich Simon's strong claim that music, and especially Mozart's music, is the best way to express the meaning of glory ("Resurrection in a Post-Religious Age," 152–53).

4. ETHICAL AUTHORITIES: 1 CORINTHIANS 7

1. This use of "autonomous" appears close to the first of four senses noted by Paul Helm on p. 7 of his 'Introduction' to *Divine Commands and Morality*. For a discussion of the ways the term may have many meanings, see chap. 4 of Keith Ward's *Holding Fast to God*.

2. *Euthyphro* 9c-11b. Socrates speaks of the relationship between the holy (*to hosion*) and the god-beloved (*to theophiles*) in this section. Because the former turns out to be part of justice (11e), the discussion has implications for the relationship between morality and religion. Or so it is commonly taken. (Nicholas Denyer has, however, suggested another approach to me. Think of what makes a convention courteous. It is that it pleases the recipient; but the recipient may be pleased only because the courtesy was shown. The circularity of "I like it because it's a courtesy, and what makes it a courtesy is that I like it," might apply too to holiness and what the gods are pleased about. Holiness would thus be a matter of human conventions toward the gods.) For a defense of Euthyphro's religious approach to ethics, see Peter Geach, *God and the Soul*, 117–29 (reprinted as chap. 11 in Helm).

3. See Moore, *Ethics*, 63ff., and Frankena, *Ethics*, 28–30. Much of the discussion in the Helm collection takes its start from the "Euthyphro dilemma."

4. Nowell-Smith, "Morality: Religious and Secular," 97.

5. See James Rachels, "God and Human Attitudes," and the preface and introductory chapter of Don Cupitt's *Taking Leave of God*.

6. Nowell-Smith has been criticized by A. Boyce Gibson, "Morality, Religious and Secular: A Rejoinder": "What is extraordinary is what Nowell-Smith believes Christians to believe. For if there ever was a religion which challenged the morality of rules, it was Christianity." See also J.R. Lucas's discussion of Nowell-Smith in Ramsey, *Christian Ethics*, 126–32. For comments on Cupitt (n. 5, above) see Keith Ward, chaps. 4–6.

7. See Baruch A. Brody, "Morality and Religion Reconsidered."

8. Adams's defense is "one of the most fully worked-out Divine Command Theories of recent years" (Helm, *Divine Commands*, 7). Adams's basic view is presented in "A Modified Divine Command Theory of Ethical Wrongness" and "Divine Command Metaethics Modified Again." See also his "Moral Arguments for Theistic Belief" and "Autonomy and Theological Ethics."

9. Robert Young raises some problems in the third section of his "Theism and Morality." Questions about the theory of meaning that Adams invokes are raised by J. Wesley Robbins in "Are the Things That We Call 'Wrong' Contrary to the Commands of a Loving God?"

10. The inclusive label "Judeo-Christian" may seem inappropriate here when so much of the difference between Jew and Christian has been made by the latter to turn on the issue of legalistic morality (see Sanders, *Paul and Palestinian Judaism*, 33–59). But of course the issue of knowing how to obey need have nothing to do with legalism; and indeed Christians may learn much from their Jewish co-believers about the complexities of argument over the applicability of divine commands. However, although this issue is common to both traditions, apostolic authority is a different matter, and I later restrict discussion on this to Christian morality.

11. I have in mind J. C. Hurd, Jr., *The Origin of I Corinthians*, on the content of the Corinthian letter to Paul (154–69) and on the relationship alluded to in v. 36 (169–82); on the latter question, see also Whiteley, *Theology of Paul*, 218–22 ("Partners in Celibacy"); and for other issues J. K. Elliot, "Paul's Teaching on Marriage." For more references, see n. 20 below.

12. See section 3, "The Varied Modes of Exhortation," in chap. 2 of Furnish, *Theology and Ethics in Paul*.

13. There is reference to the Spirit of God in v. 40. The role of the Spirit in Paul's ethics is undoubtedly important; however, it is hard to maintain that the Spirit is given any independent moral authority in 1 Cor. 7. Paul instead reinforces his own advice with the claim that he believes himself to have the Spirit of God (see Furnish, 230 ff.).

14. Cf. Titus 1:5ff., where the "charge" or "order" to Titus requires that certain conditions be met in the appointment of elders. Gerhard Delling comments that "*diatassesthai* is obviously part of the apostolic office" (*TDNT*, VIII, 35).

15. The theme of imitation in Paul has been much discussed. Since the major references all link Paul with Christ (see Furnish, 218–24), the theme has

been seen as a way to express either emulation of particular qualities of Christ or else the believer's incorporation into Christ as the source of ethical life (see Furnish, 219; Whiteley, 211–13). It may be significant that in the veiled imitation language of 1 Cor. 7:7, Paul could not very well insist on a *universal* imitation of his own or of Jesus' example of celibacy. Chaucer's Wife of Bath makes the point rather strongly, though for her own purposes:

> For hadde God comanded maydenhede
> Thanne hadde he dampned weddyng with the dede;
> And certein, if ther were no seed y-sowe
> Virginitee, wher-of thanne sholde it growe?

(*Prologue of the Wife of Bath's Tale*, 69–72. It is from her mouth, incidentally, that the quotation at the beginning of this chapter comes. Though Chaucer has her read scripture from her own perspective, the quotation is not a bad summary of one important feature of 1 Cor. 7.)

16. This means my emphasis differs from Peter Richardson's treatment of the chapter as the expression of a conscious (though lenient) apostolic authority (" 'I Say, Not the Lord': Personal Opinion, Apostolic Authority and the Development of Early Christian Halakah"). Although Paul cannot forget his authority any more than the Corinthians can think his letter just any piece of correspondence, he does not appeal to *that* authority in his specific judgments in the chapter. In fact, the only statement that is *apostolic* is in v. 17, where what Paul decrees in all the churches is the most general rule to walk according to God's call. (*Pace* Richardson's section IV, there is no reference to church *custom* in v. 17 — what would the custom be? — but only to Paul's decree.)

17. C. K. Barrett (*First Corinthians*, on 7:7) thinks that *thelô* in v. 7 expresses a "wish that is capable of realization, . . . almost a command." To make sense of a near command to the married that they be celibate like Paul in spite of everything else Paul says to the married, Barrett must make the true content of the clause following *thelô* the wish for "all men to live in obedience to God." Although Paul wishes and ordains this in v. 17, it is not the content of his wish in v. 7a, where celibacy is in view (that, after all, is the point of the *alla* immediately following). So I read *thelô* as nothing like a command at all, but only the expression of Paul's preference.

18. Moulton and Milligan point out that Paul's use of *epitagé* for divine commands "is in accordance with its technical use in dedicating inscriptions" (*Vocabulary of the Greek Testament*, 247).

19. For possibilities, see Barrett, *First Corinthians*. Delling thinks that Paul wants to demote marital relations from the obligatory to the permissible, so speaks *kata sungnômên* and adds v. 7 as well (*TDNT*, VIII, 37).

20. So most commentators: see Furnish, 51f. Peter Richardson prefers to think that Paul has in mind a prophetic saying of the risen Lord rather than a tradition from the earthly Jesus (" 'I Say,' " 71.) For our purpose the majority opinion holds most interest: it allows Paul to work with established sayings whose authority would be widely recognized, and thus sharpens the issues.

On the relationship between Paul and Jesus on divorce, see Dungan, *The*

Sayings of Jesus, part II. Dungan's treatment of the issue of authority differs from mine, for he concludes that it is Paul who correctly interprets Jesus' original saying as forbidding remarriage but not divorce.

21. See Furnish, 51–65: because Paul does not appeal to the sayings of Jesus as a primary source for his ethics, the "words of the Lord" carry their authority in the context of the believer's life of faith. Whiteley links the lack of sayings to the importance of Christ's whole life, mediated through the church and in Paul himself; hence the importance of imitation (n. 15, above).

22. For a discussion of Paul's leniency, see Richardson's article (n. 16 above).

23. John Drane claims that 1 Cor. 7:19 is on the face of it contradictory of Galatians: in Galatians Paul had rejected all forms of legalism, but now by claiming that "keeping the commandments of God is everything," Paul reintroduces "the *form* of legal language" and slides in 1 Corinthians into the legalism he had rejected (*Paul: Libertine or Legalist?*, 165). But if Drane is right, 1 Cor. 7:19 contradicts itself, as well as Galatians, for Paul says that circumcision is nothing. (Cf. F. F. Bruce's judgment of "doubtful cogency" on Drane's point, *Paul: Apostle of the Heart Set Free*, p. 215, n. 14).

24. See, however, Hurd and Whiteley, n. 11, above. (Note that the RSV translation of v. 36 suggests that the problem concerned engaged couples, not a father's relationship with a betrothed daughter or partners in a celibate "marriage.")

25. I recognize the ambiguity in *mallon chrêsai* (v. 21). Are slaves to use their slavery as God's call in spite of opportunity for freedom, or use rather the opportunity to change their condition? (For discussion of opinions, see Allo, on 7:21). Were this the only example of Paul's approval of a change in condition, the second meaning would be problematic. But because the slavery/freedom image is used in the case of the sanctioned separation of partners in a mixed marriage (*ou dedoulôtai*, v. 15), this is evidence that Paul means to approve taking an opportunity of freedom.

26. Some commentators read *peri tou idiou thelematos* in a very specialized sense: Gottlob Schrenk says it must be translated, to have power "over one's own sexual impulse" (*TDNT*, III, 60). Whatever the merits of this reading, the general point remains that the control is exercised from within the agent, not imposed by an external force.

5. THE BURDEN OF THE WEAK: 1 CORINTHIANS 8-10

1. C. S. Lewis, *Studies in Words*, 192–93. For the omitted words, see below, n. 22.

2. Diets rich in animal protein and saturated fats have long been associated with heart and gastro-intestinal diseases in the Western world. That it is wasteful of resources to eat meat has been argued by Frances Moore Lappé in *Diet for a Small Planet* (New York: Ballentine Books, 1982), 69–71: it takes sixteen pounds of grain and soy feed to produce one pound of beef for human consumption.

Among those Christians arguing for a modified diet, the Mennonites have been prominent: see, for example, the cookbook *More With Less*, commissioned by the Mennonite Central Committee, Akron, Pennsylvania (Scottdale, Pa.: Herald Press, 1976). And for a critique of Christian attitudes toward creation and ecological problems generally, see John Passmore, *Man's Responsibility for Nature: Ecological Problems and Western Tradition* (London: Duckworth, 1974).

3. See Henry Cadbury, "The Macellum of Corinth," 134–41; and further comment from John Hurd, *Origin of I Corinthians*, in a long note on p. 144. Whereas Hurd thinks most meat would have been suspect, Barrett thinks that it would have been possible for Corinthian Christians to live on an ordinary diet without having to purchase very often "goods with a religious history" ("Things Sacrificed," 40–59).

4. To use Barrett's words, "Things Sacrificed," 41.

5. Ehrhardt, 267–90, and Barrett, "Things Sacrificed," 41–45. The *Didache* forbids idol meat, but *Barnabas* interprets the dietary laws so as to allow all foods (chap. 10).

6. The association of immorality with idolatry is an ancient theme. Since nothing hangs on the rest of the decree for this study, I ignore the other prohibitions, "blood" and "things strangled."

7. Pierce, 78.

8. Ehrhardt (278) and Hurd (280) both believe that Paul himself ate idol meat in Corinth.

9. *Origin of I Corinthians*, 146.

10. See Hurd, 126–42; and Barrett, "Things Sacrificed," 53 (cf. his *First Corinthians*, 16).

11. The slogan first appears in 1 Cor. 6:12; see Barrett, *First Corinthians*, on 6:12.

12. Barrett points out that the first question begins with "for," not the objecting "but," and that Paul does not answer the questions. Barrett prefers the explanation that Paul is reinforcing his reasoning from vv. 28–29a, that it is for the sake of the other person's conscience that one should abstain. "If I were to suppose that I must abstain on account of my own conscience, then I should have submitted myself to the judgement of another, and given up my freedom" (Barrett, *First Corinthians*, on 10:29). However, this sense can be taken from the text only by supposing Paul to say, . . . "for sake of the other man's conscience, because my freedom *ought* to be determined by his conscience rather than my own." And then it is still open to Paul's reader to raise the objection that I deal with. For references to a variety of interpretations of these two questions, see Hurd, p. 130, n. 2.

13. Jonathan Draper has pointed out to me that the *Didache*'s approach is exactly the opposite: gentile Christians are encouraged to observe whatever of the dietary laws they "are able to bear" (*ho dunasai bastason*, 6:3), so here weakness is a *failure* to be observant.

14. *Origin of I Corinthians*, 117–25.

15. Ehrhardt, 278; cf. Barrett's account of T. W. Manson's similar view ("Things Sacrificed," 46).

16. Cf. H. J. Cadbury's opposite word, "overconversion," to refer to the problems of those who adopted positions more extreme than Paul's own ("Overconversion in Paul's Churches").

It is possible that the category of the "weak" may also include those on the edge of conversion but not there yet. Paul becomes as weak to these weak in order to win them (cf. chap. 6, below).

17. Dodd, *Romans*, 219f.

18. See Charles A. Baylis's comments in *The Encyclopedia of Philosophy*, under "Conscience."

19. Another example of this common interpretation of 1 Cor. 8 and 10 may be had in John Gladwin's remark on the passage: "We must attend to the needs of other people's consciences in our behaviour when such issues arise" (*Conscience*,17).

20. This paragraph and the next reports material from C. A. Pierce, *Conscience in the New Testament*.

21. Christian Maurer, *TDNT*, under *sunoida, ktl.* Margaret Thrall criticizes Pierce in "The Pauline Uses of Suneidesis," arguing that in Paul *suneidêsis* can assess the actions of others and direct future behavior. It ought to be noted that a past experience can be future-directive without its attaining thereby a full-blown moral status: *suneidêsis* may therefore be forward-looking without having to be a moral conscience in the modern sense.

22. *Studies in Words*, chap. 8. Lewis follows Pierce's account, but provides many examples of the development of "conscience" in English as well as the corresponding Greek and Latin terms. The words "not consciring, but" were omitted from the quotation on p. 104, above, but are easily replaced once Lewis's meaning is known.

23. Maurer, *TDNT*, under *sunoida*.

24. Lewis, *Studies in Words*, 192.

25. Pierce may be right about the meaning of *suneidêsis*, but he cannot be right in his reading of 1 Cor. 10:25–29a. He begins, as we have noted in section II, above, with the assumption that Paul would have had bad feelings over the eating of idol meat; and as a result Pierce tends to treat the "weak" as persons with whom Paul could identify himself (*Conscience in the New Testament*, 80). In counseling them not to raise questions about unidentified meat, Paul wishes only to save them from the pain that would ensue if they knew for sure what they were eating. This turns Paul's advice into a counsel of prudence: Pierce unabashedly likens it to the proverbial expression "What you don't know won't hurt you" (p. 76).

It would of course be strange moral reasoning to move from a claim that you cannot feel bad about something you do not know to the advice that it is permissible to do an action of a type wrong in itself as long as you do not bother to determine whether this act is in fact of that type. (It is wrong to cheat on my income tax. I suspect that this particular claim is not allowed — but is it permissible to make the claim as long as I do not actually look up the regulations?) Fortunately we need not attribute this reasoning to Paul, for Pierce's analysis does not fit the text. Were he right, Paul would have written 10:28–29a entirely differently. For Paul says that in this case the observer does the identifying for you: he points out that you are about to eat idol meat. On Pierce's view, that would be sufficient to cause you bad feeling, and you would have to refrain because of your own *suneidêsis*. But Paul, as we know, assumes that your *suneidêsis* can remain clear.

Pierce has been misled by his basic assumption about Paul's own attitude to the eating of idol meat. Once Paul's genuine freedom to eat has been accepted, one can give a truer account of the weak in 1 Cor. 8 than Pierce offers (cf. my Section V.i above). Moreover, we are saved from Pierce's awkward attempt to base the freedom to eat on a liberated catchword of "conscience" from some Corinthians: in so doing he opens himself to the charge that these Corinthians use "conscience" in the moden antiauthoritarian sense that Pierce wants to deny was operative in Paul's time.

26. Since writing this section, I have worked out in more detail the ways in which *suneidêsis* functions in 1 Cor. 8 (as self-awareness) and in 1 Cor. 10 (as bad feeling): see my " 'Conscience' in 1 Corinthians 8 and 10."

27. I owe this point to Peter Richardson, "Pauline Inconsistency".

28. This shift in emphasis between 1 Corinthians and Romans calls into question Hans Conzelmann's comment on 1 Cor. 8:7. Correctly observing that Paul does not advise how the weak conscience is to be strengthened, Conzelmann notes:

> There is no pedagogical passion. This is an example of the Christian humanity which allows our brother to stand as the man he is, not as the man he ought to be according to some ideal standard. This makes it possible for Paul to examine situations in their individual particularity and to define conduct likewise in terms of individual history as the exercise of the particular freedom of the moment, without relativizing the norm. (I *Corinthians*, p. 147, n. 17).

This, I suggest, is an appropriate comment on Romans 14, where Paul stresses mutual acceptance without any attempt to change the beliefs of the other person. But the humanity and love that accept the Corinthian brother need not reject the possibility of educating his weak conscience. That Paul does not discuss education may mean only that he thinks it more important to save the weak from wounding than to instruct them in Christian truths. Once protected from attack, they can be nursed along in the faith — and indeed must be. How could Paul be content to let stand as they are those who lack the knowledge of 1 Cor. 8:4–6?

6. FOR AND AGAINST ACCOMMODATION: 1 CORINTHIANS 9:19-23

1. For comments on the "rhetorical mastery" of the passage, see Bornkamm, "Missionary Stance," 194–95. Bornkamm, however, sees only three groups, not four, in vv. 20–22a: he equates the Jews and those under law, in spite of his comment that "being under the law" does not denote a merely natural and

historical peculiarity (p. 195) — as would presumably being the member of a particular race.

2. Barrett notes the definite article, *tois pasin*, which "groups together all the examples" (*First Corinthians*, on 9:22).

3. Perhaps "the majority": cf. 1 Cor. 10:5 and 15:6.

4. *Kerdainô*, to "gain" or "win," may well be used by Paul from the context of Jewish proselytizing, where it meant "to win persons over for God." See D. Daube, *The New Testament and Rabbinic Judaism*, 348 and 355–61; Richardson, "Early Christian Sources."

5. Note the use of the article here: "he must be referring to a particular occasion, perhaps that of Timothy's circumcision" (Barrett, *First Corinthians*, n 9:20).

6. Paul does not say "*as* weak," but this must be his meaning. He does not consider himself weak (cf. Rom. 15:1 and our analysis of the problem of the weak in Corinth in chap. 5, above) any more than he thinks himself under law.

7. That is, a sharer in the benefits or gains of the gospel. Calvin remarks that Paul here *extends* what he says to all Christians, lest the Corinthians "get it into their heads that what Paul did was something that applied to him alone, because of the office he held" (*First Corinthians*, on 9:23). Richardson treats accommodation as an *apostolic* practice in "Pauline Inconsistency." From my later discussion of the possible justification for accommodation, it will be seen that I prefer Calvin's reading, though it is hard to extract from v. 23 alone. The fact that many share in the gospel does not entail that they each share in the same way.

8. *Pantôn* may be either masculine or neuter; since the *pasin* that immediately follows it is most naturally masculine, it is probably best to use that sense in reading the phrase as "free from all men."

9. Though this phrase is missing in some ancient authorities and the received text, it "probably fell out by accident in transcription, the eye of the copyist passing from *hupo nomon* to *hupo nomon*" (Metzger, *Textual Commentary*, on 9:20).

10. Or perhaps, following Barrett, he himself is not "God's lawless one" but is "Christ's law-abiding one" (on 9:21). On this phrase, see Dodd, "*Ennomos Christou*," and Bammel, "*Nomos Christou*."

11. In 2 Cor. 11:22, Paul calls himself an Israelite, of Abraham's seed, and a Hebrew; the first two of this trio are repeated in Rom. 11:1. Perhaps the best known description of his heritage is Phil. 3:4ff. However, in 1 Cor. it is hard to discover any acknowledgment of his Jewishness: when he mentions Jews he usually refers to Greeks in the same breath in order to play down differences (1:22–23; 10:32; 23:13). And his use of *pateres hêmôn* in 10:1 includes the Corinthians in some way: the Israelites are "our" ancestors.

12. So Barrett, on 9:20, 21.

13. So Paul must speak again in his own defense in 2 Cor., emphasizing that he has been straightforward in his dealings and speech (1:12, 17f.; 2:17; 4:2; 6:3, and so on).

14. Chrysostom and Origen use *sugkatabainô* in commenting on Paul's behavior, but this word does not appear in the NT except in its root sense of "go down with," and then only at Acts 25:5. See Richardson and Gooch, "Accommodation Ethics," pp. 91–93.

15. A well-known expression of the puzzle comes in the paradox Meno sets Socrates: no one can learn anything, because if they know it, learning is unnecessary, whereas if they don't know it, they will be unable to recognize it as what they ought to know (cf. *Meno* 80d). The *Oxford English Dictionary*, incidentally, gives as its third definition of accommodation, "Adaptation of a word, expression, or system to something different from its original purpose." Although that will suit my pedagogic accommodation, note that epistemological accommodation is wider: someone else's expression may be picked up with its meaning undisturbed to serve communication.

16. We may find it almost anywhere. Paula Milne, in her devastating portrayal of the fantasy life of a teenage girl, has an adviser to the lovelorn counsel this accommodation: "And remember, take advice from an old hand. It's not what you say but how you look, that's what counts. So don't try to impress him with your mind. No clever stuff, right? Just agree with whatever he says and look pretty. It's the only way, believe me" (*S.W.A.L.K.* [London: Thames Methuen, 1983] 56).

17. I do not mean to advocate the impossible task of believing only what has been proved true by some infallible method. There may be groundless beliefs, beliefs accepted on authority, beliefs rejected not because they are proved false but because they are inconsistent with other beliefs we hold strongly — and many other categories of not strictly provable beliefs. Nonetheless in all these cases we do offer reasons for believing, even if the reasons are not always the same. In this sense we do have regard to the truth of our beliefs.

18. Bornkamm recognizes this. "Paul could not modify the gospel itself according to the particular characteristics of his hearers. The whole of his concern is to make clear that the changeless gospel, which lies upon him as *anagkê* (9:16) empowers him to be free to change his stance" ("Missionary Stance," 196).

19. Mark 6:22 // Matt. 14:6. Thayer separates the sense of "causing pleasure" from the sense of "serving" in the word (*Greek-English Lexicon* under *areskein*).

20. Those who doubt that Paul delivered anything like this speech need not doubt its aptness as an example of accommodation; the claim is one of type and instance.

21. Two examples: Bornkamm's very title, "The Missionary Stance of Paul in I Corinthians 9 and in Acts," and Henry Chadwick's opening reference to Paul's "principles of evangelism" in "All Things to All Men," 261. Bornkamm, however, recognizes (in spite of his title) that Paul intends to "characterize a practical stance" rather than to "describe several ways of adjusting his preaching" (202); and Chadwick soon moves to discuss not evangelism but Paul's style of argument in his letters.

22. See the second and third puzzles in section I above; and Richardson, "Pauline Inconsistency," 350–51.

23. The quotations from Chadwick are from pp. 264, 272, 275, 271 and 275 in that order; and from Longenecker, pp. 234, 236, and 244.

24. Longenecker, 233, and Chadwick, p. 364 n. 3. Chadwick is a little more guarded in his defense, being more interested in describing the method than in evaluating. To call someone an "ingenious" controversialist is to commend mental agility rather than to endorse the use to which it is put.

25. Bornkamm does make this clear: see n. 21, above.

26. Bornkamm's understanding of strong and weak is different. He thinks it significant that Paul could not say he had become strong to the "strong," because participation in pagan cultic meals took accommodation too far ("Missionary Stance," 203). Paul may have had other reasons for leaving "to the strong I became strong" out of his list in 9:22 (he does not use this label at all in 1 Cor. 8–10, as I noted in chap. 5, section V.i), but his omission does not necessarily mean that he identified himself with the theological position of the weak. Perhaps someone really "strong" on the issue of idol meat could not properly say that he or she had become *as* strong.

27. Because of this I do not restrict the issue of accommodation to apostles alone, as does Peter Richardson: see n. 7, above.

28. Contrary to Dodd, who thinks the law of Christ "is such that it can be stated in the form of a code of precepts to which a Christian man is obliged to conform" ("*Ennomos Christou*," 100); see chap. 4, n. 21, above.

29. The word "love" does not of course appear in 7:35. But Paul exhibits *agapê* toward the Corinthians in seeking their advantage; and because it is their own advantage that is important, love for themselves (in this sense) may guide their conduct. They are also to imitate Paul in showing the same regard for others. Love for Christ is present in the verse in the aim of so living as to wait without distraction on the Lord. Further, the idea of the "seemly" may be related to the desire to please others, for it is a social value (see chap. 4, section V, above).

30. The issue is a large one, best handled by others. I observe only that in the references cited in n. 11, above, Paul does not specifically call himself a Jew; the only place he uses that term of himself is in Gal. 2:15. But there he stands apart from Judaism: Peter and he are Jews "by nature" as distinct from gentiles; but they have died to law in Christ, achieving a new identity and manner of life. Richardson has pointed to Paul's association of the term "Judaism" with transient charateristics, and his reservation of "Israel" for the people that love God and seek to do God's will (*Israel*, 147).

31. Paul does not explicitly invoke the self-regarding limit to accommodation. But it may be present in 9:23 in his desire to accommodate in order to share for himself in the benefits of the gospel. And he is conscious that he must retain his freedom over his body lest he himself turn out to be disqualified (9:27).

32. In "Pauline Inconsistency."

33. In "The Missionary Stance of Paul," 204–5.

34. The letter is quoted in Bede, *A History of the English Church and People* (trans. L. Sherley-Price. Harmondsworth: Penguin, 1968), I. 30. An example of confusion possibly related to such accommodation might be King Redward's apostasy. He "tried to serve both Christ and the ancient gods, and he

had in the same temple an altar for the holy Sacrifice of Christ side by side with an altar on which victims were offered to devils" (Bede, II.15).

35. *Pensées* (trans. John Warrington. London: Dent, 1960), 95.

7. PARTIAL KNOWLEDGE: 1 CORINTHIANS 13

1. The idea that faith and hope will cease in the life to come may be found in Calvin, who equates faith with the knowledge we have of God in this life, and hope with perseverance in that faith (*First Corinthians*, on 13:13). Héring believes that faith and hope will lose their meaning in the consummated world '(*First Corinthians*, on 13:13); Schmitals seems to agree (*Gnosticism*, 144). Stauffer regards the triad as stylistically impressive, but since faith and hope do not belong with love, "Paul has here sacrificed precision of thought to loftiness of expression" (*TDNT*, under *agapaô*).

But this view is rejected, with an explanation something like the one I have reported, by Bultmann (*TDNT*, under *elpis*); by Barrett (*First Corinthians*, on 13:13) and Conzelmann (*I Corinthians*, on 13:13).

It may be worth noting that, because hope is future-directed, it is a virtue that cannot exist in an atemporal state. That is not incompatible, however, with a state of perfection. As Plato remarks in connection with *erôs*, a desire that is fulfilled may nevertheless continue to wish for the persistence of its fulfillment in the future (*Symposium* 200d).

2. It could not be argued for this interpretation that Paul thinks *gnôsis* to be only a pretended knowledge of God, and that the destruction is of the pretense alone. For Paul himself claims to know in a way that will be destroyed. It should be noted that by the time he comes to v. 12, Barrett has dropped the secret character of knowledge in order to speak of *all* knowledge of God in the present age as incomplete and unclear. There seems little reason, however, to make the knowledge of v. 8 special and the knowledge of v. 12 general.

G. Kittel seems to open another way to solve the puzzle by making v. 12 refer to *prophetic* speaking and seeing. He connects the mirror image and the idea of *ainigma* with OT prophets who were afforded less clarity of vision than was Moses (Num. 12:8). Paul's meaning becomes this, that Christian pneumatic or prophetic seeing is the partial knowledge that will be done away with. But by implication this makes Christian knowing less clear than that afforded to Moses, surely a strange way to read 1 Cor. 13 (*TDNT*, under "*ainigma/esoptron*").

3. Bultmann thinks that with *gnôsis* in v. 8 and *ginôskô* in v. 12 Paul is adapting gnostic usage, but Paul then robs the notion of knowledge of its gnostic significance by claiming that God knows Paul fully: our knowledge of God is thus gained though God's knowledge of us, not by our effort (*TDNT*, under *ginôskô*). Even this view would not destroy the generality of Paul's critique, however.

For an approach to the meanings of Paul's terms for knowing, see Moises Silva, "The Pauline Style as Lexical Choice."

4. Conzelmann makes a point of using this term (*I Corinthians*, on 13:9).

5. The infant who is immature in chap. 3 is innocent in chap. 14. For the child-adult image in Hellenistic rhetoric, see G. Bertram, *TDNT*, under *nêpios*, and Hugedé, *La Métaphore du miroir*, 177–82. Hugedé rejects the suggestion that Paul takes over the image from its use in mystery religions; it belongs rather to popular diatribe.

6. Hugedé, chap. 3, following Dupont, *Gnosis*, chap. 3, and Behm, "Das Bildwort vom Spiegel." The idea that mirrors in antiquity were invariably imperfect is still repeated (see Grosheide, *First Corinthians*, on 13:12), in spite of the implication of James 1:23–24 that looking in a mirror provides adequate information about one's face.

7. Contrary to W. Michaelis, *TDNT*, under *horaô*. Although the passage does not expressly make God the object of the eschatological vision, the inference of face-to-face seeing cannot be otherwise. It is true that there is no grammatical object for the verb "to see": but I discuss this in section II.iii of this chapter.

8. There is debate whether the verb means "to reflect in a mirror" or "to look in a mirror." For the first, see Liddell, Scott, Jones, *A Greek-English Lexicon*, under *katoptridzô*; and Dupont, "Le chrétien," as well as his *Gnosis*, 119–20. For the second, see Kittel, *TDNT*, under *esoptron, katoptridzomai*; and Hugedé, chap. 1.

9. Plato may be thought to be the champion of the direct over the indirect with his devaluing of written language against the spoken word (written words look intelligent but when you question them, they can only say the same thing over again [*Phaedrus* 274ff.]; and poems cannot be questioned whereas people can be [*Protagoras* 347f.]). But although they have this failing, records of conversation have a different virtue: they may promote understanding by allowing a detailed examination of claims and arguments, which is presumably in part why Plato bothered to write.

10. See Elie Wiesel, *Night* (London: Hill and Wang, 1960), and William Styron, *Sophie's Choice* (New York: Random House, 1979).

11. See Martin Buber, *I and Thou*.

12. Paul's image cannot be made to yield a *complete* account of the believer's present knowledge of God. Because the metaphor is visual, it does not take speaking into account: but words are important in the relationship between the believer and God, both in God's speaking to someone and in prayer addressed to God. Again, the emphasis in the metaphor is on the viewer's perception of images, which ignores the possibility of reciprocal viewing and knowing: but the God who is imperfectly perceived has complete knowledge of the viewer. Such limitations in the metaphor may distort the account of Christian experience I offer here. For instance, it might be argued that in prayer the believer is, contrary to the metaphor, in *direct* relationship to God. Nevertheless, although the believer may realize that on God's side the experience is direct, from the believer's side there is not yet any direct knowing.

13. The comparison between Paul's mirror and Plato's cave is made by Bassett (had Paul known Plato's cave, he would have made Plato's point: "I Cor. 13:12," 235) and by Perry (Plato's prisoners "see only 'baffling reflections in a

mirror,' and the real nature of things as things as they are in themselves is hidden from their sight" ("I Corinthians xiii.12a," 279).

There are two questions here, one historical and one comparative. On the historical question — Did Paul know Plato? — it seems difficult to attain much certainty. It may be that Platonic influence on popular philosophy made itself felt remotely on Paul; but that possibility does not affect my interpretation greatly. The comparative question deserves a little more comment. We should ask exactly in what respects the mirror and the cave are to be compared, because the contexts in which the images appear are so different. Paul's simple image expresses the character of our knowledge of God in this life, whereas Plato's developed parable in *Republic* (7:514ff.) encapsulates a complex vision of epistemology, metaphysics, and political philosophy. Both locate full reality beyond the physical world and make that reality the object of complete knowledge. What is known now is in some sense a reflection of that reality. But whereas Plato has an encompassing theory of Forms to account for all human knowledge, Paul's image is concerned solely with knowledge of God. Platonic philosophers may hope to attain a vision of the Forms in this life, after an arduous ascent motivated by *erôs*, their striving for the good and beautiful; once they see the Forms they must descend again to the cave, to express politically the values they have grasped. For Paul, there is no ascent in this life, no privileged knowledge of God for the few. Love as *agapê* is (as we shall see in section III of this chapter) expressed now but experienced fully only in the face-to-face knowledge of the eschaton. Paul is willing to say that our present epistemic condition is one of partial (that is, imperfect) knowledge, whereas Plato's philosophical interest generates a more complete account of epistemic states in which he restricts knowledge to the apprehension of unchanging realities, claiming that our awareness of the world can have only the status of belief.

The images of cave and mirror are best connected, then, in the relationship between the ontological status of objects and the corresponding cognitive awareness of those objects. Plato, Paul, and many others agree that mirror images, like shadows, are derivative and dependent; they do not give us real objects. The move from that judgment on their status to the inferiority of our cognitive awareness of them is a Platonic move — but it is not a patented device, and there is no reason why Paul should not have been able to hold a similar opinion.

14. It has been claimed that Paul is influenced by pagan practices of divination through mirrors, with a young child as medium to discern the future. But Paul speaks of seeing not our own futures but God; and the point of the comparison with the child is not clairvoyance but the imperfection of childish perception. See Hugedé, 75–95. For an example of a child medium from more recent literature, albeit fiction, see Wilkie Collins's famous nineteenth-century mystery novel, *The Moonstone* (Harmondsworth: Penguin, 1969), First Period, chap. 3.

15. For these ideas and others, see Dupont's report, *Gnosis*, 135.

16. Ibid., 137.

17. *La Métaphore du Miroir*, 141–48.

18. References in Dupont, *Gnosis*, 135, n. 1, include Num. 12:8; Deut. 28:37; 3 Kings 10:1; Prov. 1:6.

19. The question of Pauline consistency on this topic will be approached in different ways. Some will be inclined to think that his argument in 1 Cor. 13:8-13 is ad hominem: desiring to deflate Corinthian conceit, he professes a humility for himself designed to impress the Corinthians but not to be taken as a serious claim about Paul himself. His flashes of temper, his concern over his reputation, and his jealousy for the truth of the gospel all betray a tenacity of conviction that cannot sit comfortably with professions about the imperfections of his knowledge. Another approach might, in similar vein, acknowledge Paul's inconsistency but choose to stress the importance of his claims about our present knowledge of God. It might remind us that Paul's insights about the equality of male and female in Gal. 3:28 and 1 Cor. 7 are significant and to be pursued, in spite of their uneasy alliance with some of his specific directives about women. Still another approach would look carefully at the kinds of matters on which Paul claimed certainty, the topics on which (at least as far as his extant letters show) he did not say very much, and the ways in which he took his own Judaism to hold puzzles to be worked out in the light of his new experience of Christ. Certainly in the tensions Paul experienced between the arrival of a new age and its lack of consummation in his (or in any) historical time, we find fruitful ground for his theme of partial knowledge. Paul would insist on the knowledge to be found in the gospel (the mystery is revealed), but he also insists that there is much that we do not yet know of its consummation. We have seen how little and how much there is to be said of Pauline resurrection in chap. 3, above; his certainty about the future does not tempt him to the speculation so common among more epistemologically indulgent believers. In this life he is absent from the Lord, and he walks not by sight but in faith, in the freedom of the Spirit according to God's call, rather than in the settled structures of the past. He prays without ceasing but does not know how he ought to pray; and even as death approaches, he cannot claim to have finished: he wishes still to win Christ, to know him, to attain somehow to the resurrection and perfection that is not yet his.

20. As Gregory Vlastos points out, mainly against A. Nygren, in "The Individual as an Object of Love in Plato." See also J. A. Brentlinger's essay "The Nature of Love."

21. See Gooch and Mosher, "Divine Love."

22. *TDNT*, under *agapaô*.

23. Fackenheim, *God's Presence in History*, 73.

24. See Plantinga, *God, Freedom and Evil*, 28.

25. This is included, as anonymous, among the ten "most often quoted limericks of all time" by Bennett Cerf, *Out on a Limerick* (New York: Harper, 1960), 20.

Bibliography

Adams, Robert Merrihew, "Autonomy and Theological Ethics." *Religious Studies* 15 (1979) 191–94.

_____. "Divine Command Metaethics Modified Again." *Journal of Religious Ethics*, 7 (1979) 71–79. Partially reprinted as "Divine Command Metaethics as Necessary A Posteriori" in Helm, ed., *Divine Commands*.

_____. "A Modified Divine Command Theory of Ethical Wrongness." In *Religion and Morality: A Collection of Essays*, Gene Outka and John P. Reeder, Jr., eds., Garden City, N.Y.: Anchor Books, 1973. Reprinted in Helm, ed., *Divine Commands and Morality*.

_____. "Moral Arguments for Theistic Belief." In Delaney, ed., *Rationality and Religious Belief*.

Allo, Ernest Bernard. *Saint Paul: Première Épître aux Corinthiens*. Paris: Gabalda, 1956.

Baillie, John. *The Idea of Revelation in Recent Thought*. Oxford University Press, 1956.

Bammel, Ernest. "*Nomos Christou*." In *Studia Evangelica*, vol. 3, F. L. Cross, ed. Berlin: Akademie, 1964.

Barrett, Charles Kingsley. *A Commentary on the Epistle to the Romans*. London: Adam and Charles Black, 1957.

_____. *A Commentary on the First Epistle to the Corinthians*. Second edition. London: Adam and Charles Black, 1971.

_____. *A Commentary on the Second Epistle to the Corinthians*. London: Adam and Charles Black, 1973.

_____. "Things Sacrificed to Idols." In his *Essays on Paul*. London: S.P.C.K, 1982.

Bassett, Samuel E. "I Cor. 13:12, *blepomen gar arti di' esoptrou en ainigmati*." *Journal of Biblical Literature*, 47 (1928), 232–36.

Beare, Francis W. *Colossians*. The Interpreter's Bible, vol. 11. Nashville: Abingdon Press, 1955.

Behm, Johannes. "Das Bildwort vom Spiegel, I Korinther 13, 12." In *Reinhold-Seeberg-Festschrift*, vol. 1, Wilhelm Koepp, ed. Leipzig: A. Deichertsche, 1929.

Betz, Hans Dieter. *Galatians: A Commentary on Paul's Letter to the Churches in Galatia*. Hermeneia. Philadelphia: Fortress Press, 1979.

Bornkamm, Gunther. *Early Christian Experience*. London: SCM Press, 1969.
_____. "The Missionary Stance of Paul in 1 Corinthians 9 and in Acts." In *Studies in Luke-Acts*, L. E. Keck and J. L. Martyn, eds. Nashville: Abingdon Press, 1966.
Brentlinger, John A. "The Nature of Love." In *The Symposium of Plato*, translated by Suzy Q. Groden and edited by John A. Brentlinger. Amherst: University of Massachusetts Press, 1970.
Brody, Baruch A. "Morality and Religion Reconsidered." In *Readings in the Philosophy of Religion: An Analytic Approach*, Baruch A. Brody, ed. Englewood Cliffs, N.J.: Prentice Hall, 1974. Reprinted in Helm, ed, *Divine Commands and Morality*.
Bruce, F. F. *Paul: Apostle of the Heart Set Free*. Grand Rapids: Eerdmans, 1977.
Buber, Martin. *I and Thou*. Translated by Walter Kaufmann. Second edition. New York: Scribner, 1970.
Bultmann, Rudolf. *Der Stil der paulinischen Predigt und die kynisch-stoische Diatribe*. Forschungen zur Religion und Literatur des Alten und Neuen Testaments, 13. Göttingen: Vandenhoeck & Ruprecht, 1910.
_____. *Theology of the New Testament*. Vol. 1. Translated by Kendrick Grobel. London: SCM Press, 1952.
Cadbury, Henry J. "The Macellum of Corinth." *Journal of Biblical Literature*, 53 (1934) 134–41.
_____. "Overconversion in Paul's Churches." In *The Joy of Study*, S. E. Johnson, ed. New York: Macmillan, 1951.
Calvin, John. *The First Epistle of Paul the Apostle to the Corinthians*. Translated by John W. Fraser. Calvin's Commentaries, edited by D. W. Torrance and T. F. Torrance. London and Edinburgh: Oliver and Boyd, 1960.
Chadwick, Henry. "All Things to All Men." *New Testament Studies*, 1 (1954–55) 261–75.
Conzelmann, Hans. *I Corinthians: a Commentary on the First Epistle to the Corinthians*. Translated by James W. Leitch. Hermeneia. Philadelphia: Fortress Press, 1975.
Craig, William Lane. "The Bodily Resurrection of Jesus." In *Gospel Perspectives: Studies of History and Tradition in the Four Gospels*, vol. I, R. T. France and David Wenham, eds. Sheffield: JSOT Press, 1980.
Cullmann, Oscar. "Immortality of the Soul or Resurrection of the Dead?" In *Immortality and Resurrection*, Krister Stendahl, ed. New York: Macmillan, 1965.
Cuppitt, Don. *Taking Leave of God*. London: SCM Press, 1980.
Dahl, Murdoch E. *The Resurrection of the Body: a Study of I Corinthians 15*. Studies in Biblical Theology, 36. London: SCM Press, 1962.
Daube, David. *The New Testament and Rabbinic Judaism*. London: Athlone Press, 1965.
Davies, William David. *Paul and Rabbinic Judaism: Some Rabbinic Elements in Pauline Theology*. Third edition. London: S.P.C.K, 1970.
_____. Meyer, Paul W.; and Aune, David E. Review of *Galatians: A Com-*

mentary on Paul's Letter to the Churches of Galatia by Hans Dieter Betz. *Religious Studies Review*, 7 (1981) 310–28.

Delaney, C. F., ed. *Rationality and Religious Belief*. Notre Dame, Ind.: University of Notre Dame Press, 1979.

DeWitt, Norman Wentworth. *St. Paul and Epicurus*. Minneapolis: University of Minnesota Press, 1954.

Dodd, C. H. "*Ennomos Christou*." In *Studia Paulina: in honorem Johannis de Zwann septuagenarii*, J. N. Sevenster and W. C. van Unnik, eds. Haarlem: De Erven F. Bohn, 1953.

_____. *The Epistle of Paul to the Romans*. Moffat New Testament Commentary. London: Hodder and Stoughton, 1942.

Downing, F. Gerald. *The Church and Jesus*. London: SCM Press, 1968.

_____. *Has Christianity a Revelation?* London: SCM Press, 1964.

Drane, John W. *Paul: Libertine or Legalist? a Study in the Theology of the Major Pauline Epistles*. London: S.P.C.K, 1975.

Dungan, David L. *The Sayings of Jesus in the Churches of Paul: The Use of the Synoptic Tradition in the Regulation of Early Church Life*. Oxford: Basil Blackwell, 1971.

Dupont, Jacques. "Le chrétien, miroir de la gloire divin d'après II Cor. III, 18." *Revue Biblique*, 56 (1949) 392–411.

_____. *Gnosis: La connaissance religieuse dans les Épitres de Saint Paul*. Bruges: Desclée de Brouwer, 1949.

Ehrhardt, Arnold. *The Framework of the New Testament Stories*. Manchester University Press, 1964.

Elliott, J. K. "Paul's Teaching on Marriage in I Corinthians: Some Problems Considered." *New Testament Studies*, 19 (1972–73) 219–25.

Ellis, E. Earle. "The Structure of Pauline Eschatology." In his *Paul and His Recent Interpreters*. Grand Rapids: Eerdmans, 1961.

_____. " 'Wisdom' and 'Knowledge' in I Corinthians." *Tyndale Bulletin*, 25 (1974) 82–98.

Fackenheim, Emil L. *God's Presence in History: Jewish Affirmations and Philosophical Reflections*. New York: Harper and Row, 1972.

Fischer, James A. "Pauline Literary Forms and Thought Patterns." *Catholic Biblical Quarterly*, 39 (1977) 209–23.

Flew, Antony. "Can a Man Witness His Own Funeral?" *Hibbert Journal*, 54 (1956) 242–50.

_____. and MacIntyre, A., eds. *New Essays in Philosophical Theology*. London: SCM Press, 1955.

Frankena, William K. *Ethics*. Second edition. Englewood Cliffs, N.J.: Prentice Hall, 1973.

Furnish, Victor Paul. *Theology and Ethics in Paul*. Nashville: Abingdon Press, 1968.

Geach, Peter. *God and the Soul*. London: Routledge and Kegan Paul, 1969.

Gibson, A. Boyce. "Morality, Religious and Secular: A Rejoinder." *Journal of Theological Studies*, n.s. 13 (1962) 1–13. Reprinted in Ramsey, ed., *Christian Ethics*.

Gladwin, John. *Conscience*. Grove Booklet on Ethics, 18. Bramcote: Grove Books, 1977.

Gooch, Paul W. "Authority and Justification in Theological Ethics: A Study in I Corinthians 7." *Journal of Religious Ethics*, 11 (1983) 62–74.

_____. " 'Conscience' in I Corinthians 8 and 10." *New Testament Studies*, forthcoming.

_____. "The Ethics of Accommodation." *Tyndale Bulletin*, 29 (1978) 93–117.

_____. "On Disembodied Resurrected Persons: A Study in the Logic of Christian Eschatology." *Religious Studies*, 17 (1981) 199–213.

_____. "Margaret, Bottom, Paul and the Inexpressible." *Word and World*, 6 (1986) 313–25.

_____. "The Pauline Concept of the Resurrection Body." *Crux*, 8 (1970–71) 18–29.

_____. "Reply to Professor Reichenbach." *Religious Studies*, 18 (1982) 231–32.

_____. "St. Paul on the Strong and the Weak." *Crux*, 13 (1975–76) 10–20.

_____, and Mosher, David L. "Divine Love and the Limits of Language." *Journal of Theological Studies*, n.s. 23 (1972) 420–29.

Grosheide, Frederik Willem. *Commentary on the First Epistle to the Corinthians: the English text with introduction, exposition and notes*. Grand Rapids: Eerdmans, 1953.

Gundry, Robert H. *Sôma in Biblical Theology, with Emphasis upon Pauline Anthropology*. Society for New Testament Studies Monograph Series, 29. Cambridge University Press, 1976.

Güttgemanns, E. *Der leidende Apostle und sein Herr*. Forschungen zur Religion und Literatur des Alten und Neuen Testaments, 90. Göttingen: Vandenhoeck & Ruprecht, 1966.

Helm, Paul, ed. *Divine Commands and Morality*. Oxford University Press, 1981.

Héring, Jean. *The First Epistle of Saint Paul to the Corinthians*. Translated from the second French edition by A. W. Heathcote and P. J. Allcock. London: Epworth Press, 1962.

Hick, John. *Philosophy of Religion*. Third edition. Englewood Cliffs, N. J.: Prentice Hall, 1983.

Hooker, Morna D. " 'Beyond the Things Which Are Written': An Examination of I Cor. iv.6." *New Testament Studies*, 10 (1963-64) 127–32.

_____. "Paul and Covenantal Nomism." in *Paul and Paulinism*, M. D. Hooker and S. G. Wilson, eds. London: S.P.C.K, 1982.

_____. *Pauline Pieces*. London: Epworth Press, 1979.

_____. "Were There False Teachers in Colossae?" In *Christ and Spirit in the New Testament. Studies in Honour of C.F.D. Moule*. B. Lindars and S. S. Smalley, eds. Cambridge University Press, 1973.

Hugedé, Norbert. *La Métaphore du miroir dans les Épîtres de saint Paul aux Corinthiens*. Neuchatel: Delachaux et Niestlé, 1957.

Hurd, John Coolidge, Jr. *The Origin of I Corinthians*. London: S.P.C.K, 1965.

Jeremias, J. " 'Flesh and Blood Cannot Inherit the Kingdom of God' (I Cor. XV, 50)." *New Testament Studies*, 2 (1955–56) 151–59.

Jewett, Robert. *Paul's Anthropological Terms*. Arbeiten zur Geschichte des antiken Judentums und des Urchristentums, 10. Leiden: Brill, 1971.

Kittel, Gerhard, ed. *Theological Dictionary of the New Testament*. Translated and edited by Geoffrey W. Bromiley, 10 vols. Grand Rapids: Eerdmans, 1964–1976.

Lewis, C. S. *Studies in Words*. Second edition. Cambridge University Press, 1967.

Lewis, H. D. *Persons and Life After Death*. London: Macmillan, 1978.

———. *The Self and Immortality*. London: Macmillan, 1973.

Lohse, Eduard. *Colossians and Philemon*. Hermeneia. Philadelphia: Fortress Press, 1971.

Longenecker, Richard. *Paul: Apostle of Liberty*. New York: Harper and Row, 1964.

Lucas, J. R. Untitled discussion of "Morality: Religious and Secular" by P.H. Nowell-Smith. In Ramsey, ed., *Christian Ethics*.

Martin, Ralph. *Colossians and Philemon*. New Century Bible. London: Oliphants, 1978.

Metzger, Bruce M. *A Textual Commentary on the Greek New Testament*. London: United Bible Societies, 1971.

Moore, George Edward. *Ethics*. Second edition. Oxford University Press, 1966.

Morton, Andrew Q.; Michaelson, S.; and Thompson, J. David. *A Critical Concordance to I and II Corinthians*. The Computer Bible, vol. 19. Wooster, Ohio: Biblical Research Associates, 1979.

Moule, C. F. D. "St. Paul and Dualism: The Pauline Conception of Resurrection." *New Testament Studies*, 12 (1965–66) 106–23.

Moulton, J. H., and Milligan, G. *The Vocabulary of the Greek Testament*. London: Hodder and Stoughton, 1929.

Munck, Johannes. *Paul and the Salvation of Mankind*. London: SCM Press, 1959.

Nowell-Smith, Patrick H. "Morality: Religious and Secular." *Rationalist Annual*, 1961. Reprinted in Ramsey, ed., *Christian Ethics*.

Orr, William F., and Walther, James A. *I Corinthians*. The Anchor Bible. Garden City, N.Y.: Doubleday, 1976.

Penelhum, Terence. *God and Skepticism*. Philosophical Studies Series in Philosophy, vol. 28. Dordrecht: Reidel, 1983.

———. *Survival and Disembodied Existence*. New York: Humanities Press, 1970.

Perry, A.S. "I Corinthians xiii.12a: *blepomen gar arti di esoptrou en ainigmati.*" *Expository Times*, 58 (1946–47) 279.

Pfitzner, Victor C. *Paul and the Agon Motif*. Supplements to *Novum Testamentum*, vol. 16. Leiden: Brill, 1967.

Phillips, Dewi Z. *Death and Immortality*. London: Macmillian, 1970.

Pierce, C. A. *Conscience in the New Testament*. Studies in Biblical Theology, 15. London: SCM Press, 1955.

Plantinga, Alvin. *God, Freedom and Evil*. Grand Rapids: Eerdmans, 1978.

———. "Is Belief in God Properly Basic?" *Nous*, 15 (1981) 41–52. Reprinted in Delaney, ed. *Rationality*.

———. and Wolterstorff, Nicholas, eds. *Faith and Rationality: Reason and Belief in God*. Notre Dame, Ind.: University of Notre Dame Press, 1983.

Price, H. H. "Survival and the Idea of 'Another World.' " *Proceedings of the Society for Psychical Research*, 50:182 (1953) 1–25.

Rachels, James. "God and Human Attitudes." *Religious Studies*, 7 (1971) 325–37. Reprinted in Helm, ed., *Divine Commands*.

Ramsey, Ian T., ed. *Christian Ethics and Contemporary Philosophy*. London: SCM Press, 1966.

Reichenbach, Bruce. *Is Man the Phoenix? A Study of Immortality*. Grand Rapids: Christian University Press [Eerdmans], 1978.

_____. "On Disembodied Resurrected Persons: A Reply." *Religious Studies*, 18 (1982) 225–29.

Richardson, Peter. "Early Christian Sources of an Accommodation Ethic — from Jesus to Paul." *Tyndale Bulletin*, 29 (1978) 118–42.

_____. *Israel in the Apostolic Church*. Society for New Testament Studies Monograph Series, 10. Cambridge University Press, 1969.

_____. " 'I Say, Not the Lord': Personal Opinion, Apostolic Authority and the Development of Early Christian Halakah." *Tyndale Bulletin*, 31 (1980) 65–86.

_____. "Pauline Inconsistency: I Corinthians 9:19–23 and Galatians 2:11–14." *New Testament Studies*, 26 (1979–80) 347–62.

_____, and Gooch, Paul W. "Accommodation Ethics." *Tyndale Bulletin*, 29 (1978) 89–93.

Robbins, J. Wesley. "Are the Things That We Call 'Wrong' Contrary to the Commands of a Loving God ?" *Journal of the American Academy of Religion*, 49 (1981) 89–97.

Robinson, John A. T. *The Body: A Study in Pauline Theology*. Studies in Biblical Theology, 5. London: SCM Press, 1952.

Sanders, Edward P. *Paul and Palestinian Judaism*. London: SCM Press, 1977.

Schaff, Philip. *The Creeds of Christendom*. 3 vols. Grand Rapids: Eerdmans, 1966.

Schmithals, Walter. *Gnosticism in Corinth: An Investigation of the Letters to the Corinthians*. Translated by John E. Steely. Nashville: Abingdon Press, 1971.

Scroggs, Robin. *The Last Adam: A Study in Pauline Anthropology*. Philadelphia: Fortress Press, 1966.

_____. "Paul: *Sophos* and *Pneumatikos*." *New Testament Studies*, 14 (1967–68) 33–55.

Sevenster, J. N. *Paul and Seneca*. Supplements to *Novum Testamentum*, vol. 4. Leiden: Brill, 1961.

Sider, Roger J. "The Pauline Conception of the Resurrection Body in I Corinthians xv. 35–54." *New Testament Studies* 21 (1974–75) 428–39.

Silva, Moises. "The Pauline Style as Lexical Choice: *Ginôskein* and Related Verbs." In *Pauline Studies*. Essays presented to F. F. Bruce, edited by D. A. Hagner and M. J. Harris. Exeter: Paternoster Press, 1980.

Simon, Ulrich. "Resurrection in a Post-Religious Age." In *Life After Death*, edited by A. Toynbee, A. Koestler et al. London: Weidenfeld and Nicolson, 1976.

Stacey, W. D. *The Pauline View of Man*. London: Macmillan, 1956.

Stowers, Stanley Kent. *The Diatribe and Paul's Letter to the Romans*. SBL Dissertation Series, 57. Chico, Calif.: Scholars Press, 1981.

Thackeray, H. St. John. *The Septuagint and Jewish Worship: A Study in Origins*. London: The British Academy, 1921.

Thayer, Joseph H. *A Greek-English Lexicon of the New Testament*. Grand Rapids: Zondervan, 1970.

Thrall, Margaret E. *The First and Second Letters of Paul to the Corinthians*. Cambridge Bible Commentary: New English Bible. Cambridge University Press, 1965.

———. "The Pauline Use of *Suneidêsis*." *New Testament Studies*, 14 (1967–68) 118–25.

The Translator's New Testament. London: British and Foreign Bible Society, 1973.

Trevor, G. H. "The Apostle Paul's Contribution to the Philosophy of Religion." *Bibliotheca Sacra*, 72 (1915) 177–207.

Vlastos, Gregory. "The Individual as an Object of Love in Plato." In his *Platonic Studies*. Second printing. Princeton University Press, 1981.

Ward, Keith. *Holding Fast to God: A Reply to Don Cupitt*. London: S.P.C.K, 1982.

Whiteley, D. E. H. *The Theology of St. Paul*. Second edition. Oxford: Basil Blackwell, 1974.

Wilckens, Ulrich. *Weisheit und Torheit: eine exegetischreligiongeschichtliche Untersuchung zu I Kor. 1 und 2*. Tübingen: Mohr, 1959.

Wolfson, H. "Immortality and Resurrection in the Philosophy of the Church Fathers." In *Immortality and Resurrection*, Krister Stendahl, ed. New York: Macmillan, 1965.

Wuellner, W. "Haggadic Homily Genre in I Corinthians 1–3." *Journal of Biblical Literature*, 89 (1970) 199–204.

Young, Robert. "Theism and Morality." *Canadian Journal of Philosophy*, 7 (1977) 341–51. Reprinted in Helm, ed. *Divine Commands*.

Index

Abraham, 45, 65
accommodation
    epistemological, 128, 130, 134, 138
    practical, 129, 131, 134–135, 138, 140
    theological, 129, 130, 133, 138
    vs. conversion, 129, 141
Adam, 69, 84
Adams, R. M., 88
angels, 80, 116, 175 n. 40
apostles, 24, 25, 49, 132
Apostolic Decree, 106, 107, 115
Aquinas, Thomas, 58
Aristotle, 99
Ascension, 75, 76, 80
Augustine, 12, 49, 58
authorities, ethical, 85–86, 92-96
authority, apostolic, 2, 93–94, 107, 124, 136, 177 n. 16

Barrett, C. K., 18, 44, 48, 81, 108, 144
Bassett, S. E., 152
boasting, 21, 23, 25–27, 40, 46
Bornkamm, G., 140
Bottom, 27, 28, 37
Buber, M., 149

Calvin, 16, 48–51, 58
cave, Plato's, and Paul's mirror, 186 n. 13
Chadwick, H., 133–34
Chaucer, 85, 177 n. 15
circumcision, 95, 97, 100, 106
commands, divine, 87–88, 95–97
    modified by Paul, 97–98
    nontheological justification of, 99

concept hunting, 21
concepts, anachronistic, 61
conscience, 8, 117–120, 180 n. 25
Conzelmann, H., 17, 48, 49
courtesy, 112, 117, 121, 124, 126, 127, 175, n. 2
Cruncher, Jerry, 58
Cullmann, O., 54

Dahl, M. E., 70
Daniel, 67
dead, speaking of the, 52, 53, 80
deontological ethics, 85, 87
Dickens, 58
divisions in Corinth, 18–21, 23, 33, 38
Dodd, C. H., 116
Dostoevsky, 158
dualism, 53–57, 60, 62, 72, 78, 83, 84, 140
Dupont, J., 152

Easter, 75, 77
Elijah, 54
Elisha, 54
Ellis, E. E., 83, 84
emotion in Paul's language, 18–20
Epictetus, 8
ethics of belief, 31, 130
evil, problem of, 157–161
Ezekiel, 54

Fackenheim, E., 158
faith and reason, 16, 29–32, 37–38, 46–47

197